Cultivating the Nile

NEW ECOLOGIES FOR THE TWENTY-FIRST CENTURY

Series Editors: Arturo Escobar, University of North Carolina, Chapel Hill
Dianne Rocheleau, Clark University

JESSICA BARNES

Cultivating the Nile

THE EVERYDAY POLITICS OF WATER IN EGYPT

Duke University Press   Durham and London   2014

© 2014 Duke University Press
All rights reserved
Printed in the United States of America on acid-free paper ∞
Designed by Heather Hensley
Typeset in Quadraat Pro by Tseng Information Systems, Inc.

Library of Congress Cataloging-in-Publication Data
Barnes, Jessica, 1978–
Cultivating the Nile : the everyday politics of water in Egypt /
Jessica Barnes.
pages cm — (New ecologies for the twenty-first century)
Includes bibliographical references and index.
ISBN 978-0-8223-5741-4 (cloth : alk. paper)
ISBN 978-0-8223-5756-8 (pbk. : alk. paper)
1. Water resources development—Egypt. 2. Water-supply—
Egypt. 3. Water use—Egypt. 4. Nile river. I. Title. II. Series:
New ecologies for the twenty-first century.
HD1699.E3B37 2014
333.9100962—dc23
2014012187

Cover photograph by Jessica Barnes

CONTENTS

vii   Note on Transliteration, Units, and Abbreviations

ix   Preface

xv   Acknowledgments

CHAPTER 1   The End of a River   1

CHAPTER 2   The Nile's Nadir: The Production of Scarcity   35

CHAPTER 3   Fluid Governance: Water User Associations and Practices of Participation   72

CHAPTER 4   Irrigating the Desert, Deserting the Irrigated: Land Reclamation at the Margins   106

CHAPTER 5   Flows of Drainage: The Politics of Excess   137

CHAPTER 6   Making Egypt's Water   169

179   Notes

199   References

223   Index

NOTE ON TRANSLITERATION, UNITS, AND ABBREVIATIONS

I use a system of transliteration designed to be accessible to readers unfamiliar with the Arabic language while recognizable to Arabic speakers. In transliterating written and Egyptian spoken Arabic, I omit the diacritical marks, long vowels, and *hamzas* (') that come at the start of words. The Arabic letter *ayn* I mark with a ('). I use italics for all Arabic terms except for words that have become standardized for usage in English.

I use the following units and abbreviations in the text:

bcm   Billion cubic meters

feddan   The unit of area measurement in Egypt. One feddan is made up of 24 qirat and is equivalent to 1.04 acres or 0.42 hectares. I follow the colloquial practice of using the word *feddan* in its singular form.

LE   Egyptian pound. At the time of fieldwork, in 2007–9, the Egyptian pound was approximately 5 LE for US$1.

MWRI   The Ministry of Water Resources and Irrigation, which I also refer to as "the ministry" (*al-wizara*) or, as farmers do, as "The Irrigation" (*al-rai*).

WUA   Water user association

My heart quickens. We have been driving for hours along rutted dirt roads, but now we are on the final stretch of our journey. We park by a sign that welcomes us to Gish Abay and find a guide from the village. We descend a steep, slippery slope of red soil, a crowd of children following behind us. A light rain falls, and black-and-white monkeys scamper out of our way. At the bottom of the hill, a circular green building with a small cross on it signals our destination. The church is considered so holy that you are only able to visit if you have not eaten that day. We have, so we skirt around it and gather by a muddy pool. Water trickles out of the ground through a small opening, surrounded by stone blocks. A few people are collecting water in colored bottles and containers. At the other end of the pool, water flows slowly out into a gully, which winds off to the north, into a flat plain of short yellow grasses. Our guide says, "This is the source of the river, which then flows 6,600km to the sea."

Water seeping out of the ground may not seem all that momentous, but this spring high up in the Ethiopian Highlands marks the beginning of one of the longest rivers in the world: the Nile.[1] As I stood by the source of the Nile's primary tributary—the Blue Nile—one damp day in April 2012, I imagined the large river this small stream becomes. I thought about the channels, dams, pumps, and fields of Ethiopia, Sudan, and Egypt that it passes through on its long path to the Mediterranean Sea. I pondered the possibilities that the water opens up with its presence, the potentials it oc-cludes in its absence, and the conflicts it generates in the process.

Five years earlier when I arrived in Egypt to begin my doctoral fieldwork, I felt a similar sense of excitement as I stood on the 6 October Bridge in the center of Cairo, looking over the Nile. Traffic screeched around me and a fog of pollution hung in the air. Rimmed by high-rise buildings, dotted with boats, and only half a kilometer or so in breadth, the main channel of the Nile that passes through the city is also not all that remarkable. Yet that water provides a lifeline, feeding the fields and quenching the thirst of millions in a country where other sources of water are minimal.

This book is about the political dynamics that emerge in, through, and around this water. In April 2011, the Ethiopians began work on a major new dam across the Blue Nile. Downstream neighbors responded with alarm. How, they asked, will this dam affect the amount of water that they receive from the Nile? The dam is the latest development in a series of tense political contestations over use of a river whose basin spans eleven nations. The pronounced power asymmetries of the Nile Basin and colonial-era legal agreements over Nile waters have been the topic of an extensive literature on transboundary water management. My approach to understanding the politics surrounding this water, however, is different. Instead of looking at the dramatic politics of international treaties and large dam projects, I focus on the everyday politics of water: the mundane yet vital acts of blocking, releasing, channeling, and diverting that determine where the water flows and who receives it. This is a story about water politics, therefore, that takes the water itself, and the many ways in which that water is manipulated, as its beginning.

My analysis centers on the final stretch of the river as it passes through Egypt. This is the site of the ethnographic fieldwork that I conducted with farmers, government engineers, and international donors. It is through close ethnographic observation of how people interact with water on a day-to-day basis that I am able to access the politics of the everyday. But I do not limit the view to Egypt alone. Rather, I situate this detailed, on-the-ground analysis within the context of processes, institutions, and technologies operating outside the nation's borders, which also affect how the water of the Nile flows into and through Egypt. Thus my analysis moves back and forth across space, shifting the gaze from downstream to upstream, farmer to donor agency, local to global, international water conference to irrigation canal.

My central argument is that Egypt's water is not a given object of management but rather is made as a resource through daily practices. What do I mean by this? Take, for example, water flowing through one of the many irrigation canals that wind across the fields of rural Egypt. Seeing this water as a given object of management would be to take the flow of water through this canal as the starting point for analysis. But what if, instead, the starting point were the actions that have produced that particular volume and quality of water? The act of the gatekeeper who opened the weir at the start of the canal; the decision made in the offices of the water ministry in Cairo about that canal's water allocation; the diversion of water from the canal by one farmer to reclaim new desert land; the planting of rice by another; the visit to the district irrigation engineer by farmers campaigning for more water; the pumping of saline water from a drainage ditch back into the canal for reuse; the installation of flow control devices by an internationally funded aid project; the removal of an upstream blockage in the canal by a government excavator? Directing the focus to these everyday social, biophysical, technical, and political practices that produce particular quantity and quality characteristics across space and time is what I mean by the making of Egypt's water.

This book builds on scholarship within anthropology, geography, and other disciplines that has demonstrated how natural resources are inherently social, cultural, and political in their constitution and use. The contribution of this book is to focus attention on *how* a resource is made—the ongoing processes that take place across different scales and that produce not just a singular resource but one that is multiple in its nature. By bringing into the story not only farmers, engineers, policy makers, and international experts but also pumps and pipes, dams and ditches, the book elucidates what exactly it means to say that a resource comes into being. This approach to water opens up a wider frame of political dynamics, social relations, and technological interventions, which must be considered if the nature of water—this most critical of resources—is to be understood.

While the construction of the Aswan High Dam across the Nile marked a profound moment in the history of Egyptian control over the river, and has been a focus of scholarly attention, the making of Egypt's Nile is not a matter of a singular event but an evolving series of events. To explore these ongoing processes, this book sets the decisions made by government engineers about the daily operation of the High Dam alongside those made by farmers about the daily operation of their irrigation ditches. It highlights the significance of pipes below the surface as well as that of large dams across the river. It contrasts the times and spaces where there is not enough water with those where there is too much. It looks at the neat plans of policy makers and the messy work of digging out blocked irrigation canals. It examines the international donors' projects to improve water distribution efficiency and the ways in which they morph as they are implemented in practice. The book therefore reveals the multiscaled, everyday practices of water manipulation and use, which are where, I argue, some of the most active political contestation is taking place.

Since I completed the main body of research for this book (in 2007–2008), the Arab Spring has swept across the Middle East. In January 2011 Egyptians took to the streets to protest three decades of autocratic rule. Eventually succeeding in toppling President Mubarak, the protestors ushered in a period of political transformation. In July 2013, following further popular unrest, Mubarak's elected successor, Mohamed Morsi, was ousted by the Egyptian military. As this book goes to press, the contours of Egypt's political system are in flux. How the new authorities will reform water management practices and the agricultural sector remains to be seen. Yet the current moment presents an apt one in which to consider questions of who is able to access water, a substance fundamental to society and, in particular, to all those whose lives are directly or indirectly tied to agricultural production. With its focus on the politics of water distribution and use, this book speaks to issues that are at the heart of contemporary debates within Egypt about inequality, livelihoods, and governance of the nation's resources.

In connecting local-level daily practices around water use, regulation, and control with those taking place at national and international scales, this book offers a refreshing new take on water and will be valuable to readers interested in water politics and water resources management. More broadly, the book informs conversations about society-environment interactions within environmental anthropology, political ecology, and science and technology studies, few of which have been focused on the Middle East to date. By tracing where the water comes from, how it moves, and who moves it, this book demonstrates the importance of looking at the specific processes through which a resource comes into being. It reveals a politics that is intimately tied to the nature of the resource in question.

The book's narrative follows the flow of water through different sites. In chapter 1, I situate the reader in Egypt, at the end of the river, laying out the key actors who use, manage, and manipulate Egypt's water. I introduce my field site of Fayoum Province, frame my work within the literature of political ecology and science and technology studies, and outline the ethnographic methods that I use to access the politics of the everyday.

Chapter 2 focuses on the places of scarcity, where irrigation canals lie empty. The making of Egypt's water is as much about determining where water does not flow as determining where it does. I show how scarcity is produced through the technologies, agricultural practices, and decision-making processes, operating on a range of scales, that control the passage of water through the country on a day-to-day basis. I highlight the political disputes generated around the problem of scarcity and the ways in which different actors respond. Such responses to scarcity, I argue, comprise another set of devices for intervening in the flow of water and determining what water flows where.

In chapter 3, I examine the governance structures that water passes through. I analyze the international donors' efforts to forge a participatory management regime through the establishment of water user associations along the irrigation canals. Through an ethnographic study of one donor's project to form water user associations throughout Fayoum Province, I show how participation—a buzzword of the global water community—plays out in practice. I explore the conflicting visions of what it means to participate, the difficulty of constructing a community around a flowing resource, and the ways in which the associations evolve after their point of establishment. The chapter demonstrates the multiplicity of interests, strategies, and forms of social connection that determine who is able to exert influence over water flowing through the canals and thus help shape the contours of Egypt's water.

Chapter 4 follows the water as it flows out of the canals and over the fields. I look at farmers' efforts to reclaim desert along the margins of the cultivated zone and analyze how this process affects patterns of water distribution. I describe the quotidian practices that farmers employ to access water for desert reclamation and show how they impact the quantity and quality of water that flows on to downstream farmers. As some farmers accumulate water to develop new land, they dispossess others of the resource needed to cultivate their existing land—a source of considerable political discontent. The making of Egypt's water is closely tied to the making of Egypt's land.

Chapter 5 tracks the water as it moves from the fields, down into the soil, and into the drainage network. I highlight the places where there is actually too much water, leading to problems of waterlogging and salinization. I examine the technologies used to manage this excess water and the political relations that both shape and are shaped by a partially implemented network of subsurface drainage pipes. I analyze the process of recycling drainage water back into the irrigation system for reuse and how this influences water's quantity and quality characteristics. In tracing the flow of water and salts down and up through the soil and from drainage ditches back into irrigation canals, the chapter exposes a vertical dimension to the making of Egypt's water.

Through these chapters, the book traces the quotidian practices of accessing, monitoring, and utilizing water that shape what Egypt's water comes to be. These are the practices that determine how much water flows through each branch of the irrigation network. They set the places where water is scarce and where it is in excess, where it is good quality and where it is saline. They define which land blooms and which land lies fallow. I expand on these themes in chapter 6, returning at the end of the book to a canal in rural Egypt to discuss what is at stake in this everyday politics of water.

ACKNOWLEDGMENTS

It is difficult to pinpoint where the journey began to write this book. Perhaps it was sitting in the lecture theater as an undergraduate student at Oxford, listening to Lutfi Radwan talk about his work on irrigation in Egypt. Or the conversation with my sister, on a hill outside the oasis town of Siwa, about my dreams of living in the Middle East. Or the year studying Arabic in Damascus, when I decided that I would like to do a PhD. Or the series of events that led me to shift my fieldwork from Syria to Egypt. Whatever its beginnings, one thing is clear—the fact that I would not have reached this end point without the guidance and support of many, many people.

My thanks go first to the people of the village that I call Warda. I thank them for letting me into their homes and fields with such kindness and generosity of spirit. I thank, in particular, the extended families of those who I refer to as Abu Khaled and my neighbor, Assam. I will always remember winter evenings sitting with Om Ahmed, Nagat, Hana, Mona, and Intisar around a metal bowl of hot coals under blankets, eating roasted corn and talking as children of different sizes fell asleep on and around us.

I owe great gratitude to Habib Ayeb and Reem Saad who helped me first identify Fayoum as a field site and establish a life in Warda. I thank, also, Bianca Longhi, Xavier Puigimarti, Ahmed Abu Zeid, Ikram Abu Zeid, Zohra Merabet, Jon Bjornsson, Marina Fischer, Herrie Heckman, and Donald Benson, for their warm hospitality. In Cairo, James Baldwin, Helena Wright, Ginny Philps, Rania Kassab, Jennifer Derr, and Alan Mikhail provided much appreciated support and friendship. Lamia el-Fattal, Maurice Saade, Rick Tutwiler, Stephen Brichieri-Colombi, and Liz Wickett shared their valuable advice and candid insights.

This project would not have been possible without the affiliation that I had with the donor project, which allowed me to learn about the day-to-day workings of the Ministry of Water Resources and Irrigation. I thank the manager of the project for her openness to my research and for sharing her astute and thoughtful observations on water in Egypt. Her company brightened my days in Fayoum. I thank, also, the Egyptian project director for supporting my affiliation with the project, and other members of the Fayoum Irrigation Directorate and project staff for allowing me to attend workshops, meetings, and field visits, and sharing their expertise. I thank the ministry officials from the central office in Cairo and the consultants and staff from international and bilateral donor agencies who provided fascinating interviews and helped me plan field visits to the delta.

I began this project as a doctoral student at Columbia University, where I was fortunate to have two extraordinary mentors. Paige West encouraged me to develop my own critical voice, inspired me with her brilliant scholarship and writing, and guided me through the transition from student to academic. Timothy Mitchell helped shape this project from its formative stages, sharing his time, wonderful intellect, and deep understanding of Egypt with amazing generosity. I hope they will see the fruits of the many hours they have given me in this book. Lila Abu-Lughod, Lisa Anderson, and Frank Magilligan also provided valuable feedback on the project at different stages. I wrote this manuscript as a postdoctoral associate at Yale, under the wise mentorship of Michael R. Dove. The intellectual community of the Yale School of Forestry and Environmental Studies, Yale Climate and Energy Institute, and Dove Lab offered an exceptionally supportive and stimulating environment in which to develop my ideas from dissertation to book. I finish the book as an assistant professor at the University of South Carolina, where I feel lucky to have such a collegial environment within the Department of Geography and Environment and Sustainability Program in which to bring this project to a close.

I thank those who read and provided feedback on the manuscript in its entirety—Michael Dove, Jeannie Sowers, David Kneas, and students in Michael Dove's fall 2011 *Society and Environment* course at Yale. I thank those who provided valuable input on individual chapters of the book—Samer Alatout, Nikhil Anand, Lisa Bjorkman, Ashley Carse, Annie Claus, Tessa Farmer, Dana Graef, Annie Harper, Barry Muchnick, Beth Pillsbury, Jeff Stoike, and participants of three water workshops at Harvard, organized by Steven Caton.

I thank Valerie Millholland, Gisela Fosado, and Susan Albury at Duke University Press for their support for this project and advice through each stage of bringing the book to publication. I owe many thanks to three anonymous reviewers who read and provided detailed commentary on the manuscript through various rounds of revisions. I also thank Bill Nelson for drawing the illustrations, Elaine Otto for her copyediting work, and Celia Braves for writing the index. The research for this book was generously funded by the Wenner-Gren Foundation for Anthropological Research and the Yale Climate and Energy Institute.

Finally, I thank my family and friends. There is a beautiful passage near the start of the novel *Seasons of Migration to the North*, by Taeb Saleh, shortly after the narrator returns from studies overseas. He describes looking out of the window from his family home at a date palm, at its thick trunk and strong branches. He reflects on his sense of being not a storm-swept feather but like that palm tree, with roots. I am so grateful for my roots. I thank Florence Miller, Tara Wigley, Sarah Winchester, Beth Willis, Katy Bower, Beth Pillsbury, and Sarah Vogel for their long friendships (and in the case of Sarah Winchester, for journeying with me, along with Yshak Tsegaye, a very long way to the source of the Nile in Ethiopia). I thank Ann and John Kneas and all the other members of the Kneas family for making a home for me this side of the Atlantic. I thank my parents, Tim and Trish Barnes, and my siblings, Toff Barnes, Liddy Pleasants, and Natasha Barnes, and their families, for reminding me, always, what is important in life. And I thank my husband, David Kneas, and our children, Henry and Oliver, for making every day a happier one.

CHAPTER 1

The End of a River

Water is often talked about today in crisis terms. In popular, policy, and academic circles, managing the world's limited freshwater has become a central challenge of the twenty-first century. Millions lack access to this most basic of needs. Water supplies are being over-exploited. Deep conflicts have emerged over the division of shared waters. Climate change is altering patterns of supply and demand. Wars could be fought over water. In this context, the political dynamics that moderate access and use of water have become paramount concerns.

This book examines the processes and patterns of water distribution and use in Egypt, an arid country at the end of the longest river in the world. In doing so, it presents a novel view of water politics: a politics anchored not in an alarmist narrative of global crisis and potential wars, but in the everyday practices of managing canals, opening dams, dredging channels, turning on faucets, operating pumps, and irrigating fields. These are the practices that determine who is able to access this vital substance, and these are the sites where I argue that some of the most active political contestation is actually taking place.

As the source of 96 percent of Egypt's water, the Nile is what makes life in Egypt possible.[1] Rising in the highlands of East Africa, the river passes through Egypt on the final stretch of its long journey to the sea (map 1.1). Given that over 90 percent of Nile water is used in irrigation, this book focuses on how farmers and government officials channel the flow of the Nile to cultivate the land.[2] But it also looks at how people shape the volume, direction, and

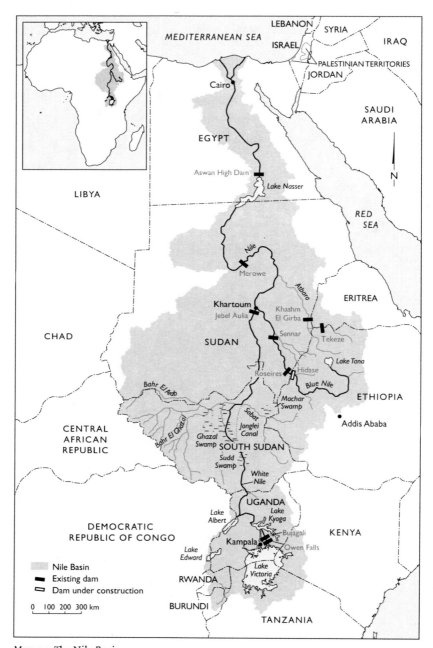

Map 1.1. The Nile Basin

nature of that flow through day-to-day acts of blocking, releasing, and diverting water. These practices mold the spaces of agricultural possibility, by determining where the water flows and where it does not. They control where water is sufficient for agricultural production, where it is too scarce to support a crop, and where it is so plentiful that it causes waterlogging and salinization. Agriculture in Egypt is as much about cultivating the Nile as it is about cultivating the land.

My main argument is that Egypt's water resources are not a given but are made through these daily practices of accessing, monitoring, and manipulating the flow of water. I build on work within anthropology, geography, and other disciplines, which has shown how natural resources are not objective facts but products of the societies that put them to use. I extend this work by focusing on the processes through which this resource making takes place. The supply side of a national water budget cannot be captured in a simple summation of rainfall, groundwater, and surface water inflow. Instead, what water comes to be is the outcome of social, biophysical, technical, and political processes that produce particular quantity and quality characteristics in any given time and place. There is obviously a "natural" dimension to water. Rain falls over the Nile source regions; water moves through a channel according to hydraulic properties of flow; pressure differentials govern the interaction between surface water and groundwater stores. But this dimension cannot be disconnected from the practices that shape how, where, and when the water flows. The politics of water lies in these quotidian practices of making water as a resource available for use.

I access this everyday politics through ethnography. Drawing on 14 months of ethnographic fieldwork at sites of water policy making, management, and use within Egypt, and at panels on Middle East water at international water conferences, I analyze the making of Egypt's water across multiple scales. This is a process that is linked to the decisions made by policy makers in government offices in Cairo, to the act of engineers opening and closing dams, to the work of farmers irrigating their fields, and to the projects of international and bilateral donors that seek to transform the technological and managerial landscape of water. These actors derive their agency, their ability to shape the nature of Egypt's water, from contrasting forms of knowledge, frameworks of understanding, and technical devices. Sometimes their goals are aligned, sometimes they are in conflict. Each one has its own interest in cultivating the Nile.

The idea that a country's water resources are made and not a given recasts the fundamental question of water resources management. Water management becomes a question not of how a country can best manage the resources that it has but of how those resources come into being. The starting point for this book, therefore, is not "How should Egypt manage its water?" but "What is Egypt's water?" The key to the sustainable management of this water lies in the engineering structures, agricultural practices, decision-making processes, and technologies that determine where water flows and how its characteristics change along the way.

I turn now to the water, which provides the central thread for this analysis, tracing the flow of water through the Nile Basin to Egypt's fields. I then introduce the agricultural system which that water supports and three overlapping, interconnected, and heterogeneous groups of actors—farmers, government officials, and international donors and consultants. In the next section, I describe my primary field site of Fayoum Province. Finally, I frame this work within the literature and describe the ethnographic methods that I use to explore the politics around everyday water management and use.

THE TRAVELS OF A WATER DROPLET

Rain pours down on a landscape of grassy hills, swampy valleys, and occasional rocky peaks rising to significant heights. It is an August day in the Ethiopian Highlands, midway through the four-month rainy season. A water droplet runs over the saturated soil into the brown, sediment-heavy stream known locally as the Abay, but more widely as the Blue Nile. The river winds a tortuous path as it descends through the highlands, at times cutting a steep-sided canyon into the basaltic plateau. Some 800km later, after descending more than 1,000m, the droplet crosses over the Sudanese border. The water slows as it approaches the backed up water behind the Rosieres Dam, 80km inside Sudan. Through the dam, the droplet continues on its course, flowing through wooded country, at first larger and more varied trees, many of them baobab, giving way to small thorny acacias. Two hundred and fifty kilometers further on, the water meets its second temporary storage point—the reservoir behind the Sennar Dam. The droplet moves through the dam and, some distance downstream, flows into the dusty city of Khartoum. In the middle of this city, at an altitude of 380m above sea level, the Blue and White Niles meet, continuing their course together. As the river flows northwards, the droplet passes between cultivated fields and pastures of grasses and acacia trees. The surroundings become increasingly arid. Following the Merowe Reservoir and Dam and a series of rapids, the channel widens, marking the beginning of Lake Nasser. The droplet moves through the lake, at some point crossing an invisible border and into Egyp-

Figure 1.1. The Nile at Aswan. Photograph by the author.

tian territory. It reaches the large gates of the Aswan High Dam. Below the dam, the Nile cuts a blue line through a narrow strip of green fields. The droplet flows past temples built thousands of years ago and through the barrages of Esna, Naga Hamadi, and Asyut. The banks become increasingly built up as the river enters the noisy metropolis of Cairo. North of the city, the water passes through the Delta Barrages and the river splits in two, forming the Rosetta and Damietta branches. If the droplet reaches the end of one of these branches, it joins the salty waters of the Mediterranean. It is unlikely, however, to get that far. More probably, at some point before it reaches the sea, the droplet will be diverted into a canal and onto a field.

This is the journey of over 6,000km that brings water from a rainstorm over East Africa to a ditch in rural Egypt. Ninety-six percent of Egypt's water comes from the Nile. Of that water, 85 percent comes from seasonal rainfall over the headwaters of the Blue Nile in Ethiopia.[3] The remainder comes from year-round rainfall over the highlands surrounding Lake Victoria, which feeds into the White Nile. Rainfall declines sharply over the river's catchment, from 2,000mm in the source regions to less than 200mm from Khartoum northwards. This creates an asymmetry between where the water of the Nile comes from (East Africa) and where rainfall is so low that agriculture is impossible in its absence (Sudan and Egypt).[4]

Egypt's allocation of water from the Nile is guaranteed through a decades-old legal document, the Agreement for the Full Utilization of Nile Waters, which Egypt and Sudan signed in 1959. According to this agreement, Sudan is legally bound to ensure that at least 55.5 billion cubic meters of water flow each year across its border with Egypt. Egypt also has the power to veto any upstream water development projects that could impact this water allocation. Ethiopia's recent launch of the Grand Renaissance Dam (also known as the Hidase Dam) project on the Blue Nile, however, in direct contravention of Egypt's veto power, signals the upstream countries' unwillingness to continue to accept the terms of an agreement to which they were not party (map 1.1).[5] Indeed over the last few years, six of the eleven basin states have signed a new Nile treaty, the Comprehensive Framework Agreement, which opens up the potential for upstream countries to initiate projects along the Nile.[6] While the treaty has yet to be fully ratified, if it comes into effect, it will mark a significant shift in the international framework of rights to Nile water.[7]

Once the water of the Nile reaches Egypt, it is subject to a set of national legal doctrines that determine the rights of access. Under article 18 of Egypt's Irrigation and Drainage Law No. 12 (1984), "All agricultural land in the Nile valley and delta has a legal right to receive irrigation water." Egypt therefore has a system of universal rights to water for all farmers for irrigation purposes. This contrasts with the system of rights based on land-ownership, as in the riparian doctrine of United States water law, or historical usage, as in the prior appropriation doctrine. It is not, though, a formal system of water rights, since the law does not specify how much water each unit of land should receive, nor is there a legal and regulatory framework for farmers to defend their rights if water fails to arrive.[8] Yet farmers do not lack a sense of entitlement. They know what water they need to grow their crops. They do whatever is necessary to access that water so as to cultivate their land.

CULTIVATING THE LAND

I started my fieldwork in Egypt in June 2007. In June, the bright heads of sunflowers punctuate the landscape. Tall stalks of sorghum sit alongside the deep green leaves of fodder maize (garawa), yellow flowers of cotton plants, and spikes of rice in flooded paddy fields. Through the ditches that snake across and around the fields, the flow of Nile water sustains these plants during summer days of clear skies and a burning sun. As the crops are harvested in late August and September, the landscape changes.

Figure 1.2. Flood irrigation. Photograph by the author.

Farmers gather the rice straw for sale and burn or plow over the remaining fields of stubby rice stalks. They load the fluffy balls of cotton into sacks and pile the brown sinewy remains of the crop. Balanced high up in palm trees, men and boys pick dates and cut fronds for use in furniture and roofing.

As the weeks pass, farmers prepare the fields for the next season. They plow and weed the soil, then add manure. The next step is to irrigate. Most farmers use a technique that engineers term *flood irrigation*. They open up offtakes from the canals and divert Nile water onto their fields. Using a series of earth dams, they channel the water around the fields until either the whole surface or the furrows between the crop rows are covered up to a certain depth, then leave the water to infiltrate the soil. Once the soil is well watered, they plant the winter crops in succession. By November, the early winter crops are ready for harvest. Each day, farmers cut maize for fodder and fuel, loading the long stalks on top of camels to transport them back to their households. Laborers move through fields of tomato plants, picking out the ripe fruit. November is also the time when the late winter crops are planted. Fields are busy with young men transplanting the onion seedlings that have been carefully tended in field nurseries, wading through flooded fields to place individual seedlings into the raised earthen banks. In other fields, farmers plant wheat seeds in rows.

Interspersed among the blocks of newly planted onions and wheat are fields of Egyptian clover (birsim). Present throughout the winter season, the clover fields soon take on a semi-shaven look. Farmers go every day to collect fodder for their livestock, cutting off handfuls of stems near the ground, creating a steadily enlarging rectangular "shaven" strip. Women and children walk home with piles of clover balanced on their heads or stuffed into saddlebags slung over donkeys.

While wheat, onions, and clover are the dominant crops, the winter landscape is not a uniform one. The wide leaves of sugar beet are a common sight, as are the leafy stems of faba beans. In some fields, white chamomile and orange moonflowers sprinkle the ground. In others, enormous local cabbages dot the fields, each over a foot in diameter.

By March the landscape is a patchwork of deep green wheat, brighter green clover, and darker green onions. Some fields are covered in a film of water, others are dry, as the farmers take turns to irrigate different parts of their land. In the fields of faba beans, the pods are beginning to develop and swell on the stems. The sugar beet is ready for harvest, and farmers load the knobby roots high in trucks. This is the time of year when a marked transition spreads across the landscape. The sea of wheat transforms from green, to greeny white, to golden yellow. The land shimmers as the golden ears of wheat move back and forth in the breeze.

The wheat and onions are harvested in April and early May. Farmers go out before sunrise to cut the wheat, leaving piles of harvested stalks in the fields to dry, before gathering them into upright bundles. Dust billows out behind the threshing machines that separate the wheat kernels from the straw. The fields of onions take on a brownish tint as farmers halt the flow of irrigation to let the fields dry out before harvest. Laborers uproot the crop, filling up red sacks, which they line along the fields. The colors change as the late winter crops are harvested; no longer the yellow of the mature wheat nor the bright orange of the moonflowers. The landscape shifts back to brown and green as farmers plow the fields and water the soil in preparation for their summer crops. The cycle begins again.

The seasonal pattern of cultivation that I observed over the year that I lived in Egypt is similar to that which takes place throughout the country.[9] It is a cyclical pattern that is integrally tied to the travels of a water droplet. Without the rain that falls on the upper reaches of the Nile Basin, none of this production would be possible. Without the canals and ditches which convey that water to the fields, farmers would not be able to cultivate these crops.

This agriculture builds on a history of cultivation that dates back thousands of years. The first settled agriculture along the Nile is thought to have begun around seven thousand years ago. Since that time, agriculture has provided an important foundation for successive civilizations (Butzer 1976; Bowman and Rogan 1999). Embedded in this landscape, however, are traces of policies, technologies, and modes of social organization that have modified the system of agricultural production over the years. In my description of Egypt's changing agricultural landscape, three elements offer windows into particularly significant recent transitions—the year-round cultivation, the patchwork of different crops, and the small size of the fields. Each of these dimensions of the cultivation system helps shape where and when Egypt's water flows and what it becomes in the process.

The reason why the fields can be cultivated throughout the year is the constant availability of irrigation water, which sustains production in the near absence of rainfall.[10] Whereas for thousands of years, Egyptian farmers ordered their agricultural calendar around the rising waters of the Nile in late July, farmers are now able to plant crops not only in the winter but also in the summer. Perennial irrigation dates back to the mid-nineteenth century, when Egypt was part of the Ottoman Empire. In 1843, Mohamed Ali, Ottoman viceroy in Egypt, began construction of the Delta Barrages.[11] These barriers held back the flow of the river, maintaining the water level during the months of low discharge before the flood. This allowed farmers in parts of the delta to tap the waters of the Nile in the hot summer months, so as to cultivate a summer crop. Following the British occupation of Egypt in 1882, the irrigation authorities continued the process of irrigation development and built a number of barrages. More were built after Egypt's independence in 1922, with the involvement of the British, who remained influential in many spheres, including the irrigation sector.[12] The most pronounced change came, however, after the 1952 revolution and birth of the Arab Republic of Egypt. The new government of President Gamal Abdel Nasser began construction of a dam of unprecedented size across the Nile. Inaugurated in 1971, the Aswan High Dam facilitated the transition to perennial irrigation on a nationwide scale and completed the system of major water control structures that is evident in Egypt today (map 1.2).

At 3,830m in width and 111m in height, the High Dam is able to hold back thirty times more water than its predecessor, the first Aswan Dam built by the British in 1902. The dam stores water from successive years of the river's seasonal high flows in Lake Nasser, and the government controls

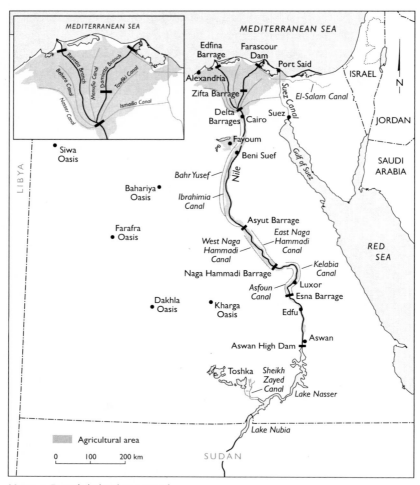

Map 1.2. Egypt's irrigation network

the release of water throughout the year. This has transformed the river's hydrograph. No longer is there a pronounced peak of flood discharge in September. No longer does the river burst its banks and inundate the floodplain on an annual basis. Instead, discharge remains relatively constant throughout the year, ranging from just above 100 million cubic meters a day to just above 200 million cubic meters a day (see figure 1.3). Water flows through the irrigation canals year round. At the same time, since the river no longer deposits nutrient-rich sediment on the fields once a year, fertilizers are a vital component of the continuous cultivation that I observed.

The second aspect of the landscape that offers a window into recent his-

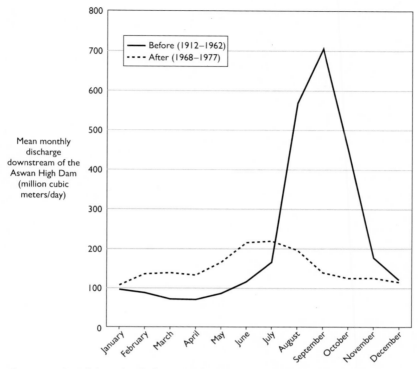

Figure 1.3. The Nile's regime before and after construction of the Aswan High Dam. *Source:* Data from S. Shalash, "The Effect of the High Aswan Dam on the Hydrological Regime of the River Nile." Proceedings of the Helsinki Symposium, June 1980.

tory and to current patterns of water usage is its diversity. Farmers decide what to plant and when to plant it. In this decision, they control a vital flux of water out of the irrigation system through evapotranspiration. This has not always been the case. Following the revolution in 1952, President Nasser introduced a series of central controls on the agricultural sector. The government dictated cropping patterns, distributed production inputs, and purchased all crops. This state-led agricultural policy was gradually reversed by Nasser's successor, Anwar al-Sadat, who came to power in 1970. Sadat's government opened the country to foreign investment, embraced a new alliance with the United States, and encouraged private enterprise in agriculture. Hosni Mubarak continued this process of liberalization after he became president in 1981. In the face of a growing financial crisis in the late 1980s, Mubarak signed an agreement with the International Monetary Fund and World Bank in 1991 to embark on a structural adjustment program of economic reform.[13] Under pressure from the United States Agency for International Development (USAID), the government started to transition away from state intervention in agriculture. By the early 1990s, it had eliminated almost all input subsidies, compulsory cropping patterns, and crop procurement.[14]

While agricultural liberalization has given farmers the freedom of crop choice, they also now face much higher prices for fertilizers and pesticides, which is a matter of widespread discontent. In the wake of Egypt's January 2011 revolution, this discontent has found fertile ground. A newly founded farmers' union and other civil society groups have called for the new regime to reinstate governmental supports for the farming sector (Ezzat 2011). Officials in the Ministry of Agriculture have responded by talking about the need to reintroduce subsidies on agricultural inputs and to use cooperatives to help farmers increase their productivity (Hussein 2011). It is still too early to know whether this rhetoric will translate into new policies, but the lack of actual change to date has left many skeptical about the likelihood of agricultural reform (Viney 2012). Thus for the time being, farmers remain constrained by high fertilizer costs and uncertain markets, but free to decide what to grow and, consequently, when and how they irrigate their land.

A farmer's decision about what to grow depends partly on market prices and family needs, and partly on the quantity and quality of water he or she is able to access. Different crops require different amounts of water. Crop needs range from 450mm–650mm over the course of a growing season for grains like wheat, sorghum, and barley to 700–1300mm for cotton and 1,500–2,500mm for sugarcane (Brouwer and Heibloem 1986). Crops also vary in their tolerance to water salinity. Some crops, like sugar beet and cotton, can grow happily when irrigated with saline water (with an electrical conductivity over 4dS/m); other crops, like maize and faba beans, experience a 50 percent yield loss in these circumstances (Ayers and Westcot 1994). Farmers may not think about crop water requirements in terms of millimeters of water per growing season or the electrical conductivity of the water, but they are well aware that some crops have to be irrigated more frequently than others and that some can cope with salty water and others cannot. Thus crop choice is shaped by the water that flows to and through the fields and, in turn, helps shape that flow as crops transpire different volumes of water back into the atmosphere.

The third aspect of the landscape that reveals a trace of history and helps explain patterns of water distribution is the small size of the fields. As part of his Arab socialist agenda, President Nasser implemented a land reform program that had a profound impact on land distribution. Previously, 0.1 percent of the landowners had owned 20 percent of the cultivated land, while 75 percent of the landowners had owned just 13 percent of the cultivable land, in individual holdings of less than one feddan. (The feddan is the Egyptian measure of area, which is roughly equivalent in size to an acre.) The land reform eliminated most of the biggest estates of more than 200 feddan. Almost two million laborers and tenant farmers benefited from the redistribution of seized land, receiving an average of 2.4 feddan each.[15] Although the government passed Law No. 96 in 1992, which revoked the tenancy supports that the earlier land reform had provided and enabled some large landowners to repossess land, the landscape remains primarily one of small farms.[16]

Hence water moves through multiple hands in its passage through Egypt's landscape, each individual helping to determine the fate of that water. Ninety-five percent of the farms are less than five feddan, and the average sized farm is two feddan. Most farms are not contiguous but made up of scattered plots, which farmers have either inherited or bought over time. This means that farmers may have to tap into the network of Nile water distribution at multiple points to irrigate their land. Approximately 50 percent of farming households are landless and so they either rent or sharecrop land (IFAD 2005, 3). Some farmers who own land also rent additional plots from other farmers or family members. While the farms are small, almost all farmers grow crops for both home consumption and market sale. Most farming families also have nonagricultural sources of income from family members working in government, trade, transportation, industry, or tourism (Hopkins and Westergaard 1998; Saad 2004). Although small farms predominate, larger commercially oriented farms of Egyptian and international agricultural investors are of growing importance, especially in the new areas of agricultural expansion in the desert. With more capital at their disposal, these farmers often use sprinkler or drip irrigation to distribute Nile water through their fields.

In Egypt, the word for farmer is *fellah* or *muzari'*. The former carries with it connotations of "peasant," but is the term that farmers generally use to describe themselves. The latter term strictly means "he who cultivates the land" and is the more formal term used in policy documents and official settings. What distinguishes both terms, though, is their masculine gender—a gender that obscures the fact that women also farm. In households where both men and women are present and healthy, the men generally assume a dominant role in irrigation and agriculture as the women are busy

Figure 1.4. Picking onion seedlings. Photograph by the author.

with household work, such as cooking, cleaning, and childcare. Nonetheless, there are certain agricultural tasks that wives, sisters, and daughters take primary responsibility for, like weeding and picking onion seedlings, harvesting chamomile, and collecting fodder for livestock. The degree of female participation in farming activities varies by region. Women are more of a presence in the fields in the delta than they are in the south of the country. It also varies by socioeconomic class. In poorer households, women typically play more of a role in agricultural production than they do in richer households. In rural households where the man is not present, however, either because he has died or is working elsewhere, women are left responsible for cultivating and irrigating the family's fields. In cases where those women have male relatives or can afford agricultural laborers, they may delegate some of the day-to-day tasks in the fields, but they remain the primary agricultural decision makers.

So those who use the vast majority of Egypt's water are farmers working small pieces of land, deeply embedded in national and international networks of migration, trade, and communication. This group is far from homogeneous. Lines of difference and groupings of interest run through the farming population, shaped by many factors including wealth, gender, regional identity, size of holding, religion, and political affiliation. Yet the need to access sufficient water to sustain their fields is an objective shared by all. I turn now to the second group of actors in this book—the water bureaucrats—many of whom also come from farming families and so, depending on the context, can play the role of either the water user or the water official.

WATER BUREAUCRACIES

The tall, pale yellow building of the Ministry of Water Resources and Irrigation's central offices stands on the western bank of the Nile in Cairo. Over its multiple floors, the hierarchies of bureaucracy are manifest. The high-level officials have large air-conditioned offices that look over the river, allowing them to survey the resource on which their job depends. Their offices are marked by emblems of authority: large desks with gold name placards; chairs for visitors arranged around coffee tables; orderly filing cabinets; certificates of workshop participation on the walls; thick carpets on the floor; and purring air-conditioning units. Sharing the same floors are the international consultants who manage donor-funded water projects. Their offices benefit from the same cool flow of conditioned air but are less formal in their layout. Stepping out of the elevator onto another level of the building, you enter a different world. The corridors are dirty and poorly maintained. Offices are crammed with five or six desks, windows flung open to capture a faint breeze, fans working overhead. Sheaves of paper are piled up in loose bundles on rickety shelves.

This is the government agency that I focus on in this book.[17] Under Law No. 74 (1974), the Ministry of Water Resources and Irrigation is responsible for managing a network of more than 30,000km of canals, ten major barrages, and more than one hundred large pumping stations. Maintaining the quality of water that passes through this network is also part of the ministry's role, under Law No. 48 (1982). In addition, 18,000km of drainage canals and 450,000km of subsurface drainage pipes fall within the ministry's jurisdiction. The system of water distribution is therefore a highly centralized one. The ministry's influence stops, though, at the point where the water flows out of the canals and into the irrigation ditches, known as mesqa, which are managed collectively by the farmers. The point of water usage thus ultimately lies in the farmers' hands.

The ministry's main objective is to ensure that everyone receives water of sufficient quantity (kemia) and quality (no'ia). This means controlling the daily distribution of water through the operation of a series of control structures, keeping track of water quality parameters, and treating the water when necessary. Maintenance of the infrastructure is a central part of this work. Every January, during the "winter closure" (al-sadde al-shitwiya), the ministry cuts off the flow of water progressively to different parts of the irrigation network so that it can conduct maintenance work, such as rebuilding banks, repairing offtakes, mending pipes, and dredging canals.

Throughout the book, I refer to the Ministry of Water Resources and Irrigation as "the ministry," which is how people shorten its name in Arabic (al-wizara). When farmers refer to the ministry, though, they have a different abbreviation. They call it al-rai, which means, literally, "the irrigation." To farmers, the importance of the ministry lies not in its position as part of a larger state bureaucracy but in terms of what it delivers.

In my analysis of the ministry as a key player in this account of water politics, I emphasize the contrasting perspectives held by employees occupying different positions within it. The ministry is a large, heterogeneous, and complex bureaucracy, with numerous departments, authorities, sectors, public contracting companies, and research institutes. The ministry divides the country into twenty-two directorates, which are subdivided into forty-eight inspectorates and 167 districts. In each directorate, the undersecretary (wakil al-wizara), who represents the central ministry, and director general of irrigation (mudir al-'am) manage the flow of water through the main and branch canals, using a staff of inspectors (mufatish), district engineers (muhandis), technicians (fanni), and gate keepers (bahhar). The vertical relations between the ministry staff are heavily ingrained. As one expatriate consultant joked to me, "Everyone here thinks in pyramids, as they have been doing for thousands of years!" These hierarchical relations are made and maintained through quotidian practices (Gupta and Ferguson 2002): the positioning of seats during meetings (the undersecretary and director general up on a stage, looking down on everyone else); the markers of dress (a district engineer wearing a suit and carrying his papers in a briefcase); and the mode of interaction (senior officials keeping others waiting as they almost invariably arrive late for meetings). Yet social connections both reinforce and transcend this hierarchy. Relationships within extended families or between neighbors, for example, provide opportunities for individuals to access power and influence beyond that which their position would normally allow, enabling them to "jump scales" (Smith 1992). Rather than being made up of a rigid set of stacked levels, therefore, the ministry incorporates multiple overlapping relationships, moderated by professional skills and personal connections.

The Ministry of Water Resources and Irrigation is one of Egypt's more influential ministries. It stakes a claim to being one of the oldest in Egypt, tracing its origins back to the Public Works Department, which was established by Mohamed Ali in 1836.[18] It is not, however, the only ministry involved in water management.[19] The Ministry of Foreign Affairs represents Egypt's interests in the Nile Basin negotiations, on-field water management falls under the authority of the Ministry of Agriculture and Land Reclamation, and the Ministry of Drinking Water and Sanitation supervises drinking water provision and wastewater treatment. This division of responsibility over water is a source of significant tension; each ministry is keen to maximize its authority. As the operator of the Aswan High Dam and network of control structures, though, the Ministry of Water Resources and Irrigation ultimately plays the largest role in shaping what happens to Egypt's water. At the same time, the making of Egypt's water lies not only in Egyptian hands, as discussion of the next group of actors—the international donors—illustrates.

WATER FUNDERS

International involvement in the design and financing of water-related initiatives in Egypt has a long history. During the years of the British occupation, in the late nineteenth and early twentieth centuries, Nile control was at the heart of the British colonial project. The colonial administration expended considerable funds to establish an irrigation infrastructure that would support cotton production for textile mills back in Britain (Tvedt 2004; Derr 2009; Cookson-Hills 2013). Following the 1952 revolution, Egypt turned to the World Bank, Britain, and France to finance its first major infrastructure project—the Aswan High Dam. In a pivotal geopolitical moment, these donors withdrew from the project after three years of negotiations, leaving the Soviet Union to step in in their place (Bishop 1997). The World Bank renewed its relations with Egypt a few years later, granting its first loan in 1959 for improvements on the Suez Canal. Since that time, the bank has financed a number of projects focusing on water management and rural development. The bank remains, however, a relatively small actor in comparison to the other international donors (IEG 2009, 9–14). The dominant player, since the mid-1970s, has been the United States, which expanded its economic assistance program significantly after the signing of the Camp David Accord between Egypt and Israel in 1979 (Momani 2003). A number of European countries and Japan also maintain bilateral aid programs, and the European Union recently became a major donor (ADE 2010). Water is an important focus for donors' poverty alleviation and development efforts. Not only does it fulfill a basic livelihood need, but it is a foundation of Egypt's agricultural sector, which contributes 14 percent of the GDP and provides employment for 31 percent of the labor force.[20]

Egypt is now the third highest recipient of aid for water-related projects in the world. Between 1990 and 2004, Egypt received an average of US$168 million a year in water aid, constituting 7 percent of the annual average development assistance to the country over that same period.[21] Donor projects (mashari') have become an integral part of the everyday workings of the Ministry of Water Resources and Irrigation. Such is the degree of donor influence that one expatriate consultant described the ministry as "suffering from projectitus," which she explained as being "a sense that you need a project to do anything."

Key policy documents bear the name of the Ministry of Water Resources and Irrigation but are actually the outcome of many hours of consultancy labor and project funding. Take, for example, the National Water Resources Plan, a thick publication with crisp white pages, packed full of data, maps, and analysis (MWRI 2005a). On the glossy blue cover, the name of the ministry stands out at the top, above the title *Water for the Future*. After a preface from the minister of water and irrigation, the report provides a detailed overview of the nation's water resources, the policy framework for water management, and an in-depth study of strategies for "facing the challenge." It is, in tone, content, and title, a *national* plan. Yet the plan emerged not through a national planning process but through a Dutch-funded project.[22] Despite its title, the National Water Resources Plan is more linked to the work of international consultants than to the government's vision of its water resources and the future of those resources. As one Dutch consultant acknowledged to me, "No one in this ministry feels ownership of the plan. They can't translate it into their everyday work. . . . It is still seen as a project."

Whole units within the ministry owe their origins and continual existence to project budgets. In line with some of the main contemporary trends in international water management, there are special units focused on farmer participation (the Irrigation Advisory Service), rural women (the Gender Focal Point), integrated water resources management (the National Water Resources Plan Unit), public awareness (the Water Communication Unit), water use efficiency (the Irrigation Improvement Sector), and decentralization (the Institutional Reform Unit). When projects come to an end, the units sometimes atrophy in the absence of a budget necessary to support them. Other times, the ministry folds them into its day-to-day operations, and the markers of donor support—the well-furnished offices, promotional brochures, and up-to-date equipment—gradually fade.

Egypt's water, therefore, cannot be disconnected from those who fund water development projects and who help shape what this resource comes to be. "The ministry hasn't made any decisions for ten years," one international consultant commented to me. While this is clearly an exaggeration, it is indicative of the leverage that donors hold over ministry policy. The ministry orients its activities to fit the donors' priorities because, in the consultant's words, "If the donors want to do something, that means there will be money." This money funds dam construction, canal maintenance, pipe laying, pump installation, and weir repair to control the passage of water through the irrigation network. It finances workshops, training sessions, and outreach activities to implement changes in water governance. It is this flow of dollars and Egyptian pounds that molds and maintains the network of water flows.

Hence one of the central themes of the book is the role played by international advisors and funders in the making of Egypt's water. As Ben Orlove and Steven Caton write in their review article on water, it is no longer possible to study water without recognizing "the profound presence and involvement of the transnational community of water experts" (2010, 411). Numerous international financial institutions, international and regional organizations, bilateral donors, and international nongovernmental organizations are engaged in water-related projects in Egypt. Working alongside these funding organizations are the international management consultancy companies that provide the expatriate consultants who generally run the projects, under the leadership of a project director from the ministry and with a team of national consultants and staff.

In this book, I refer to this group of actors, collectively, as the "donors." This is how members of international development community often refer to themselves.[23] I use this collective term for ease of presentation, not to suggest that the donor community is a homogeneous one. Indeed the various donor agencies have markedly different approaches to water management, and cooperation between them is limited. As one consultant said to me, "Every donor has a niche."

The aid agency staff and consultants who run water projects draw on their experience managing projects in other parts of the world to inform their practice in Egypt. At international conferences and training workshops they discuss water management models with other policy makers, funders, and advisors. At the Fifth World Water Forum in Istanbul in 2009, a large billboard at the entrance to the conference hall proclaimed in English and Turkish, "Istanbul welcomes the Water Community": clear white words in a swathe of blue, framed by an outline of the Istanbul skyline. The idea of a global water community—a notion that many participants in the conference also alluded to—is striking. The community constitutes what Michael Goldman (2007) calls a "transnational policy network on water," made up not only of international organizations like the World Water Council, which organizes the world water forum every three years, but also representatives of states, international financial institutions, development agencies, think tanks, water corporations, and nongovernmental organizations.[24] It is a community to which membership is defined by a particular type of expertise. As someone who has studied water management at an academic institution in the United States and written a doctoral thesis on the topic, I am implicitly part of this network. So, too, are the ministry officials who have doctorates from European or American institutions. Yet most of those who staff the ministry lie outside these circles of engagement, as do the farmers who use the majority of Egypt's water.

This international group of donors, scientists, and consultants does not work alone in its efforts to improve water management in Egypt. The "water community" is an assemblage of social, biophysical, and technical worlds, an amalgam of human and nonhuman (Callon 1986a; Latour 2005). Alongside the experts are the texts, instruments, and materials that allow them to promote their particular vision of water management. This is an example of what Callon, Lascoumes, and Barthe (2009) term a "research collective." International agreements on water, such as the Dublin Statement on Water and Sustainable Development, set the parameters of *good* water management. A plethora of project documents, workshop minutes, and consultancy reports corroborate how those principles apply to the Egyptian context. Technical instruments, such as participatory water management, water pricing, and private-public partnerships, offer a menu of options for dealing with water-related problems, which are in line with current dominant paradigms in resource management. Materials like training manuals, funds, and machinery enable the translation of these ideas into practice. Influence lies not only with the experts but in the tools that they put to use in helping shape Egypt's water.

What happens to the water of the Nile as it passes through Egypt is therefore an outcome of the complex interplay between these three overlapping groups of actors—water funders, water bureaucrats, and water users. I

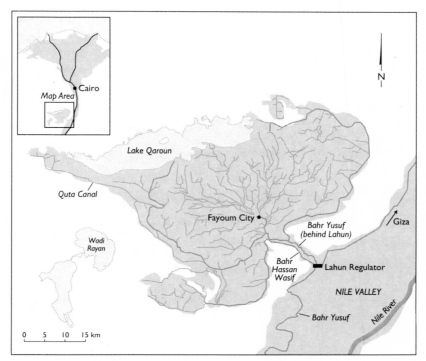

Map 1.3. Fayoum Province

introduce, now, my field site of Fayoum, where I explore how these groups interact around water and the everyday political dynamics that emerge through these interactions.

A LEAF OFF THE STEM

Fayoum buds like a small leaf off the green stem of the Nile valley. Located in a depression just west of the valley and 80km southwest of Cairo, this region of 430,000 feddan supports a population of 2.5 million (map 1.3).[25] Fayoum is one of twenty-nine provinces, known in Egypt as governorates (muhafiza). Nile water flows into the province at Lahun (25m above sea level) and drains down into Lake Qaroun, an expanse of blue—40km in length and up to 10km in width—that lies at the base of the depression (44m below sea level). Approximately 80 percent of Fayoum's population lives in rural areas and works in agriculture. The farms are small; 49 percent are less than one feddan in size and 34 percent are between one and three feddan (Moharram 2003, 43).

Fayoum's share of the Nile, which amounts to about 2.5 billion cubic meters a year, enters the province through two channels. The first is the

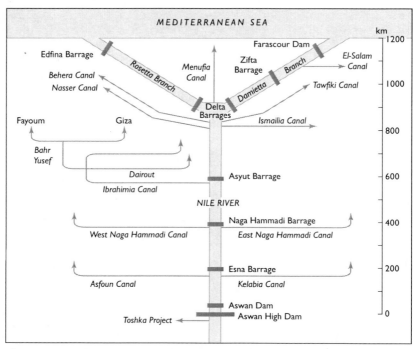

Figure 1.5. Egypt's canal system and the major control structures on the Nile.

Bahr Yusuf, a meandering channel thought to have been formed by the work of the Nile in flood some 70,000 years ago. While its origins are natural, human modifications of the Bahr Yusuf date back almost four thousand years to when it was first widened and deepened by King Amenemhat I. Around 300 BC, Ptolemy I built a barrage with sluice gates across the channel at Lahun.[26] Today a modern descendant of this ancient barrage still sits across the Bahr Yusuf, and downstream of it, the channel that is officially named the Bahr Yusuf Behind Lahun (*khalf al-lahun*) leads into the depression. The other route for water flowing into Fayoum is the Bahr Hassan Wasif, its straight line revealing its origins in the work of a mechanical excavator rather than flowing water. The two canals draw from a larger canal, also somewhat confusingly named the Bahr Yusuf, which winds its way approximately 200km up the western edge of the Nile valley. This canal is fed by water from the Ibrahimia Canal, which in turn taps the Nile just upstream of the Asyut Barrage (see figure 1.5).

Once the water enters Fayoum, officials within the Fayoum Irrigation Directorate distribute it through a network of main and branch canals. Farmers are responsible for management of the mesqas (irrigation ditches), which draw from this network through government-constructed points of offtake.[27] Fayoum's irrigation system differs from that of the Nile valley and delta in two important respects. First, due to the province's basin-shaped topography, water flows by gravity from the canals onto the fields. This is a point of contrast with the rest of Egypt where farmers have to pump water up to their fields from the canals. Second, the rotation system that divides water between the farmers takes place at the mesqa level rather than at the branch canal level. This means that whereas in other parts of Egypt, branch canals have water flowing through them for a set number of days and then are dry for a period, in Fayoum the branch canals are always (in theory) full. Water flows continuously from the branch canals into each mesqa. The farmers along each mesqa then cooperate to divide that water between them according to a rotation system (mutarfa), which specifies who will receive each of the 10,080 minutes of irrigation water in a week. Every farmer has access to a certain number of minutes of weekly irrigation water, depending on the size of his or her landholding.[28]

Sometimes people describe Fayoum as a microcosm of Egypt; it draws from a single source, the Bahr Yusuf, as Egypt draws from the Nile, and drains into Lake Qaroun as Egypt drains into the Mediterranean. Others, though, highlight Fayoum's gravity irrigation as a marker of the province's unique nature. I do not see Fayoum as being all that exceptional. Although some differences exist in the techniques of water distribution and access, the disparity is narrowing as more and more Fayoumi farmers start using pumps to supplement their gravity supply. Furthermore, the goal of farmers in Fayoum is no different than that of farmers elsewhere in Egypt—to access the water that they need to irrigate their fields. The ministry officials in Fayoum share the same responsibilities as those in other provinces for managing the irrigation system. Thus I use my ethnographic data from the fields of Fayoum and offices of the provincial irrigation directorate to ground my analysis of everyday water politics in Egypt.

WATER'S POLITICS, SCALE, AND MATERIALITY

This book draws on two main strands of literature: political ecology and science and technology studies.[29] Political ecology is an interdisciplinary field of research, which highlights the politicized nature of human interactions with the environment (see, for example, Rocheleau et al. 1996; Escobar 1999; Forsyth 2003; Robbins 2004; Biersack and Greenberg 2006; Peet et al. 2011).[30] Political ecologists see processes of environmental change as being integrally tied to socioeconomic and political dynamics, which operate on a range of scales. They emphasize the power relations that mediate control over and access to resources. Within a political ecology framework, environmental conditions and resource distribution are not static or prearranged but the contingent outcome of a series of political engagements. Whereas earlier scholars of cultural ecology explored how societies are shaped by their adaptation to the environment (e.g., Steward 1955), political ecologists study how those environments themselves are shaped by society. Contrary to critiques leveled at political ecology (e.g., Vayda and Walters 1999), this scholarship does not focus on politics to the exclusion of ecology. Rather, political ecology rests on the assumption of a dialectical relationship between nature and society (Watts and Peet 2004). In other words, political ecologists open up the category of the "environment" (by showing how politics shapes ecology), while not denying the impact of environmental dynamics on social relations (i.e., the fact that ecology shapes politics). One of the major contributions of this scholarship has been to demonstrate how many of the landscapes previously perceived as natural are, in fact, intensely managed and manipulated.[31] A related body of literature has shown how resources—those aspects of landscapes that are used for particular ends—are not a given but rather come to exist through technical, physical, and cultural practices (Ferry and Limbert 2008; Richardson and Weszkalnys 2014).

Thus I examine the water of the Nile not as a preexisting object of management but as a resource that comes into being through politically moderated interactions between multiple actors. This process is mediated by the technologies that allow different actors to control where, when, and how the water flows. Scholars of science and technology studies have long argued for the importance of taking technical artifacts seriously (Winner 1980; Pinch and Bijker 1984; Latour 1992). Technologies can be used for multiple purposes. They modify the relations between social groups. Paying close attention to technical artifacts can hence yield insights into the history and development of societies, and the contested terrain of politics and ethics (Bijker 2007; von Schnitzler 2013).

Technology is not, however, something external to society, which molds social and political relations in a deterministic way. A central tenet of the literature on the social construction of technology is the two-way relationship between society and technology. Society shapes technology as much as technology shapes society (Pinch and Bijker 1984; Callon 1986b; Hughes 1987; Bijker 1995; Kline and Pinch 1996). In the case of an irrigation system, therefore, rather than the technical component being fixed and neutral, it emerges through the interplay of social groups (Mollinga 2003). Technologies of water distribution and use are embedded in discourses and perceptions, sensory regimes and memories, practices and policies (Limbert 2001). Although I do not use a compound term such as *sociotechnical* (Uphoff 1986; Latour 1999) or *technopolitical* (Mitchell 2002), this understanding of technologies as deeply social and political—in their design, use, and development—runs through the book.

Consider, for example, a pump by a canal. At first glance, the pump may appear to be a technical object. It is made of steel. It runs on diesel. It performs a clear function: to lift water from the canal and deliver it to a field. It has a political effect, allowing the farmer to cultivate his land, earn an income, and thereby gain advantage over a farmer who cannot afford a pump to access the same amount of water. Yet look a bit closer and the pump emerges as more than an amalgam of its parts. The farmer has modified it since it came out of a factory in India, replacing part of the axle with a piece of rubber to prevent two metal parts from grinding against each other. It does not sit by the canal all the time. Instead, every time the district engineer makes his rounds, the farmer hides the pump in a nearby field. The pump has a colloquial name. The farmer calls it a *makina*, a machine, the same word he uses to describe the motorcycle that he uses to get to the fields. Thus the technology for lifting water is actually embedded in and generated by multiscaled social, cultural, economic, and political relations.

Since the early 1980s, irrigation studies have highlighted the fact that irrigation is more than just a technical matter. Irrigation systems incorporate multiple overlapping and co-constituting dimensions of hydrology, engineering, farming practices, organizational structures, sociocultural relations, and spirituality (Coward 1980; Chambers 1988; Pfaffenberger 1990; Lansing 1991; Uphoff et al. 1991; Zimmerer 2000; Gidwani 2002; Mollinga 2003). More recent articulations of a similar argument, applied generally to water rather than irrigation, come from within geography, anthropology, and science and technology studies. This literature sees water as a hybrid, which captures elements that are at once material and symbolic, natural, social, and cultural (Bakker 2002; Raffles 2002; Swyngedouw 2004; Helmreich 2011; Barnes and Alatout 2012; Sultana 2013). Building on this scholarship, I outline below the approach that I use to study water: a close focus on the everyday politics of water management, a multiscalar analysis, and an attention to water's material characteristics.

Everyday Politics

As a resource central to human livelihoods, water holds particular political import. Variably distributed in space and time and paying no heed to national boundaries, water generates plenty of points for politicized interaction. The dramatic compound *hydropolitics*, which is employed widely in both scholarly and policy work, reflects this close association (Waterbury 1979; Elhance 1999; Allan 2002a; Sneddon and Fox 2006). In fact, water is so significant that many think disputes over its use could generate interstate conflicts. This is a topic that has been hotly debated, especially with regards to the Middle East. Some argue that water wars have already taken place or are imminent (Starr 1991; Bulloch and Darwish 1993; Gleick 1994; Libiszewski 1999; Toset, Gleditsch, and Hegre 2000); others reject the notion (Wolf 1998; Allan 2002b; Selby 2005; Sowers and Toensing 2010). Despite the academic critique, though, the term still has widespread currency in both popular and political circles.[32]

Water is not only political in that its lack can lead to political conflict but also in the ways in which its manipulation can be used for political purposes. Projects to channel, dam, or reorient water's passage are visible manifestations of state power. Libya's Great Manmade River, the Panama Canal, or Three Gorges Dam in China, for example, like Egypt's Aswan High Dam, are undoubtedly projects with hydrological goals but which also serve to demonstrate those states' technical expertise. Such projects bolster not only the geopolitical position of the host state but, in many cases, that of other nations who have helped finance those projects.

Yet while the water politics literature has brought important attention to the ways in which water constitutes a nexus for contestation, in much of this scholarship the water itself is absent. As Karen Bakker (2012, 617) writes, "In the standard approach, water is largely framed as a backdrop to politics: an inert resource, struggles over the control of which are often the source of (at times violent) human conflicts." In relegating water to a backdrop, this literature fails to consider where the water actually comes from and how, when, and where it flows. My argument in this book is that the politics of water lies precisely in these daily practices of moving, blocking, storing, redirecting, and utilizing water. This is a politics that Wiebe Bijker (2007, 123) describes as "Politics with a lower-case 'p': not the politics of politicians, but a broad range of politics from micro to macro scale, and relating as much to the power of humans, as to the power of ideas and things." It is a politics that takes place in the everyday, a realm of practice that is often the site of some of the most significant political action (Scott 1987; Özyürek 2006).

To examine this politics, I employ an ethnographic lens. I direct this lens not only at those who manage water but also at the knowledge and technologies they use and the water itself. This means adopting an ethnographic approach whether with farmers in their fields, engineers by dams, policy makers in government offices, consultants in donor workshops, or international water experts at conferences. I position the book, therefore, alongside other ethnographic works on water (Lansing 1991; Gelles 2000; Alley 2002; Orlove 2002; Raffles 2002; Mosse 2003; Strang 2004; Rodríguez 2006; Rademacher 2011; Muehlmann 2013). By painting a detailed picture of how water flows through diverse sites, the book reveals the day-to-day political dynamics through which this resource comes into being.

Scales of Water

Water inhabits multiple scales. It is at once local (a farmer's irrigation ditch), national (Egypt's water supply), international (the Nile Basin), and global (the hydrological cycle). Yet much of the social science literature on water is characterized by a single scale of analysis. Many scholars have focused on the international dimension and explored the political dynamics of sharing transboundary water resources (for the Middle East, see Waterbury 1979; Bulloch and Darwish 1993; Hillel 1994; Kliot 1994; Scheumann and Schiffler 1998; Amery and Wolf 2000; Allan 2002b; Waterbury 2002). This literature has provided insights into the negotiations between national policy makers over shared waters and the internal political factors driving countries' water development strategies. But in general it has given little consideration to the practices and perspectives of those who actually use the water.[33] At the other end of the scalar spectrum, there is an extensive literature on local water management. This literature has examined patterns of water use within particular communities or along individual canals (Geertz 1983; Hopkins 1987; Guillet 1992; Gelles 2000; Mosse 2003; Trawick 2003; Baker 2005). It has emphasized the processes of cooperation that emerge around water, providing ample evidence to refute Hardin's (1968) Tragedy of the Commons thesis. Yet in their small-scale focus, these studies have often failed to connect community dynamics to wider processes of water distribution and use.

In this book, therefore, I bring together local, national, and international realms, drawing on the example set by other multisited ethnographies (e.g., Tsing 2005; West 2006; Escobar 2008). I track water as it infiltrates the soil of an Egyptian farmer's field, but also as it appears in a colorful graphic on a PowerPoint slide at an international water conference. I move back and forth across space, from local to global, nation to river basin, surface to subsurface. This is an analysis that draws together the dynamics of water policy making in government offices with those of water management and use in the fields, by asking how water moves and is moved through space and time.

Scale is not only a methodological tool, however. It is also an ontological proposition, a particular way of understanding the world (Sayre 2005). In his book *In Amazonia*, Hugh Raffles writes, "It is by transgressing the conventions of human space that rivers reveal the poverty of scalar categories. They are, as Bruno Latour has written of railroad tracks, 'local at all points,' while being, definitively, unstoppably translocal" (Raffles 2002, 181). There is something about water that runs counter to the idea of a world ordered into local, national, and global spaces. Scholars have highlighted the fact that scale, as a notion of the world as a nested hierarchy, fails to capture the complexity of multiple sociotemporal configurations (Delaney and Leitner 1997). Water, as it flows across space, provides an apt illustration of this.

Yet rather than using water's slippery nature as a reason to reject scale altogether, as some scholars have called for (Marston, Jones, and Woodward 2005), I maintain that a multiscalar approach is a valid one for analyzing water politics. Scale matters. It sets the bounds of interaction, the possibilities of dissent, and the potential for influencing a course of action. A ministry official's voice in Cairo carries authority in part because she can talk about *national* policy making. To an international donor schooled in participatory approaches to development, a farmer's perspective, as proprietor of the *local* realm, holds particular import. A report written by a multinational agency can make bold recommendations and declare that countries adopt those recommendations precisely because it comes from an *international* source.

At the same time, as Neil Smith (1992) argued, these scalar categories are not absolute but are socially produced. Indeed practices and discourses of water management are one of the ways in which politically significant scales are generated, consolidated, and maintained (Biro 2007; Harris and Alatout 2010). A donor project to establish water user associations aims to build a *local* realm of water management. The ministry's practices of engineering the flow of water through the country help create Egypt's *national* space. The lectures, workshops, and debates about water taking place in conference halls around the world work to forge an *international* domain of water expertise.

I therefore use the flow of water as a starting point and follow the water through different scales of analysis. In doing so, I demonstrate the multiple actors who seek to influence where the water goes and what it becomes.

Water's Materiality

Recent years have seen a "material turn" in the environmental literature, as in many fields of social science scholarship (Bakker and Bridge 2006; Richardson and Weszkalyns 2014). This has brought a renewed focus on materiality, defined by Noel Castree (1995, 13) as "the ontological reality of those entities we term 'natural' and the active role those entities play in making history and geography." Materiality, here, is not an abstract concept but a way of bringing attention to the material in question and its properties (Ingold 2007). At the heart of this work is a premise that the physical nature of nonhuman things matters to understanding the social and political dynamics that evolve around them. Whether or not such things can be considered (nonhuman) actors in their own right is a matter of debate (Callon 1986a; Pickering 1992; de Laet and Mol 2000; Latour 2005), but the key point is simply that they make a difference. The material properties of a thing shape the kinds of apparatus employed to extract, process, transport, and utilize it. In the process, they variously facilitate, inhibit, or disrupt forms of society-environment interaction and set the terrain of political possibilities (Braun and Whatmore 2010; Mitchell 2011; Barry 2013).

Taking seriously the materiality of water means attending closely to water's physical characteristics—its ability to flow, reflect, absorb, collect, divide, dissolve, disperse, transform, and erode (Bull 2011). Such characteristics distinguish water from the more solid (although nonetheless far from static) forests and conservation areas that have been the focus of much of the political ecology scholarship. As a number of scholars have shown, these material qualities of water shape social and political formations, enabling certain connections while constraining others (Bakker 2004; Sneddon 2007; Hughes 2010; Anand 2011; Bear and Bull 2011).

This does not mean a return to environmental determinism, though, because materials themselves are "historical products of material, representational, and symbolic practices" (Bakker and Bridge 2006, 18). An emphasis on the materiality of water is thus not in tension with my understanding of Egypt's water as something that is made and not a given. Instead, it means tracking the water as it flows through canals, lingers behind dams, covers a field, moves down between soil particles, passes through crops, and evapotranspires back into the atmosphere. My conception of materiality, therefore, incorporates not only the climatological dynamics, hydrological processes, and agroecological practices that determine how, where, and when the water moves, but also the engineering technologies that enable, moderate, and constrain those dynamics, processes, and practices.

Throughout the book, different dimensions of water's material nature come to the fore.[34] Water's propensity to erode earthen banks influences the amount of water that engineers are willing to release through control structures. Water's fluidity affects the forms of governance that evolve around it. Water's ability to transform greens the desert while other land becomes barren. Water's capacity to dissolve and carry salts renders drainage technologies vital to prevent soil salinization. Hence water's materiality both creates and hampers various potentials for political action as different people work to mold the flow of water to meet their needs. In the final part of this chapter, I turn to the ethnographic methods that I employ to explore the spaces of political possibility that emerge in and around water.

FOLLOWING A FLOW

It is a Ramadan evening in October 2007.[35] From the doorstep of my house in the village of Warda, in the western part of Fayoum, I watch the sun go down.[36] People are heading home quickly for iftar, the meal with which they break their fast. On the other side of the road runs an irrigation ditch. This evening, there is not much water flowing through it. One of my neighbors squats beside the ditch, washing some clothes. Her daughter toddles over, and she strips her to dunk her in for a bath.

Behind the ditch is a field of clover and my neighbor Assam's plant nursery, where he grows bougainvillea, oleander, cacti, and ornamental shrubs. The sun makes its way down—a warm yellow, pinks to purples. Young boys from Assam's household return from the fields with the herd of sheep and goats that they have been watching graze. Some jostle to drink from the ditch; others kick up the dirt. Men walk by on their way back from the fields with their sons, leading water buffalo, cows, and donkeys home for the night. Assam's brothers, who work with him in construction, arrive home from work, three deep on a motorcycle.

The sun dips below the horizon, leaving the sound of iftar in the air, pots clapping, raised voices, light spilling out from houses over the street. Now the palm trees form silhouettes against the purply blue sky. It is quiet save the sound of people in their houses. There is no traffic on the dirt road and no noise from the asphalt road. Even the dogs are silent, momentarily content, sneaking inside to grab tidbits from the meal.

I first arrived in Warda in the spring of 2007. Warda is a village of some 3,000 people near the western edge of Fayoum Province. The village dates back to the 1940s when a member of one of Fayoum's large landowning families, Ibrahim Wali, bought land in this area. A handful of sharecropping families came to farm Wali's land, eager to escape the more densely settled areas further east. Over time, these families gradually purchased land from Wali's descendants. The village expanded, and new families moved in. In the mid-1970s, a French potter built a house in the village, followed by a steady stream of Egyptian and foreign artists, poets, authors, translators, and academics. As the news has circulated of this peaceful location, free of Cairo's traffic and polluted air, Warda has become a popular location for weekend houses for expatriates working in the city. Golden mud-domed villas have sprouted up around the village, cloistered behind high walls. Branches of purple bougainvillea and white jasmine trail over the edge of those walls, hinting at the lush gardens, elegant patios, and swimming pools that lie beyond. The villas dwarf the flat-roofed cement homes of the farming families, which they sit alongside. These houses are not walled in. Instead, they have wide front porches, where people sit in the early evening, enjoying the cooler air and calling out to passersby, "Ahlan, tishrabi shai!" meaning "Welcome. Come and have tea!"

I chose Warda as the base for my fieldwork for pragmatic reasons. Since the government restricts access to rural Egypt for foreigners, Warda was one of the few places where I could live as a foreign woman without arousing the attention of government authorities. Over a twelve-month period from the summer of 2007 through 2008, I rented a house that one of the builders in the village, Assam, built for me next to his house. As a neighbor and living in Assam's house, I was welcomed into Assam's household, which was a constant hive of activity, occupied by his mother and father, wife, three brothers, their wives, and eighteen children.

The presence of the Cairean and expatriate community makes Warda in some ways an anomaly. The village has markedly less garbage in its streets than other villages in Fayoum. Its supply of drinking water and electricity is more reliable. Almost every farming family has a member working in the construction industry, helping build new villas, or employed as a guard, cook, housekeeper, or gardener in one of the two hundred or so existing villas. In other ways, though, Warda is not so different from other villages in

Egypt. Certainly the fact that farming households have an additional non-farming source of income is not atypical.

Although I was unlike most of the other expatriates who visit Warda in my desire to spend time with the local people, visit their houses, and learn about agriculture, many of the villagers seemed to welcome this interest. My ability to speak Arabic and my conservative dress helped these interactions. I developed relations, in particular, with two of the largest extended families in the village—the family of my neighbor, Assam, and that of Abu Khaled, an older, respected member of the community who was introduced to me by a professor from the American University of Cairo at the start of my fieldwork. During the year that I lived in Warda, and on subsequent visits in April 2009 and November 2011, I spent a considerable amount of time with both families, joining them for meals and cups of tea, attending family celebrations, and visiting family members in neighboring villages.

Fields surround Warda on every side. As a single woman, however, it was not altogether easy to "go to the field" (ruh al-ghayt). While women do carry out agricultural work, the fields in this area are a male-dominated space. When I walked through the fields on my own, any encounters I had were mediated by people's surprise at what a foreign lady, an agnabiya, was doing there. I therefore largely limited my time in the fields to either going to visit farmers whom I knew or accompanying them when they went to work. It would have been inappropriate, though, to go with male farmers on a daily basis. I also did not wish to impose on farmers, who invariably insisted on hosting me as a guest in their fields and preparing tea and food, which they otherwise might not have taken the time or money to do. So I focused, instead, on being in the fields during times in the agricultural calendar when particular work was taking place, such as the weeding of onions, onion transplant, collection of chamomile flowers, or peanut harvest. Sometimes I would participate, if it was a task that girls or women typically help with; other times I would just observe.

While my gender posed some constraints to my fieldwork, it also served in my favor. People in the United States often ask me if it was difficult to work as a woman in Egypt. On the contrary, I was treated with respect and was grateful for the care people took to ensure my safety and well-being. As a woman, I was able to access women's spaces within their homes. As a foreigner, I was able to sit and talk with groups of men to whom I was not related, in a way that would not be common for rural women from Fayoum.

Over the time that I lived in Warda, I gained insights into the priorities and perspectives of the men, women, and children involved in farming. My observations from interacting on a daily basis with people from the village helped me see beyond the singular "farmer" category that appears in water policy documents to a diverse population, concerned on a day-to-day basis with what will be for dinner, the price of bread, cost of agricultural chemicals, market for different crops, paying bills, saving for the next child's wedding, planning the following child's engagement, dealing with health problems, buying medicine, solving interfamily disputes, resolving unhappy marriages, and caring for young children. In fact I found that farming households generally talk much more about these issues than they do about water.[37] As a substance that runs through all aspects of daily life, water is so apparent and obvious it does not need constant discussion. The conversations that people had during times of water-related problems, though, provided especially valuable data, such as when the supply was low in the summer, a canal was blocked, or a mesqa needed repairing.

My story is not, however, only about those who use water in the fields. To access other points in the network of water management and manipulation, I became affiliated with a donor-funded water project. Unlike most of the donor projects, which are run out of the Cairo headquarters of the ministry, this project was based in the offices of the Fayoum Irrigation Directorate in the provincial capital of Fayoum City. During my affiliation (from June 2007 through July 2008), I spent between three and four days a week with the project. Some days I stayed in the office, talking to project staff and observing conversations between farmers visiting the office and ministry personnel. When workshops, meetings, and training sessions took place involving project staff, consultants, ministry officials, and farmers, I attended and observed. Other days I accompanied project staff or ministry engineers on their trips to the field to meet with farmers. This allowed me to see some of the variety within Fayoum Province and to visit different rural communities in a way that would not have been possible as an independent researcher. At the same time, arriving in a white pickup truck, emblematic of the ministry, farmers who I met through these visits inevitably saw me either as part of the bureaucracy that delivers their water, so with anger or hope depending on their particular situation, or as a donor, with funds or influence potentially at my fingertips. The conversations I had in these contexts were moderated by these associations. Nonetheless, the meetings were rich sites for observation of the interactions between farmers and ministry officials.

Due to a good relationship with the foreign project manager and her Egyptian counterpart (both female), I was accepted by the project staff quite unproblematically. Nobody seemed to see me as a threat, and my incessant note taking was seen as a curiosity rather than a challenge. Most in the project bracketed me as a "gender person." Being a woman, they assumed that I would be interested primarily in women's issues, which is what they understand gender to mean. In return for my affiliation with the project, I conducted a survey of fifty male and female farmers and wrote a report on gender and water in Fayoum for the project. At first my association with the gender component of the project made it easier for me to accompany the female project workers on their trips to the field, but over time I forged relations with the male project staff and so was able to go with them to meet with male farmers as well.

Affiliation with the donor project helped me make contact with high-level officials in the central offices of the ministry in Cairo for interviews. In addition, the project manager facilitated my access to the community of donors working on water issues in Egypt and international water consultants who advise and manage those projects. Interviews conducted with these people in 2007–2008, and during follow-up trips in 2009 and 2011, allowed me to explore the perspectives of those who interact with Egypt's water in different ways, through making policy decisions and funding water projects. In donor project offices, I gained access to some of the extensive literature of project reports, commissioned studies, evaluations, and workshop minutes on water-related topics.[38] I also visited other donor-funded projects in the Nile delta and met agricultural investors working in that area.

The final component of my research sought to gain an insight into the dialogue taking place within the international water policy network and how that dialogue affects water-related initiatives in Egypt. I conducted participant observation at the Fifth and Sixth World Water Forums in Istanbul and Marseille (in March 2009 and March 2012). These weeklong events each brought together over 30,000 representatives of governments, international agencies, nongovernmental organizations, research institutes, and private water companies from around the world. In addition, I attended the Second Arab Water Forum in Cairo in November 2011, a smaller meeting of around 300 water experts, both from the region and from international organizations. In conjunction with the interviews that I conducted in Cairo with international and bilateral donors and foreign consultants working on water projects in Egypt, this piece of my research allowed me to explore how the making of Egypt's water is tied into much larger circulations of management paradigms, funding, and expertise.

CHAPTER 2

The Nile's Nadir THE PRODUCTION OF SCARCITY

The sky darkens. "Look at the sky! It's all clouds." The murmur ripples through the office of the irrigation directorate. The clouds open. Soft drops of rain fall on the dusty street outside. Everyone is excited. All work stops as people go to look out of the window, breathing in the scent of moistened pavement. Their job may be to manage water, but to these irrigation engineers, water falling from the sky remains a novelty. Children run around outside, shrieking with joy. The man next to me comments, "For us, rain is a blessing (kheir)." Four minutes later, the droplets cease and the blue skies return. Rain is a fleeting occurrence here in Fayoum. Sometimes a few drops, then gone. Occasionally dramatic storms; other years, no rain at all. As is the case throughout a huge swathe of Egypt south of Cairo, Fayoum receives an average of less than 5mm rainfall a year. Yet while little water falls as rain, through the center of this arid land flows nearly 60 billion cubic meters of water a year—the waters of the Nile on the final stretch of its long journey to the sea. Abundance side-by-side with scarcity.

The idea that water is scarce in the Middle East is one that has received considerable attention in international circles, academic analyses, and the press. If scarcity is measured in figures of water availability per capita, as it is in one of the most popular indicators developed by Malin Falkenmark (1989), then the twin specter of a limited water supply and rapidly growing population poses an imminent crisis.[1] At the same time, recent years have seen many of the international institutions adopt more nuanced understandings of water scarcity. There is a new recognition that social, political, and economic factors impact both how much water is available for use (supply) and how it is used (demand) (World Bank 2007). There are now multiple definitions of scarcity that distinguish between biophysical and economic water scarcity (Gleick et al. 2002; Rijsberman 2006) and raise the need to look beyond national indicators to regional and local patterns of water access (Alatout 2000). Critical studies have revealed that rather than being a natural characteristic, water scarcity may be the outcome of certain government policies (Barnes 2009), technological choices (Gyawali and Dixit 2010), or regulatory regimes (Bakker 2000). Scarcity may be socially constructed for political ends, as part of a project of nation-building (Alatout 2008), to protect particular groups of farmers' interests (Budds 2008), rationalize resource privatization (Kaika 2003), or justify large infrastructural developments (Mehta 2005; Jairath 2010). This literature has highlighted the need to ask questions about who uses water and for what purpose.

In this chapter, however, I look not at the *construction* of scarcity but at the *production* of scarcity. I use the latter term to focus on the physical acts that result in water not flowing to a particular site.[2] Scarcity is not generated in the realm of discourse, by the way in which people talk about scarcity, but through very material interactions with the flow of water. This is not to say that constructions are insignificant. Framing Egypt's water as scarce is politically advantageous on several levels. Egyptian politicians can use scarcity to argue for an increased supply of water from the Nile; farmers can use scarcity to lobby for more water. Indeed the construction and production of scarcity are closely interlinked. How we see the world shapes how we interact with and transform it, which in turn influences what we see (Demeritt 2002). Yet drawing attention to what I call the production of scarcity helps elucidate the everyday practices that actually determine what water flows where. In line with scholarship on the production of nature, which has shown how nature is not external to society but an outcome of social and economic relations (Smith 1984; Roberts and Emel 1992; Castree 1995), the presence or absence of water is not a given but is produced through particular sets of social, technical, and political interactions (Bakker 2000; Birkenholtz 2009).

I seek a close understanding of how water scarcity is variously experienced by following the flow of water through Egypt's landscape on a daily basis. To appreciate the times and places where water comes to be insufficient, there is a need to understand where the water comes from and how it moves through the system. This requires looking across multiple scales at the techniques of control, modes of use, and places of blockage and at the actors who are able to exert agency at these different scales. It is in the quantities and directions of flow, in the levels of water in different sections of the canal system, that the politics of resource scarcity surface.

This chapter examines the technologies and decision-making processes that generate a situation that farmers call *mafish mai*, no water.[3] I start with farmers in the fields of Fayoum. This is the place where they face scarcity.[4] A farmer goes to irrigate and finds his ditch empty; the crops wither; a harvest falls short; his daughter's wedding plans are put off until the next year. In the first part of the chapter, I trace the roots of that scarcity to acts of water manipulation at local, provincial, national, and international scales. The second part of the chapter examines some of the ways in which government officials, international donors, and farmers are working to solve scarcity through a range of devices that seek to intervene in the flow of water in different ways.

Through this analysis, I show how the process of making Egypt's water is as much about determining where the water *does not* flow as it is about where it *does*. This is a process in which society and nature, politics and ecology, are deeply intertwined. Different groups within society employ a variety of technologies to mold the flow of water through the landscape. In turn, the use of those technologies and resultant patterns of water distribution shape social, political, and economic relations.

FLOWS OF SCARCITY

Exhausted Waters, Fatigued Farmers

Abu Ragib's fields lie a kilometer or so north of the branch canal. A meter-wide mesqa (irrigation ditch) links his fields to the canal. Water flows continuously into the mesqa through a narrow slit between two blocks of concrete built into the canal's bank, which engineers refer to as a Fayoum-type broad crested weir. (In some other offtakes, a pipe instead of a weir channels water from the canal into the mesqa.) The width of the opening is set by the ministry, which is responsible for installing the offtakes. Ministry engineers determine that width, according to the area of land that is to be irrigated through the offtake. Abu Ragib's irrigation turn comes every Friday, between 1 and 3 P.M. Just beforehand, he walks up the mesqa to his neighbor's land. At the stroke of 1, as his neighbor blocks off the flow of water onto his land, Abu Ragib removes the dam of mud, sticks, and rocks that he has built across the mesqa.[5] The water starts to flow down to his land. Breaking a gap in the earth bund that borders his field, he directs

Figure 2.1. Irrigating a field. Photograph by the author.

water onto his crops. For the next two hours, through a process of building up and breaking down earthen dams, Abu Ragib floods his fields, piece by piece. This is how farmers in Fayoum access water that has fallen as rain on East African slopes and been channeled over thousands of kilometers through the Nile and a network of canals. This is the point at which they experience scarcity.

Three moments, a common theme: scarcity. I am observing a large meeting in a government building in Fayoum City. The head irrigation officials are sitting on a stage in front of about forty farmers. A woman at the back of the room, wearing a blue *galabiya* (the long tunic commonly worn by men and women in rural Egypt), stands up. She tries to speak but gets shouted down by others who are also trying to express their grievances. She waits a minute, then walks up to the front, where the head officials are sitting. She is irate. For two years she has had no water in her canal. No water (*mafish mai*)! She tells the officials that she has had no option but to buy water.[6]

The second moment, another meeting, this time in the reception room of a *sheikh al-balad* (a village leader who is appointed by the Ministry of the Interior). We are sitting on armchairs, once ornate and grand, now dirty and worn out. I am with community organizers from the ministry, who are here to explain to this village leader about the water user associations that the ministry is establishing (see chapter 3). The man interrupts the community organizers' explanation. "All I want is water, that's all, so that I can get the land ready for cultivation." He raises his voice, frustrated. "If you went to the canal now, you would see that there is no water in the canal. We've been complaining for ages (min zaman). We're tired. I myself am tired. We're at our wits' end!"[7]

The third moment, a conversation with a friend of mine, Abu Khaled. We are talking over cups of sweet tea one summer evening. The crops are not doing well, he tells me, because of the heat. It is hotter than it has been in the past. There is not enough water. The crops are tired.

Each of these farmers faces a situation of scarcity. There is mafish mai, no water. This does not necessarily mean that the canals are empty. There may still be a low flow along their muddy base, among the weeds. But it does mean that when the farmers' irrigation turn arrives—when they go to claim the number of minutes to which they are entitled in the rotation— they open up the mesqa, but no water comes. Or not enough water comes to flood their fields. The farmers' crops do not get to drink. People are tired; their water is tired; their crops are tired.[8] This is not a gendered problem. Both male and female farmers face scarcity. It is also not a problem in Fayoum alone. According to a national survey, 71 percent of farmers find the water in their mesqas to be insufficient during summer months (El-Zanaty 2001, 7).

Scarcity is written in the landscape in fields left barren, without the water needed to cultivate them. In other places it is written in more subtle ways: newly planted olive trees where formerly there was a field of cotton; sorghum instead of rice; a less water-needy crop in place of one that requires more water. Scarcity is relative. For some farmers, it can mean that they are unable to grow any crops at all; for others, it can mean that they are not able to grow their crops of choice.

There is a pattern to this scarcity. Those at the ends of the canals are generally those who receive the least water. But even upstream farmers growing water-intensive crops like rice may consider their water to be scarce. In one meeting between farmers and ministry officials, a man started to complain about how his rice was suffering because of a lack of water. Someone at the back of the room interrupted him: "He talks about rice, but we don't have rice or wheat. I don't want to grow rice. I just want to cultivate my land!" Those at the ends of the canals ("below" [taht] as they say in Arabic) may have no water at all. Those at the heads of the canals ("above" [fowq]) are fortunate to receive the water first, but still may not have enough water to grow the crops they would like. Both face a type of scarcity.

There is a temporality to the tiredness. Some people face scarcity year-round: notably two of the three moments cited above were from winter months. But problems are much more widespread in the summer, when high temperatures mean that crops require more water than they do in the winter. Potential evapotranspiration (which is the amount that a green crop would use if limitless water were available) in Fayoum during July (224.8 million m³) is almost four times more than it is in December (56.4 million m³) (Wolters et al. 1989, 115). Many farmers, as a result, only have enough water to cultivate part of their land during the summer. Some are unable to cultivate their land at all.

The root of this scarcity lies in the particular constellation of technical apparatus and decision making that determine the flow and also the lack of flow in each time and place. An empty ditch in Fayoum may be linked to actions taken at a number of points within the irrigation system: along the mesqa, at the point of offtake from the canal into the mesqa, along the branch and main canals, or at the entry of water into Fayoum. To highlight the linkages between these actions and the materialization of scarcity, I take each of these points in turn.

First, if a farmer accesses water from the mesqa outside his turn in the rotation, he takes another farmer's water, causing localized scarcity. The farmer whose turn it is goes to the mesqa and finds it empty or the flow much depleted. This is quite common, especially in the summer, and is a source of conflict between farmers. Once walking in the fields with Abu Khaled, we came across a woman looking out over a field of sorghum and watching her two cows graze. Abu Khaled approached her, angrily, without any sort of greeting. "It won't do to cut off someone else's water! *Ma yan-fash!* It is wrong, *'aib.*" The woman responded that she had no choice; she was worried about her crops dying. As we walked away, Abu Khaled told me that this woman, who is responsible for farming seven qirat (just under a third of a feddan) as her husband is working in Saudi Arabia, took another farmer's water. He says people quite often take water out of turn in the summer, but it is just not acceptable. Everyone has their turn.

The second place where scarcity may be generated is at the point where the mesqa draws from the irrigation network. If the breadth of the weir crest or diameter of the pipe offtake is too narrow, not enough water will flow out of the canal to feed all the land along the mesqa. This can happen when the ministry's records for how much land is being cultivated from

Figure 2.2. Rice cultivation in eastern Fayoum. Photograph by the author.

an offtake are inaccurate. Where there is informal agricultural expansion along a mesqa (see chapter 4), for example, this is not reflected in the government's records, and therefore the offtake crest or pipe will be too small to channel water sufficient to irrigate all that land.

Third, tracing back from the point of offtake, scarcity in one part of Fayoum may be linked to the way in which water is distributed around the province through the main and branch canals. Diversions to reclaim desert lands generate scarcity on downstream reaches (see chapter 4). Farmers' crop choice also has a significant impact, given the marked variation in crops' water needs. High rates of extraction on upstream parts of canals for water-needy crops reduce the amount of water flowing on to downstream farmers.

Rice is a particularly significant crop in generating patterns of inequality along canals. Requiring more than $7,000\text{m}^3$ of water per feddan over its growing season, in comparison, for example, with sorghum, which needs less than $3,000\text{m}^3$, rice is a scarcity machine (FWMP 2006a, 9). Driving around Fayoum in June, the rice paddies are conspicuous, the green blades of rice poking above a glistening layer of water that covers the soil. Since the removal of government crop quotas as part of the agricultural liberalization program in the 1980s, rice has become a very popular cash crop.

The area cultivated with rice has doubled. Farmers can make large profits from growing rice; many also think that growing such a water-intensive crop leaches excess salts from the soil and so improves soil quality (they refer to rice cultivation as "washing" [*ghasal*] or "cleaning" [*nuzuf*] the land) (Barnes 2013b).

Only along the upstream reaches of the main canals, in the eastern part of Fayoum, is there enough water for rice cultivation. To access the water necessary to flood their fields, rice farmers sometimes persuade ministry officials to widen their mesqa offtake. Other times, they find a way to obtain water unofficially by buying or renting a pump and using it to lift water directly from a branch canal or drainage ditch. Although not all the water applied to the rice fields is lost in evapotranspiration—some drains back into the system—downstream farmers still feel the impact of these high rates of withdrawal. Not only does rice need a lot of water but its growing season falls in the summer months when pressure on water resources is most pronounced. On canals where lots of farmers grow rice along upstream sections, there is little water left for farmers downstream to grow anything.

Officials in the Fayoum Irrigation Directorate are particularly keen to use rice to explain water scarcity as it refocuses discontented farmers' wrath onto their peers. I attended one meeting in which the atmosphere deteriorated rapidly. The farmers in the room were angry. One man strode up to where the ministry official was sitting at a table and towered over him, shaking his fist. "We have a calamity (*karsa*) on the canal!" he yelled. "We are at the end. We are dying!" The official tried to appease the crowd, but could not resist mentioning their culpability. "I know you have a water problem. I've seen it myself," he said. "I know there is no water in the canal. A big part of the problem comes from The Irrigation [the ministry]. But also a big part of the problem is the people. For example, lots of people grow rice. Some say they only grow a qirat of rice, but they are actually growing a feddan. One feddan of rice would grow three feddan of other crops!" The crowd erupted in more shouts. Those who are able to access enough water to grow rice, one way or other, are not willing to relinquish it.

High rates of water extraction for rice cultivation have become such a problem that the ministry has introduced a policy to decrease the area of rice cultivation by a third, from over 1.8 million feddan to 1.2 million feddan. Using quotas and fines to deter farmers from cultivating rice outside sanctioned areas, the policy successfully limited cultivation to just 1.1 million feddan in 2010. The following year, however, in the aftermath of the revolution, neither ministry officials nor the police were willing to go out into the fields and enforce the ban. As a result, the cultivated area rebounded back to 1.8 million acres, creating renewed stress on the water supply (Mansour 2011). Since then, officials have reaffirmed the new government's commitment to rice area controls, but the degree to which they will enforce this policy is yet to be seen (Mansour and Beillard 2012).

Another way in which scarcity may be linked to how water moves through the province is if there is a rupture in the line of flow somewhere along a main or branch canal. Since part of the irrigation system relies on the reuse of drainage water (see chapter 5), if a pumping station that lifts water from a drainage ditch is not working for some reason, then this can lead to a lack of water in an irrigation canal. Blockages have a similar effect. Sometimes these blockages are deliberate. The ministry may block off a canal for maintenance work or to channel water into the drinking water supply system.[9] Farmers may (illegally) dam a canal using the trunk of a palm tree to raise the level of water in their canal section so that more water flows into their offtake. Other times the blockages are unintentional. Weeds, sediment, and solid waste accumulate over time and can end up clogging a canal. Now that there is no longer a period of high flows each year to scour out the riverbed and irrigation channels, removing sediment is a constant challenge for the ministry. The ministry has replaced the erosive power of the annual flood with excavators, which move along the canals during the annual maintenance period, removing blockages. This maintenance is critical to sustaining the flow of water. Where the maintenance regime fails, though, the obstructions grow and impede the flow of water to certain canal sections.

Moving back a step further in the system, the fourth potential point of scarcity generation lies at the Lahun Regulator (see map 1.3). This is the place where the ministry decides how much water should enter Fayoum and how much should continue on to other provinces. This is a decision based on a national scale of analysis, which weighs Fayoum's water needs in contrast to those of other provinces. The idea that there is simply not enough water flowing into Fayoum for all the farmers is commonly stated by both farmers and officials in the province. They are well aware of Fayoum's position as a downstream (taht) province. "We are a province at the end of the Bahr Yusuf Canal. Water comes a long way before it reaches Fayoum," said one engineer in response to a farmer's complaint about water shortages. "Fundamentally, the water coming from the top is little, so what can I do?" said another engineer. It is not surprising that the local officials are keen to locate the source of the water problem out of their hands and to displace responsibility onto others. By positioning themselves as lacking in agency over the making of the resource, they seek to divert the farmers' displeasure onto others.

The central ministry only has a limited volume of water available to allocate between the provinces. It makes those allocation decisions based on its estimates of each province's water needs. So it may be that the ministry simply does not know how large the demand for irrigation water is within Fayoum and thus how much water the province needs. As the ministry calculates water requirements according to the cultivated area with official water use rights, but some farmers cultivate land without official permits (see chapter 4), the province's water will inevitably flow out over an area larger than that for which it is intended. Yet even if the ministry did know the full extent of Fayoum's water demands, it is by no means certain that it would increase the province's water allocation. Policy makers' prioritizations are shaped not only by their calculations of water needs but also by the political weight of different provinces.

Thus there are multiple points where people carrying out everyday acts can generate scarcity. Each of these acts contributes to the making of Egypt's water by determining the times and spaces of resource absence and presence. Agency, in this case, comes from the knowledge of where and how to intervene in the flow of water to get it to flow to a particular site and away from another. The ability to exert control derives from access to different means of intervention, from use of a pump to entry to a meeting at which key water distribution decisions are made. Some interventions are small in scale, like building an earth dam or planting a field of rice, while others engage in larger scales of practice, such as an order to a regulator operator on a canal that feeds a whole region. To fully understand the situation of *mafish mai*, no water, though, requires a closer look at how water moves through the Nile system and the ways in which different actors work to monitor and regulate that movement.

Leveling the Flow

The flow of water through Egypt is inseparable from the operation of the barrages, regulators, weirs, gates, and pipes that control its journey. Along the course of the Nile, operators adjust the settings on the gates to moderate the passage of water through a series of barrages (see figure 1.5). The ministry draws water from upstream of each barrage and diverts it into twenty-four main canals. The gate operators receive their instructions from the Central Administration for Water Distribution, which calculates the volume of water that each irrigation directorate is to receive. In theory, the central administration computes day-to-day requirements according to the cropping patterns submitted by the agricultural departments. In practice, the quality of that data is limited, so the process tends to be a more approximate one, based largely on historical allocation patterns, adjusted according to complaints received in the past. Donors have sponsored initiatives to improve the distribution system, but communication problems between and within the ministries of agriculture and irrigation still hamper the ability to match supply closely with demand.[10] A water expert from USAID told me about a conference he helped organize that brought together water managers from two provinces. The director of one irrigation directorate asked an official from the central administration, "Why do you send us water in October? The farmers don't need water then." The official responded, "Well no one told us!"

Within the irrigation directorates, the ministry distributes water based on the level of water in each canal section. This height measurement is a proxy for the volume of water flowing down the canal. Using marble gauges (rukhame) mounted on the weirs, water managers and users monitor where the water is flowing. These height measurements are the basis for determining what adjustments should be made to the system so that each area receives sufficient water.[11]

District engineers play a central role in the daily operation of this system. I first met Hassan, a former district engineer, in June 2007 when he was seconded to the donor project that I was affiliated with. Always well dressed, in clean slacks and neatly pressed shirts, Hassan comes from a large village in Fayoum and a modest background. Now in his early thirties, Hassan has worked for the ministry since he graduated with a degree in engineering from Fayoum University. He was only twenty-three, fresh out of college, when he was appointed district engineer for Quta, the westernmost irrigation district in Fayoum. Although the position holds quite a lot of authority, it is not atypical for district engineers today to be young and inexperienced. Hassan found the work satisfying and liked being able to, in his own words, "make a difference." After four years on the job, though, he was fed up with the long hours, poor wages (less than LE300 a month), and farmers' complaints. Hassan transferred within the ministry and is now a supervising engineer in the ministry's Irrigation Advisory Service, at the same time as he studies for a master's degree.

One warm day in March 2008 I traveled with Hassan around the district of Quta. Hassan told me that his most important job as district engineer was to check the water levels. Each day the bahhars (gatekeepers) would call him and report the levels at critical points along the canal, which Hassan would then convey to the irrigation inspector. As we drove, Hassan explained, "So if the inspector saw that he was giving me [he talked about it in a personalized way, as though it were his water] good water—say 25 [by which he meant a water level of 25cm above the crest of one of the cross weirs that are located along the canal] —at the start of the canal, but at the end it was only 18, he would ask where this water had gone and I would go out and investigate any blockages or violations."

We stopped the car to look at a weir. The water lapped at the faded marble gauge mounted on the front of the weir, just around the 26 mark. We continued on to the end of the branch canal. As we stood there looking at the canal, a man approached us, angry. "I have my irrigation at 2am in the morning, but no water comes!" he said. Hassan responded that he had just looked at the gauge and it showed that the level was 26. The man replied, "That is only today, but here at the end of the canal we have a big problem." Farmers know what the level of water in the canal should be. Some read the gauges regularly to verify that they are receiving their full allocation; others simply observe how high the water is against the banks. Another man saw us and started shouting, "The water is terrible, zift! My onions have been ruined. All the crops are finished, khalas!" He thrust a bunch of withered onions into Hassan's hands. The green shoots had white spots on them, which Hassan identified as an indicator of water stress, and the bulbs were smaller than they should be at this stage in the season. The man entreated us to do something, to show officials in the ministry what was happening because of his lack of water.

We drove away, the withered onions on the seat between us, carrying with them the man's words of anger. Things were different when Hassan was the district engineer, he reassured me. In the summer he would make sure that the gauge was between 25 and 27, whereas before it had fallen to 12 or 15. In the winter it would generally be 35. One of the years he was district engineer, it even rose to 53, so high that the canal overflowed. It was the first time that people at the end of the canal had complained of having too much water, he said proudly.

We headed back upstream to the point where the branch canal draws from one of the main canals that distribute water around Fayoum. A concrete barrier with two metal gates marks the start of the canal. We met the head bahhar, Ahmed, who is responsible for turning the large wheel that opens and closes these gates. Greeting us with a warm smile, Ahmed in-

Figure 2.3.
Bahhar by a weir.
Photograph by
the author.

vited us into his small hut and sent a boy to bring us sodas. He and Hassan worked closely together when Hassan was the district engineer. Hassan mentioned that we had just been to the end of the canal and the water
seemed to be low. "Who told you the water was low?" Ahmed asked, testily.
He went to a cupboard and brought out a large ledger, its corners worn with
age. Opening it, he showed me the neatly written columns of figures and
pointed to the entry for the end of the canal from that morning: 26. Hassan responded that he also saw it was 26 there, but that the farmer whom
we met said the previous days it had been low. Ahmed looked dubious.
Then, after a pause, he acknowledged that maybe it had been lower the last
couple of days. There was a holiday, so he and his colleagues were away from
work. In their absence, there was nobody to raise the metal gates. Hassan
told Ahmed about the man with his onions, but Ahmed was dismissive.
The man's onions cannot have died from a lack of water, he said. They must
have died from a disease because the farmer failed to treat them properly
with pesticide.

As we left Ahmed's office, Hassan remarked that the bahhar does not like to admit that he might have been wrong or not doing a good job in managing the water levels. When he was the district engineer, he would often check the levels at this point where the water flows into Quta. He would always hide his car and record the water level before going to see Ahmed. Otherwise he knew that Ahmed would invite him in and offer him tea, while two of his helpers would go and open the gates, so that he would not be able to complain that the water was too low. "It was like a game of cat and mouse," Hassan said.

This interaction between multiple actors in the field demonstrates how the process of measuring the distribution of water is about more than just reading and reporting. To the district engineer, bahhar, and farmers, it is impossible to *know* the water without subscribing to a certain metrological network—a network that comprises not only a unit of measurement but a set of technologies for making those measurements (Latour 2005, 229). Translating the availability of irrigation water into a figure for the water level in a particular canal section, reducing the complexities of water flow into digits, allows that information to circulate through different realms. Water level (*mansub al-mai*) becomes the metric of scarcity. It is a metric that can be accessed by a number of people. Both water users and water managers check the water levels. The district engineer's job is to maintain a certain water level throughout his district; he is assessed by his superiors in terms of the number of farmer complaints lodged. The head bahhar's job is to respond to the high officials' orders to open and close irrigation gates; in doing so, he sets the water level at the start of the canal. The farmer's job is to farm his fields; he uses the measure of water level as an explanation for crop failure, proof of the ministry's inability to fulfill its role, and a reason to lobby for more water.

Some donors have tried to introduce a competing metrological framework, which they think will lead to more efficient water management. In the 1980s, USAID funded a project to install a telemetry system that would instantly transmit water level data from 800 remote units, located throughout the irrigation and drainage network, to 24 field offices and a master station at the ministry headquarters.[12] In place of a system of eye on a marble gauge, voice on a telephone, and pen on a piece of paper, the telemetry system uses a water logging device, data over the airwaves, and figures on a computer screen to monitor water flows. Today, however, the telemetry section occupies a rundown office on the first floor of the ministry; the large maps of the canal system, dotted with small bulbs indicating the monitoring stations, are faded, the bulbs unlit. In front of the maps on a stand marked with a USAID logo sits a computer mouse, immobile. Much of the telemetry system is no longer working, and water levels generally continue to be measured manually and reported over the phone by the ministry officials based in the field.

What Latour's discussion of metrology elucidates is that the system of measurement is a process of doing work, of making something local—how much water there is in the canal at a certain place—into something that can travel—a figure. This sheds light on why the donor-introduced telemetry system is no longer operating. The fact that the ministry has largely returned to its system of recording water levels in a ledger and reporting them over the phone is not a reflection of the ministry's incompetence in maintaining this sophisticated system after the donor funding is withdrawn. Rather, it is an indication of how monitoring water levels is about much more than just seeing how much water there is in a canal. It is about officials being judged by superiors on how well they are doing their jobs; should they be judged to be doing badly, they are fired. It is about farmers assessing whether they are receiving the water that the system is designed to provide; if not, they complain. Thus it is not really surprising that for some within the ministry, a manual system is more convenient. Figures in a ledger can be smudged; the time of measurement is flexible; the metric of scarcity remains in the hands of those in the field, one step removed from the supervisors back in the head office.

The donors have also targeted their recommendations for efficiency improvements at the unit of measurement within the metrological framework of water distribution. "If we move from level to flow measurements," one Egyptian working for the Dutch embassy explained to me, "we can distribute water better. Measuring levels makes the ministry more vulnerable." The level of water in a canal is only a good indication of how much water is flowing down a canal if all the other parameters that determine flow rate (channel width, shape, roughness, and slope) remain the same. But these parameters are not constant. A direct measurement of how much water is passing through each canal is therefore a more accurate basis for determining water distribution. Under another USAID-funded project, the ministry shifted to a system of volume-based allocation at the main canal intakes, barrages on the Nile, and division points between directorates.[13] The minister also issued a decree (No. 450 of 12/3/2000), which stated a plan to convert water distribution within the directorates from a system based on levels to one based on volume. But the ministry has not yet expended the money—estimated at around 250LE per feddan—to install the necessary weirs, calculate the discharge coefficients, and train the irrigation staff in how to operate a discharge-based system (MWRI 2005a, ch.5, 15). So far as farmers are concerned, therefore, water levels continue to be the metric of scarcity.

When I was doing my fieldwork in Fayoum, the issues that I have discussed up to now were those that I heard in everyday conversations about water scarcity. Water scarcity was about levels being too low, other canals getting all the water, or canals and offtakes being blocked or modified illegally. What was interesting to me, though, was that neither water users nor local officials seemed to draw a link between their water levels and the broader system from which that water comes.[14] Their focus was on actions and decisions taking place around them—an arena in which they are more likely to be able to exert a direct influence—rather than at the national scale. Although officials would sometimes say that Fayoum should receive more water, when I asked the mid-level staff in the provincial irrigation directorate about who makes decisions on water distribution throughout Egypt and how the control structures on the Nile work, they were unable to reply. The Aswan High Dam does appear in conversation as The Dam (al-sad) or The High Dam (al-sad al-'ali), but more as a symbol (Egypt's great achievement) than as the ultimate regulator of flows. Farmers know where their water comes from, but it seems that they do not necessarily relate the plenty or lack of water in their canals to the workings of this wider network.[15]

Hence it was not until I left Egypt and was reading some old newspapers that I learned what had been going on 600km to the south during my time in Fayoum. In the summer of 2007, rainfall was above average in the source regions of the Nile. Seasonal flows down the Nile later that year were the highest since 1946 (Leila 2007). At the same time that I was hearing farmers in Fayoum complain of water scarcity, Lake Nasser was full to overflowing. Faced with a water level in the reservoir of over 181.5m above sea level, the ministry diverted 1.1 billion cubic meters (bcm) of water (equivalent to almost half Fayoum's annual water allocation) into the desert west of Lake Nasser through a spillway. So as Fayoum canals were lying near empty and farmers' crops were withering, water was evaporating from the surface of the desert. In the next section, I look to the everyday practices taking place at another scale, at the ministry's ultimate control point—the Aswan High Dam—to probe how it is that the making of Egypt's water produces both scarcity and excess within one system simultaneously.

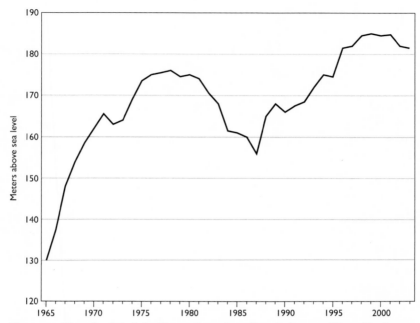

Figure 2.4. Water levels in Lake Nasser. *Source:* Data from D. Conway, "From Headwater Tributaries to International River," *Global Environmental Change.*

Turning on the River

Lake Nasser forms a dramatic sight, its deep azure water set against a back-drop of desert. In places, the shoreline rises in rugged cliffs; in others, the rocky beaches are gentle, dotted with palm trees. At the northern end of Lake Nasser lies the Aswan High Dam. The dam works as a particular kind of control device, introducing a point of delay between source—rain—and destination—field. The Nile would not flow through Egypt were it not for the rain that falls on the East African Highlands. At the same time, though, it is the ministry opening the dam that makes the Nile flow on its final stretch to the sea.

In disconnecting Egypt's water supply from its source, Lake Nasser buffers Egypt from variability. But the lake can only buffer so much. With one year of low rainfall, or a couple of years of high rainfall, the reservoir's vast volume absorbs that variability. Yet given a prolonged set of low or high rainfall years, the lake levels reveal the cumulative impact. This is what happened during the 1980s. Year after year of below average rainfall in the source region only partially replenished the reservoir, and water storage in the lake fell by more than half (Stoner 1994, 197). The ministry was alarmed, its vulnerability revealed. During the 1987–88 agricultural season, it was only able to release 52.9bcm—at least 3bcm lower than its typical release and significantly less than the country's needs.

Since that time, the ministry has therefore adopted a cautionary principle, operating the High Dam with the goal of keeping the water level in Lake Nasser as high as possible.[16] A full Lake Nasser is a visual confirmation that the nation's water supply is secure. Although more plentiful annual rainfall during the 1990s has replenished the lake's storage (see figure 2.4), the ministry is determined to protect against the risk of successive dry years. This policy may also be driven by senior officials' unwillingness to let farmers grow accustomed to higher flows. They know that Egypt may well see a drop in Nile flows in coming decades if rainfall declines in the Nile source regions under climate change, as some models predict.[17] They also know that if upstream states pursue hydro-development plans, it will affect evaporative losses in the basin and, consequently, Egypt's water allocation. So they do not want farmers to get used to a volume of water that they may not be able to provide in the future. Hence each year the ministry releases just 55.5bcm through the dam gates (MWRI 2005a, ch. 5, 2). This is the amount of water that should flow into the country each year according to the Nile Waters Agreement. But since Sudan has yet to fully use the 18.5bcm to which it is entitled, 55.5bcm is significantly less than the water that Egypt receives. Rather than releasing all the water that enters the country in a year, the ministry chooses instead to store a portion of the flow in Lake Nasser. This maintains the reservoir's reserves and keeps the lake at a high level. As a result, each year that the rains are abundant in the upper reaches of the Nile Basin, the reservoir is so full that it is unable to store the additional inflow.

Faced with a lake close to overflowing, the ministry could raise the gates of the High Dam to pass more water through the irrigation network. This would certainly please many farmers. But it cannot do this, officials say, for risk of flooding infrastructure or fields in places where the river banks do not rise far above the water level. The ministry is also concerned about excessive erosion along the banks of the Nile.[18] Maintaining banks that are eroding at a rate of up to 3cm a year using perpendicular dikes and stone walls is quite costly (Ahmed and Ismail 2008). So long as discharge downstream from Aswan is kept below 250 million cubic meters a day, erosion is limited. But if the discharge were to rise higher than that, the costs of bank erosion would be considerable (El-Kadi et al. 1995, 267). Thus the material nature of water—its propensity to erode the banks of a channel that it passes through—influences the ministry's decisions about how much water it should allow to flow through the High Dam and on down the Nile.

The ministry's response to rising lake levels is therefore to use the desert as an outlet. Satellite images of Egypt reveal a strange sight; a diversion of water that you would not notice if touring around Egypt's agricultural lands or up the Nile. Over 50km west of Lake Nasser lies a huge spread of blue in the yellow of the desert. There is no green rim to this blue, for the water here is evaporating, not irrigating. This expanse of water pooled in a series of depressions in the Western Desert, known as the Toshka Lakes, is revealed in its full scale only in this view from space. Indeed, I only learned about the lakes when I saw a Google Earth image taped to the wall of a foreign academic's office at the American University of Cairo, prompting me to ask what this water was. When the seasonal inflow from the Nile is more than Lake Nasser can store, the ministry diverts water through a spillway, which it constructed in 1978, to the desert (map 2.1).[19] The ministry first used the spillway in 1998 as the water level in Lake Nasser approached the reservoir's maximum capacity. By the end of 2001, the Toshka Lakes had reached 1,740km², covering an area a third of the size of Lake Nasser and storing 25.3bcm—almost half the amount that flows through Egypt's canal system each year. Lower rainfall in the years following this gave the ministry less cause to utilize its spillway and the lakes shrank; by 2006 they covered an area of 900km² and held 12.6bcm (Chipman and Lillesand 2007). The diversion in 2007 caused the lakes to expand once again.

Thus while many canals of Fayoum lie empty, 600km to the south water evaporates from the surface of the Toshka Lakes at an estimated rate of 2.5m a year (El-Bastawesy et al. 2007). The ministry diverts this water to evaporate from the desert rather than pass through the gates of the Aswan High Dam due to its concerns about the potential costs of allowing it to continue its journey down the Nile to places like Fayoum. This concern stems from the damage that an increased flow of water could incur on the conduits that transport water through the country. In this case, it is not so much a lack of infrastructure that produces scarcity but a particular configuration of infrastructure (the weak earth banks, the canal-side roads) and the material nature of water (its tendency to erode) that almost requires it.

Hence as the Egyptian government continues to press upstream countries of the Nile Basin to increase its water allocation and farmers in Fa-

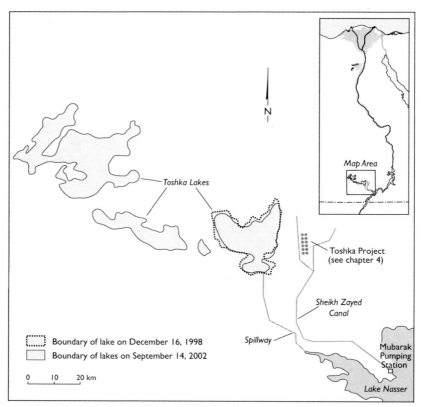

Map 2.1. The Toshka Lakes. *Source:* Lake boundaries derived from J. Chipman and T. Lillesand, "Satellite-Based Assessment of the Dynamics of New Lakes in Southern Egypt," *International Journal of Remote Sensing.*

youm leave their fields fallow for lack of water, the water that Egypt is unable to store or pass through its irrigation network evaporates from the desert. The evaporated droplets represent abundance rather than scarcity. As one expatriate who has worked in Egypt for a long time acknowledged to me, "Egypt's big challenge is how to store the water. Egypt can't store as much water as it gets." He added, furtively, "In some ways, Egypt gets *too much* water."

The knowledge of how the ministry manages water levels in Lake Nasser through diverting water into the Toshka Spillway does not circulate all that widely. I never heard farmers talking about the merits of the ministry disposing water in the desert. Nor did I hear officials in the Fayoum directorate discussing how their task of meeting farmers' needs would be easier if, rather than just having an annual water allocation of 2.5bcm to work with, they received some of the billions of cubic meters of water that are evaporating from the desert. The first I heard of the diversions that were taking place during my fieldwork was by reading a newspaper. So unlike the water levels in the canals, which are part of a metrological system of marble gauges that can be easily accessed by people working on multiple scales—from farmers and bahhars in a field, to officials in a regional office, and policy makers in Cairo—the diversion of water into the Toshka Lakes is tied into a different kind of metrological framework. Since the land around Lake Nasser is very sparsely settled, there are few local people present to observe how the shoreline varies from year to year. Instead, knowledge of how much water there is in the reservoir is tied to twice-daily measurements of water levels at a gauge board mounted on the High Dam. The dam is a site of national security, which is guarded by the military and, with the exception of the tourist viewing area, open just to those with special access. Thus the only people able to read the figures on the gauge board are officials in the Public Authority for the High Dam and Aswan Reservoir. They average the two measurements and transmit the data daily to high-level decision makers in Cairo over the phone and in written reports. The decision makers then determine how much to raise or lower the gates of the dam and send an order back to the staff in the High Dam Authority.

Information about water levels in the reservoir does not circulate beyond a close network of government officials until the ministry issues its press releases, timed and worded to communicate a reassurance that the country is safe. In the 2007 case, these releases included a brief announcement in July saying that the ministry was planning to open the Toshka Spillway in anticipation of a higher than average flood (SIS 2007); a follow-up announcement in August, asserting that the flood was under control (IPRSID 2007a); and a final announcement in October saying that the flood was on the wane and that it never posed any danger (IPRSID 2007b). So although the ministry's diversions into the Toshka Spillway are based on a measure of water level, just like the diversions between canals throughout the irrigation network, in the case of Lake Nasser, this is a different kind of water level—a level that circulates beyond a small group of officials by people reading a newspaper, not a marble gauge.

Some donors, expatriate water consultants, and engineers think there may be more efficient ways of managing the country's inflow.[20] If the water level in Lake Nasser were kept at a lower level, it would mean that during years of high inflow the reservoir would be able to accommodate the extra water, so there would be no need to spill it into the desert. Furthermore, a lower lake level would mean a smaller surface area and, as a result, lower evaporative losses (which currently amount to about 10bcm a year) (MWRI 2005a, ch.4, 16). Yet despite these experts' recommendation, the ministry has made no moves to change its management system. What this policy recommendation cannot capture is the government's sense of security—its concern that the country's primary source of water be sufficient to feed 8 million feddan of land, almost 82 million bodies, and the nation's industries every year without fail. This may in part explain the ministry's reluctance to change how it manages outflow through the High Dam. Such political considerations underscore the way in which Egypt's water comes into being, producing abundance in some areas and scarcity in others. I turn now to some of the ways in which various actors are working to intervene at different points in the system so as to solve the problem of scarcity.

SOLVING SCARCITY

The regional panel on the Middle East and North Africa at the Fifth World Water Forum in March 2009 is marked by the trays of stuffed dates sprinkled with ground pistachio nuts and powdered sugar that sit on tables outside the conference hall. Even in an anonymous conference center in Istanbul, the people of the Middle East are keen to show their hospitality, a hallmark of their identity. Alongside the dates lie buttons and key rings bearing the logo of the Arab Water Council. There is a pile of the regional situation reports that the Arab Water Council has prepared over the course of a series of meetings to highlight the key water-related issues in the region. Inside the conference hall, six maroon armchairs are arranged in a semicircle on the stage, behind small coffee tables with bottled water and saucers of mints. A large screen stretches from one side of the stage to the other, bearing the logo "bridging divides for water." The panelists file in, among them the Iraqi water minister and the president of the Arab Water Council, who until eight days previously was also minister of water in Egypt. This is the sort of space in which the high-level policy makers of the ministry move. It is in the hallways and meeting rooms of conferences like this one that they interact with the "global water community" of policy makers from water ministries around the world, hydrologists, engineers, and representatives from the water programs of the international organizations and donor agencies. Farmers are noticeable in their absence.

Water scarcity is a central topic on the agenda. The executive director of the Arab Water Council, another senior official within the ministry in Egypt, welcomes everyone. He says, "The Arab region is located in a very

Figure 2.5. Panel on water scarcity at the Fifth World Water Forum in Istanbul. Photograph by the author.

unique place of the world, in the center of the world. Water plays a dominant role to all people there because we have a big scarcity of water. Without water, the whole region is desert!" The regional report adopts a similar tone: "The Arab world is dominated by water scarcity" (Attia et al. 2009, 13). The issue of water in the Middle East is clearly framed: it is one of limited resources, a growing population, and the need to balance increasing demands from different sectors. The report presents figures for the annual renewable water resources in the region, revealing a dramatic decline from more than 4,000m³ per capita in 1950 to 1,233m³ per capita in 1998, projected to fall to 547m³ per capita in 2050 (Attia et al. 2009, 7). The report does not mention the Falkenmark classification, but this understanding of scarcity is implicit; the projected figures mark a situation of impending "chronic water scarcity."

Two and a half years later, in a five-star hotel on the outskirts of Cairo, the conversation at the Second Arab Water Forum is remarkably similar. Almost every presentation starts with an account of the region's encroaching crisis of water scarcity, accompanied by a PowerPoint slideshow with images of the desert, rapidly plummeting lines on a graph, or alarming figures in bold. In these kinds of settings, Egyptian high-level officials are willing to admit that scarcity is a problem. By bracketing the countries of the region together and talking about scarcity as a regional rather than a national issue, the discussion shifts the focus away from how water managers in individual countries handle their resources. The naturalized vision of scarcity, as a question of nature versus demography, removes the bureaucrats' culpability.[21] Furthermore, given the presence of officials from Sudan and other Nile Basin countries at these conferences, it is in the Egyptian policy makers' interests to maintain a position of lack, so as to reinforce their government's calls for a larger allocation of Nile waters. Far removed from the farmers who could capitalize on an admittance of "a problem" to press for an increase in their supply, the officials feel free to talk about their resources being limited. In these conference rooms, everyone is talking about water scarcity.

In a national context, however, the situation is different. One month after I attended the water forum in Istanbul, I met with Peter in Cairo. Peter is a Dutch irrigation engineer who has been involved in water-related projects in Egypt for many years. We sat together and drank fresh juice cocktails in the beautiful gardens of a former Ottoman palace, which is now a Marriott Hotel. "Until quite recently you couldn't talk about water scarcity," Peter told me. "The minister said we have our water resources plan from 1997 up to 2017 and the water balance is closed so there is no problem of scarcity."[22] When a Dutch-funded project organized a workshop in 2004, the project consultants were told by ministry officials that they could not say that the workshop was about water scarcity; instead, they had to say it concerned water demand management.[23] Only in the late 2000s did the situation begin to change. Peter remembers a meeting in 2007 when the minister spoke about a dream he had had the night before. It was a nightmare. He dreamed that there was not enough water. In Peter's view, it was as though the minister suddenly realized that scarcity was an issue that had to be addressed. "Now we can talk about scarcity, but only after 2017," Peter explains. "Up until 2017 we have to say that everything is fine." Another expatriate consultant told me a similar story. "Until a couple of years ago it was taboo to talk of shortages," he said. "But now people are discussing it. The official position is that there won't be shortages until after 2017." Scarcity therefore pivots on this year—an arbitrary date that marks nothing more significant than the endpoint of the twenty-year planning horizon that the government set in 1997. Within the time period that the population can reasonably hold the ministry accountable for—the coming twenty years—the official position is that everyone receives and will continue to receive the water that they need. But beyond that, water scarcity will pose a problem.

The ministry officials' reluctance to acknowledge a water shortage in a national context indicates an unwillingness to concede a point of weakness. To talk of scarcity as a contemporary problem would be to admit that the government is unable to provide for its people. It would show that the ministry is failing, at least in part, to fulfill its mission of distributing water to all farmers in the quantity and quality that they need. None of these concessions would be politically palatable. On the other hand, one could argue that since Lake Nasser has recently been full to overflowing, ministry officials, as guardians of the nation's water, have reason to maintain a position of abundance. "It's very difficult to talk about scarcity in the face of excess," one consultant commented to me. "Egypt has a lot of water. And if you think that most of the water is used at the end (i.e., in the delta), people in Cairo see all this water flowing past and say, 'Where is the problem?'"

Yet whether right now or after 2017, Egyptian policy makers recognize that at some point they will have to address the problem of scarcity. In workshops facilitated by donors and at international water forums, they discuss policy options for solving scarcity with international water management experts. I see these policy measures as different types of devices for intervening in the flow of water. If scarcity is produced through the everyday practices of water distribution and use, what these policy measures seek to do, essentially, is to tap into that system of distribution at various points so as to make the water flow to the places where it currently does not. Some policies focus on the sources of flow and how to boost the water supply; others focus on the points of usage and how to moderate the water demand. Some focus on the international and national scale, others on the local. While their mode of operation may be less direct, their efficiency more opaque, and their periodicity unlike that of a dam, weir, or pump, these policy measures also seek to organize how water moves through the country. They, too, help make Egypt's water.

More Water

One of the ministry's primary goals, a high-level official told me, is to "cooperate with Nile riparian countries to increase our water allocation." If Egypt had more water, scarcity would be less of a problem (a rhetoric similar to that of the irrigation officials at a directorate level). The government is therefore working to promote some projects in upstream countries that could increase Egypt's water allocation. The official described these as "win-win" projects — projects that would benefit other basin nations as well as Egypt. The Jonglei Canal on the White Nile in South Sudan, for example, would bypass the Sudd swamps, reducing evaporation losses and increasing the flow of the Nile by an estimated 4bcm a year (map 1.1). Work on the canal started in the 1970s but was halted in 1983 by political instability. In recent years, government officials have renewed discussions about the project and the potential role Egypt could play in helping fund it. The first foreign trip taken by the transitional government in early 2011 was to Sudan. At a news conference in Khartoum, an Egyptian cabinet spokesman announced that starting to build the Jonglei Canal was a "top priority" (Abu Edries Ali 2011). Within a few months of South Sudan's independence, government sources reported that "the new nation is poised to resume the Jonglei Canal project" (NSV 2011). The future of the project remains uncertain, though, despite some officials' optimism.

Alternative mechanisms of increasing Egypt's water supply lie within the country's borders, through the development of sources other than the Nile. Egypt has significant (albeit nonrenewable) groundwater reserves underlying the Western Desert and Sinai Peninsula that could be exploited further. Desalination of either seawater or brackish canal water offers another potential, but costly, option. There are also limited possibilities for rainwater harvesting along the Mediterranean and Red Sea coasts.

Yet while ministry officials talk about expanding Egypt's supply, to most donors the solution to Egypt's water scarcity lies not in the development of new sources but in the more efficient use of existing sources. "We are moving into a water crisis. Water conservation is the key issue," one Dutch consultant told me. The focus of most donor attention has therefore been on supporting the ministry in its efforts to improve the efficiency of the irrigation system. The more efficiently water is distributed through the network of canals and irrigation ditches, the less will be lost, and the more there will be available for use.

This strategy for solving scarcity is contingent, first, on the identification of where major losses are taking place. Despite the large volume of water that is lost in evaporation from the surface of Lake Nasser and the Toshka Lakes, ministry officials claim that the primary site of inefficiency is the fields. "The majority, say, 80 percent, of the losses are at the farm level," one senior official stated. Water evaporates from open ditches, leaks through the banks of unlined channels, and flows unused into the drainage network when farmers channel too much water onto their crops. Thus rather than challenge how the ministry operates the High Dam, donors have focused on the less politically sensitive question of improving local distribution mechanisms and farmers' practices. "There is so much waste on a local level," an official in the Dutch embassy remarked. "That's why we need to organize farmers. There is lots of farmer mismanagement." Improving field level efficiencies to boost the supply is a matter of managing both how water flows to the fields and how it flows away from them (for more on the latter, see chapter 5).

The American, German, and Japanese development agencies, along with the World Bank, have funded a series of projects to implement "irrigation improvement."[24] These projects introduce a suite of technical interventions to help the water flow more efficiently from canal to crop. The delta has been the focus of these efforts, since this is the area where reducing inefficiencies can lead to an overall increase in the water supply, by saving water that would otherwise pass into the drainage system and be lost to the coastal lakes or Mediterranean. (In the Nile valley, in contrast, any water that is used inefficiently returns to the Nile for reuse downstream.)

In June 2008 I traveled around the delta province of Kafr el-Sheikh with an engineer from the Irrigation Improvement Sector. Among the fields of rice and cotton, the signs of "improvement" stand out. Each phase of the Irrigation Improvement Project has promoted slightly different technical fixes for improving the system of water flow (Hvidt 1998). The common features of all improvement areas, though, in theory at least, are continuous flow in the branch canals and a single point for lifting water from the mesqa.

The first intervention is a departure from the rotation system that is found throughout Egypt except in Fayoum, whereby branch canals are turned on for a number of days, then turned off for a period. Accomplished using a downstream control gate, which closes only when the water reaches a certain level, this system of continuous flow is designed based on an assumption that if the water is always available, then farmers will not over-irrigate. If farmers only apply the water that a crop needs, then less water will flow unused into the drainage system and be lost through evaporation. Somewhat ironically, the scarcity device here is abundance.

The second intervention targets the fact that outside of Fayoum mesqas lie at a low level, so farmers have to pump water up to their fields. Clustering pumping in a single location ensures that farmers at the head of the mesqa do not take all the water, leaving downstream farmers in a position of scarcity. The small concrete blocks of the pump stations beside the

Figure 2.6.
Opening a valve
in an irrigation
improvement area
in the Nile delta.
Photograph by the
author.

branch canals mark the pumps' location. In its early phases, the project installed diesel pumps, the loud chugging noise audible from outside the pump house. The most recent phases of the project have installed electric pumps; silent and efficient, these pumps operate with a simple press of a button.

The improved techniques of channeling water from the pump to the farmers' fields vary. In some of the oldest improved areas, the mesqas stand above the field in raised concrete channels. Water from the pump station spurts out into the meter-wide channel, which replaces the earthen field ditch that the water formerly flowed through. Concrete in place of soil minimizes the loss of water from the channel and improves the efficiency of water transport. To access water, the farmer raises a metal gate and channels water onto his or her field. The second phase of the project installed underground pipes in place of the concrete channels. Pipes have the advantage that they minimize evaporation and leakage losses and do not become blocked with weeds. In these project sites, no channels or ditches lead away from the canal. Instead, water flows from the pump station between different farmers' land through a plastic pipe below the surface. Whereas farmers can easily access water from an open mesqa, in a piped system there are fixed abstraction points. To access water at one of these points, the farmer turns a wheel, which opens a valve and water flows out of the pipe into an open field ditch (marwa) that channels the water through the field. In the most recent iteration of the Irrigation Improvement Project, the project has also replaced the field ditches with underground pipes. In these areas, the fields are seamless. Water flows through a network of pipes under the field until the point where a farmer lifts a cap and out bubbles the water.

These new mechanisms of channeling water from canal to crop seek to remold the landscape of Egypt's water. To date, they are only present in the areas that donor projects have targeted for intervention. The everyday pattern of water movement through the fields is therefore tied to the decisions made by international consultants and ministry officials about which areas should be prioritized for improvement. In those areas, water now moves swiftly through a concrete channel or plastic pipe; in the areas deemed by water managers to be less important or less in need of improvement, it continues to flow through ditches of earth, leaking into the soil along the way.

Yet the success of this scarcity solution lies not in the design of these technologies and what they should accomplish in theory but in how they impact the flow of water in practice. Experience has shown that irrigation improvement measures do not always achieve what their architects hoped. As social groups appropriate these technologies in different ways, they change the way in which the technologies function—a functioning that hinges not only on technical capacity but on social, cultural, and political considerations. The downstream control gates, for example, do not generally function as intended. This is partly because the gates were not manufactured very well, but also because the project staff failed to explain to the district engineers, technicians, and bahhars how the gates work. As a result, some ministry staff put stones on the floaters or pierce them so that the gates are open all the time. Whether they do this because they do not understand the function of the floaters, or just do not agree with that function is unclear.[25] Many farmers complain that they are not satisfied with the new system of channeling water through the fields. What is an improvement from the perspective of the system (reduced losses) is not necessarily an improvement from the perspective of an individual farmer. The pipes are too narrow, farmers say, so it takes them too long to irrigate their fields. The valves are unevenly distributed through the fields, hard to open and close, and prone to breakage. Some would prefer their own pump to a communal pump, and frequent electricity blackouts render the electric pumping stations useless (Gouda 2007). Hence these measures are only partially successful in their attempt to increase water availability by making the water flow more efficiently to and through the fields.

Less Demand

At the same time as Egyptian policy makers investigate options for increasing Egypt's water supply, they also promote measures to decrease the water demand. This is in line with a paradigmatic shift within international water policy making away from supply-based solutions. Among international water experts, there is a widespread understanding that the scope for increasing freshwater supplies in many countries is limited and that the emphasis needs to shift toward reducing demand. "I urge you to think about demand management," concluded the chairman of the World Water Council in his introduction to a high-level panel on water scarcity at the Sixth World Water Forum. "We need to use less water and to manage it better."

Since farmers use most of Egypt's water, the onus for reducing demand falls on them. This emphasis is underscored by a common perception among ministry officials and international donors that farmers use water wastefully. The idea that "local people" are to blame for poor resource management is a recurrent theme in development interventions.[26] Thus at the same time as the government pursues massive desert reclamation initiatives, which will greatly increase water demand (see chapter 4), officials talk about how to reduce smallholders' everyday water use. Their key concern is how to encourage farmers to divert less water from the canals onto their fields. There are two policy options, each driven by a different assumption about what motivates farmers' behavior: economic incentives and education.

To many of the donors working in Egypt, prices are the best mechanism for moderating water demand. This is a popular idea in international water management circles and part of a broader neoliberal shift, which has been widely promoted by international donors since the 1980s.[27] "We need pricing because no pricing means wasted use," one panelist stated at the Fifth World Water Forum. "Water without a price is wasted," another remarked at the Second Arab Water Forum. "Unless we put a price on water, I don't think we'll be able to enhance water efficiency," reflected an audience member at the Sixth World Water Forum. The striking similarity of these comments from Istanbul, Cairo, and Marseille reflects the dominance of this notion that people only value things with a price.[28] The Dublin Statement on Water reflects the same rhetoric: "Water has an economic value in all its competing uses and should be recognized as an economic good" (ICWE 1992). This statement, which is part of the body of expertise that constitutes the "global water community," has been adopted by numerous international, multinational, and bilateral institutions. The necessity of treating water as an economic good has become "a mantra for water policy makers . . . repeated again and again, conference after conference" (Hoekstra and Hung 2005, 45). Only by treating water as an economic good, so the rationale goes, will the users recognize water's true scarcity value and therefore consume it more efficiently. Pricing water is, in effect, a device to make water scarce. Farmers may not perceive the water to be scarce, but they know their money to be scarce, so having to pay for water forces the farmers to handle the resource *as though* it is scarce. According to a USAID study, the introduction of water charges in Egypt (based on the actual volume of water used or on the crops cultivated and the water requirements of those crops) would reduce water demand by 3.5 percent (Perry 1996).

Yet this is a policy measure that the Egyptian government has been unwilling to adopt. Despite significant pressure from international donors, the ministry has refused to introduce pricing policies for irrigation water. "Nobody wants to sell water," I heard one engineer assure a group of farmers. "The Irrigation [i.e., the ministry] doesn't want to do this." Both officials and farmers often draw on cultural and religious reasoning to oppose water charges. "We in Egypt consider that water has a value," said one participant at the Arab Water Forum. "It has a cultural value, a social value, an economic value. Therefore it can't be priced. It's a cultural thing." In many workshops and conversations I heard people protest that under Islam, water is a gift of God, so it cannot be subject to payment. Whether or not Islam actually prohibits the introduction of water charges is a matter of debate among Islamic scholars. Some cite passages from the Quran which state that the buying and selling of water is forbidden; others argue that the Prophet's more important overriding concern for equity would be better served by making people pay for the water that they use (Faruqi 2001). The argument that there is something morally wrong with setting a price for such a fundamental resource is, however, a powerful one, which resonates beyond the bounds of a single religion. Many scholars and activists have argued that people should be entitled as citizens to access to water rather than seen as consumers who have to pay for it (Bakker 2005; Swyngedouw 2005).

Nonetheless, there are some within the ministry who agree with the idea of charging for water. For example, Hassan told me about a study tour he went on in Japan, funded by the Japanese International Cooperation Agency. One of the good things about the Japanese irrigation system, he observed, was that farmers do not overwater because they have to pay for the water they use. "If people pay for something, they will conserve it," he said. Hassan's brother, who was with us at the time, interrupted. "But this [water] is the right of the people," he said. Hassan was resolute. "The Irrigation doesn't take anything. We serve people for free. I know that if you tried to charge for water the farmer would say, 'Water comes from God. How can I pay?' But I would say to him, 'What about the main canals, weirs, and branch canals that mean that the water reaches you?'" As Hassan's comment elucidated, Egypt's water is not a given; to him, the fact that so much work goes into producing the flow of water through the irrigation network offers a valid justification for introducing water charges.

There are, however, strong political reasons underlying the ministry's reluctance to place a price on water.[29] If farmers had to pay for water, it would give them a sense of ownership over the water, which would create problems during those times when the ministry is unable to provide water of a sufficient quantity or quality. Ministry officials are also well aware that charges would be politically unpopular—a matter of particular concern in the current political climate. Nobody is likely to welcome having to pay for something that they have always received for free. Indeed the USAID study of water pricing in Egypt found that water charges would not only reduce water demand but also decrease farm incomes by about 4.5 percent (Perry 1996). Whenever I saw the topic of water pricing come up in meetings in Fayoum, it aroused a strong emotional response. Farmers made it quite clear that they would be very angry if the ministry introduced these charges. In some parts of the province, rumors have begun to circulate about water charges, with the result that farmers refuse to attend any meetings organized by the ministry. When ministry officials go out to meet with farmers in these areas, they find them reluctant to say their names or how much land they own, for fear that they will have to pay for their water use in the future.

The ministry has therefore maintained its stance against this mechanism of demand management. But it is still in broad agreement that the solution to scarcity lies in getting farmers to use less water. The route to doing this, many officials argue, is through training programs and what they call "awareness" (taw'iya). The underlying assumption is that farmers use water wastefully not because the water is free but because they are ignorant and do not know any better. This is a topic that comes up frequently in international discussions about water scarcity. People need to develop "awareness and a greater sense of responsibility toward water use," the regional report from the Fifth World Water Forum states (Attia et al. 2009, 14). There is a need for what a panelist in a Middle East session at the forum termed "capacitating the community." Only once water users are aware of resource scarcity will their contribution to managing that resource be valuable. As one member of the regional panel said, "We must believe in ordinary people, *if* they are informed, *if* they are educated."

Within Egypt, there is a widespread belief among policy makers and donors that because of the presence of the Nile, farmers do not understand that water is limited. Hence, they say, there is a need to educate farmers and teach them to use water efficiently. A USAID project in the 1990s focused on raising public awareness of water scarcity.[30] It established the Water Communication Unit in the ministry and launched a publicity campaign on scarcity. Evidently, however, the television advertisements, radio programs, newsletters, educational materials, wall charts, hats, and bumper stickers did not have their desired effect. "So many people don't realize that we have a water scarcity issue," exclaimed one donor with exasperation during an interview. "They point and say, 'Look, we have the Nile!'" In a workshop for ministry staff in Fayoum, the Egyptian consultant leading the workshop said, "We need to go to a farmer and say, 'Take care of that water. The Nile might dry up!' We need to make the farmer understand that water is limited." Ironically, just as he said this, the director general of irrigation in Fayoum, who was sitting next to me, received a call on his cellphone. "*Inshallah* by the end of the day you should get water," he reassured the person at the other end of the line. "We opened it up yesterday afternoon." Clearly whoever he was talking to was complaining about there not being enough water in a certain canal. That person had no need to be trained in scarcity.

I would suggest that most farmers do not need "raised awareness" about water scarcity. Many are keenly aware of how limited water resources are. It is to these individuals that I return now. What do those in the fields of Fayoum, those who actually experience scarcity, see as the solution? How do they respond to this scarcity on a day-to-day basis?

Farming Scarcity

One morning in July 2008 I visited the offices of the irrigation directorate, which occupy a large complex on a side street in Fayoum City. The once handsome colonial buildings, built in 1906, are now in a state of disrepair. The paint is chipped, doors are broken, and windows are cracked. A long wooden balcony runs along the second floor of the main building. In high-ceilinged offices, clerical staff, engineers, and uniformed irrigation police sit behind large wooden desks, sifting through mounds of paper, drinking tea, eating bean sandwiches, and chatting. On this particular morning, I was with Dr. Fathi, a former high-level official from the ministry. Dr. Fathi is now retired and works as a consultant for donor projects. As we entered the building, we passed a group of eight farmers leaving. The farmers were stern faced. One carried a few long stalks of browned maize. "That's maize that has reached the wilting point," Dr. Fathi commented. His tone was matter-of-fact, but I was troubled. The image was striking. The farmers were desperate. In their hands, they held a dead crop. The water that could have made that crop live was controlled by the officials sitting inside those very offices.

Farmers come to complain almost daily. Dressed in cleanly pressed *gala-biyas*, they line the hallways and wait for their chance to speak with an official, request an expanded offtake, or lodge an objection to other farmers' behavior.[31] Some come individually; others come in groups. In some cases, farmers may even make the three-hour trip to Cairo to complain at the central ministry offices. Since the revolution, farmers have been particularly forthcoming with their complaints. "Since the protests, the farmers have been very aggressive," one official told me when I returned to Egypt in November 2011. She gestured with the palm of one hand pushing down forcefully on the other. "They are used to being *pressed down*. But now when they make their requests, they are shouting. They say, 'We are free!' They are always shouting!" Expatriates working on water projects in Egypt painted a similar picture. "Strange things are happening," remarked one. "There have been lots of protests since the revolution." "Whenever people are unhappy," commented another, "they do a demonstration."

Yet frequently the farmer's complaints are futile. "We have been a lot to complain," one man told me. "And nothing happens. They say 'yes, yes,' but then don't do anything." "I go [to complain]," another man recounted, "but nobody listens to me." This is where "connections" (*wasta*) can make all the difference. For farmers who know people in positions of power, solving scarcity can be as simple as speaking to the right person. A ministry engineer told me about a large Fayoumi landowner who formerly held a high position within the government and so had ample connections. "If he just picked up the phone, water would arrive," the engineer said. But not everyone is able to call the director general on his cellphone.

If the ministry chooses to respond to a complaint, it has different options for relieving a localized scarcity. In the case of a blockage, officials can send an excavator to remove the sediment or weeds that are impeding the flow of water. If there is simply not enough water, they can open the gates of the regulator on the main canal to raise the water level in the section of canal from which a farmer draws. This alleviates scarcity, but sometimes only temporarily. As one woman recounted to me, "We go to the governor and he increases the amount of water, but after a week or two weeks it decreases again." Alternatively, ministry engineers can modify the system of water distribution by increasing the size of an offtake. This allows more water to flow into that mesqa, but also means that less water flows on down the canal to downstream mesqas, potentially generating new points of scarcity in the process.

From time to time farmers take matters into their own hands, demonstrating their own agency in their ability to access water.[32] Working either as individuals or with neighboring farmers, they expand their offtakes by breaking the crests, replacing the offtake pipes with larger ones, or installing additional pipes in the bank. This means that more water flows out of the canal into their mesqas. Siphons, which are pipes that farmers carefully position with one end in the canal and the other end dangling above the mesqa, accomplish a similar purpose. Alternatively, farmers use pumps to access extra water from a canal, drainage ditch, or shallow well.[33]

These everyday practices for accessing additional water are illegal. The ministry refers to them as "violations" (mukhalafat). It is the district engineers' job to try and prevent such violations by issuing fines and removing illegal pipes and pumps. But some district engineers are more vigilant than others in enforcing the regulations. Farmers also have various mechanisms of evading the district engineer, such as hiding pumps when they hear that a district engineer is approaching. Even when the engineers do issue penalties, they have a limited effect. An engineer told me about one time when he saw a farmer using a siphon. "I said to him, 'Take that out!'" The farmer refused. When the engineer responded that he would fine him, the farmer replied, "Go ahead!" The engineer was clearly still smarting from this challenge to his authority. So long as the fines are lower than the cost of a failed crop, though, farmers will continue to pay little attention to them.

In the field, therefore, the solution to scarcity lies in a very direct intervention in the flow: raising a water level, removing a blockage, widening an offtake, or tapping an additional source. Far from being ignorant of the Nile's limits, as some officials and donors claim, farmers are not only directly aware that scarcity exists but have their own set of mechanisms for getting water to flow to their fields. In employing these mechanisms, farmers, too, play a role in determining where Egypt's water flows and what it becomes in the process.

PRODUCING SCARCITY

Water scarcity in Egypt is clearly more a matter of distribution and access than fundamental lack. The scarcity that farmers experience when they go to irrigate their fields is a result not of the country having insufficient water but of the way in which that water is channeled around the country. There is a parallel here with studies of other types of scarcity. In his seminal work, *Poverty and Famines*, Amartya Sen (1983) argues that famine is not just a matter of there not being enough food but of how that food is distributed.[34] Although there is a "mesmerizing simplicity" to thinking about scarcity in terms of the ratio of resource to population, scarcity is not a question of what *exists* but of who can *command* what (Amartya Sen 1983, 8). Sen explains, "A person's ability to command food . . . depends on the entitlement relations that govern possession and use in that society. It depends on what he owns, what exchange possibilities are offered to him, what is given to him free, and what is taken away from him" (Amartya Sen 1983, 154). The supply of food is only one factor among many affecting whether a person will have the ability to obtain enough food to avoid starvation. Similarly, a farmer's ability to access water is at least in part determined by his or her position in a network of such entitlement relations. Whether or not the farmer has the money or exchangeable goods (a water buffalo or a sack of flour from a previous harvest, for instance) to buy a pump to supplement his supply, or bribe an official so that he can widen his offtake illegally, factors into whether or not his crops get enough water to drink.

However, there is a material dimension missing from Sen's analysis. The ability to command a resource depends not only on an individual's position in political, economic, social, and legal networks of entitlement but also on how that resource comes into being. This demands attention to the processes that produce a resource and govern its movement through space and time—an amalgam of things beyond any one person's direct control. Water scarcity is not a static characteristic—an insufficient volume in a particular time or place—but a condition integrally tied to the technologies and decision-making processes that make Egypt's water and, concomitantly, determine where the water flows and where it does not.

Underlining the material dimension to water scarcity reorients the focus toward the numerous actors who block, store, release, divert, and control the passage of Nile water from the highlands of East Africa to the Egyptian farmers' fields. These actors, who have different degrees of agency at the local, provincial, national, and international scales, employ a range of techniques to shape the flow of water. Some control scarcity quite literally — in the turning of a wheel, positioning of an earth dam, or opening of a gate. For others, those with the power to make people do as they say, scarcity lies in their words — an order to open a regulator, to implement a policy, or to introduce a new technology.

The various policy prescriptions that policy makers and international water experts propose to address scarcity constitute an array of mechanisms for intervening in the flow of water. One set of mechanisms focuses on how to increase the supply, by developing existing and alternative sources, or making the water flow more efficiently to the fields. The second set of mechanisms focuses on demand management, with the goal of getting farmers to use water more judiciously by charging for water or educating them about scarcity. Yet far from being ignorant of the problem, water users are keenly aware of scarcity and have their own mechanisms for addressing it.

The production of scarcity therefore offers a valuable lens into how and why it is that some farmers in Egypt have insufficient water while others do not. It highlights the multiscaled practices that govern the flow of water from its source to the field. These practices are a central part of the making of Egypt's water, and the tensions generated around them are a central part of water's everyday politics.

CHAPTER 3

Fluid Governance WATER USER ASSOCIATIONS
AND PRACTICES OF PARTICIPATION

It is a cool evening at the start of December 2007. The meeting is in the lecture hall of a government building in Fayoum City. The walls are beige with gold stripes; the dark green chairs, some still with plastic coverings on them, are fixed in rows. Five high-level officials from the Fayoum Irrigation Directorate sit on a stage behind a long table.

The farmers from a newly elected water user association arrive and greet the officials. The undersecretary starts the meeting. "The water user association is fundamental. It is the future," he says. He asks the farmers if they have any issues they would like to raise. "We have problems," says one farmer. Several others try to talk at the same time. They say how they need more water; parts of the canal are dry; an offtake is broken; they want to use additional pumps; they need subsurface drainage. The officials respond vaguely, making no effort to record any of these issues.

One official reads out the names of those in the water user association, and each farmer stands up in turn. Some look proud, others look nervous. A secretary passes around sodas and boxes of fried chicken. The director of the Irrigation Advisory Service summarizes the details of the memorandum of understanding between the water user association and the ministry. She takes a copy of the memorandum out of a plastic folder and signs it, saying what a pleasure it is to sign and passing it on to the undersecretary, who also signs. There is quiet applause as a new water user association is born. The undersecretary concludes by saying, "God willing, we'll be one family and solve the problems together."

In this chapter, I look at the shift in governance that international donors are promoting as a mechanism to address some of the points of failure within the irrigation network that I identified in chapter 2. The donors' belief is that involving farmers in decision making about water, through the establishment of water user associations, will help solve problems of poor canal maintenance, illicit withdrawals, inefficient distribution, and conflict. The water user associations will, they say, play a central role by prioritizing what maintenance work needs to be done, bringing problems to the authorities' attention, and resolving disputes between farmers. The water distribution system will function better with input from the water users. More farmers will receive the quantity and quality of water that they need to irrigate their fields; fewer will experience scarcity.

The establishment of water user associations is part of a broader policy shift toward a paradigm of participatory resource management.[1] The idea that water users should participate in water management is not novel; in some countries, water user organizations have a long history.[2] It is since the early 1970s, however, that participatory forms of water management have become widespread around the world, in part as a response to the disappointing performance of irrigation systems that received huge investments by governments and international agencies in the 1950s and 1960s (Garces-Restrepo et al. 2007). Indeed participation has become a buzzword within international water management circles. In a speech at the Fifth World Water Forum, the former president of the World Water Council proclaimed, "We *need* a participatory process." To add legitimacy to the statement, he listed the numerous reports from international organizations that have advocated user participation, including the second principle from the Dublin Statement on Water. International donors have taken up this clarion call and funded many projects to encourage participatory water management.

In Egypt, several donors have been promoting the establishment of water user associations (WUAs) since the mid-1980s (table 3.1).[3] By the late 2000s there were over 1,000 water user associations around the country, and the Ministry of Water Resources and Irrigation had adopted participatory water management as a national policy objective. This chapter analyzes one of these projects to establish water user associations. The Fayoum Water Users Organization Project (hereafter "the project") was funded by the embassy of the Netherlands and ran from 2007 to 2010. The project's overall objective was "to assist the Ministry of Water Resources and Irrigation in improving water management in the project area, the Fayoum, for increased efficiency and sustainable use of land and water, resulting in

TABLE 3.1 Genealogy of Egypt's Water User Associations

		Dates	Donor	Description
1980s: Pilot programs to establish mesqa-level WUAs	Egypt Water Use and Management Project	1977–1984	USAID	The recommendations that came out of this research project marked the first point when donors began to talk about the need for farmers to participate in irrigation management.
	Irrigation Management System Project	1981–1987	USAID and World Bank	These projects were oriented primarily toward the "improvement" of the irrigation system through a suite of engineering modifications. In addition, they introduced WUAs on the "improved" mesqas to help with the management of the engineering works.
	Irrigation Improvement Project			
	Phase I	1985–1989	USAID and World Bank	
	Phase II	1989–1996		
1990s: Pilot programs to establish branch canal WUAs		1994		The government passed the Farmer Participation Law No. 213 (a modification of the Irrigation and Drainage Law No. 12 [1984]), which made the development of mesqa-level WUAs a formal government policy.
	Fayoum Water Management Project			
	Phase I	1993–1996	Embassy of the Netherlands	Established pilot branch canal WUAs (at that stage known as "water boards") around Fayoum Province.
	Phase II	1996–2000		
	Phase III	2000–2005		

	Date	Project	Funder	Description
	1997–2002	Water Policy Reform Project (part of the EPIQ Agricultural Policy Reform Project)	USAID	Established pilot branch canal WUAs around the country.
2000s: Efforts to integrate branch canal WUAs into government policy	1999–2006	Water Boards Project	Embassy of the Netherlands	Established pilot branch canal WUAs around the country and sought to formalize a practical approach to WUA establishment.
	2000–2007	Water Management Improvement Project	JICA	Established one highly functioning branch canal WUA in the delta.
	2003	Advisory Panel Project Workshop on "Water Boards: From Pilot to Policy."		
	2004–2008	LIFE (Livelihood and Income from the Environment) Project	USAID	Established branch canal WUAs in the delta and Upper Egypt.
	2005–2014	Integrated Irrigation Improvement and Management—Water Boards Project	World Bank, German BMZ, Embassy of the Netherlands	Established branch canal WUAs in the delta.
	2007–2010	Fayoum Water Users Organization Project	Embassy of the Netherlands	Established branch canal WUAs throughout Fayoum Province.
	2007	Advisory Panel Project Workshop on "Water Boards: From Policy to Strategy."		
	December 2007	Ministerial Decree No. 10 acknowledged branch canal WUAs.		

economic growth and the alleviation of poverty" (FAWUOP 2007, 1). The project's main activity was the establishment of ninety-six WUAs along the branch canals of Fayoum Province.[4]

The project was based in the Fayoum Irrigation Directorate and run through the Irrigation Advisory Service, a department of the ministry formed in 1989 through a donor project.[5] The Advisory Service's role is to facilitate communication between the ministry and the farmers, so unlike other sections of the ministry, which by law can only employ engineers, it is able to hire social scientists. Engineer Dima, at that time head of the Advisory Service in Fayoum, was the project director. The manager of the project was Sarah, a foreign consultant with a master's in public administration who has spent many years working on water-related projects in Asia. She managed the team of community organizers who implemented the project activities. Some of the organizers were seconded from the ministry; others, most of them with degrees in social work from Fayoum University, were recruited specially for the project. In addition, the project employed a number of international and Egyptian consultants for short-term assignments on specific topics.

Critical studies of WUA programs around the world have highlighted the fact that WUAs are not always as participatory or efficient as their advocates claim. Intra-community power dynamics influence the effective participation of disadvantaged groups, such as women (Harris 2006), the landless (Hunt 1989), certain castes (Mosse 2003, chap. 9), or particular tribal groups (Pellissery and Bergh 2007). Inequalities may even be exacerbated by the operation of the WUAs. Furthermore, the participation of water users does not always lead to more effective and sustainable water management. Indeed it is not necessarily in water users' interest to use water more efficiently. For example, farmers may choose to grow water-intensive crops even if water is relatively scarce if those crops fetch a higher price. WUAs are open to corruption (Harris 2005) and often face difficulties in collecting the fees necessary to fund maintenance works to keep the irrigation system functioning well (Quintero-Pinto 2000; Raby 2000).

While this literature has provided a valuable critique of how WUAs operate and the degree to which they improve water management, this chapter explores a different set of questions. My fieldwork with the project offers a valuable insight into the formative stages of establishing participatory communities around the irrigation canals. Much like the making of water, the institutional structures through which that water flows are also always in the process of making.

The first part of the chapter examines three different understandings of "participation" that I observed being deployed: participation as communication, participation as role transfer, and participation as democracy building. I see these understandings not just as contrasting ways of talking about a common term but as attempts to forge different types of water users. The second part of the chapter analyzes the process of community construction, revealing how the fluidity of the resource confounds the process of forming a participatory community around it. In the third section, I explore how the WUAS operate in practice, evolving after their establishment into something less participatory than what their founders had in mind.

Through tracing these efforts to promote a particular kind of participatory water management, the chapter highlights the contestation over who makes the everyday decisions that shape the nature of Egypt's water across time and space. Such decisions include, for example, how much water is released through the gates of a weir, where excavators will work to scour out a blocked channel, when an offtake should be widened, and what action should be taken against an illegal abstraction. In establishing water user associations, the donors' vision is that these institutions will become the mechanism through which farmers participate in this decision making. Yet in practice, this chapter demonstrates the limits to this attempt to reconfigure farmers' agency and the multiplicity of interests, strategies, and forms of social connection that actually determine when, where, and how different parties exert influence over the flow of water.

THE BRIDE AND GROOM: VISIONING PARTICIPATION

Mohamed and I leave the office in a project truck. It is a bright winter's day, late in 2007. Out of the city and onto narrow, rutted country roads, we weave through fields of newly planted winter crops. We arrive in the village of Shubri as the loudspeaker from the mosque rings out with an announcement: "People of Shubri, people of Shubri, we have a meeting about irrigation in the mosque!" A group of fifteen men gather, and we sit together, cross-legged on the floor of the mosque, mosquitoes buzzing around us.

Mohamed starts by describing the project. He explains that a water user association (rabita mustakhdami al-mai) is a bit like an agricultural cooperative (gam'iya), and tells the gathered farmers that it is ministry policy to try and cover the whole country with WUAS. "Your canal feeds 7,000 feddan and about 7,000 farmers," he says. "The Irrigation [i.e., the ministry] can't talk to everyone. The association will help you, taking your concerns to the authorities (al-mas'ul). It has a kind of importance." He writes a list of the farmers' names and their landholdings and sets a time for a meeting to elect representatives to the WUA. After answering questions, Mohamed brings the meeting to a close. As we leave, he reassures the farmers, "We're here to help you. No more than that. Rather than you walking alone, we will walk with you."

This moment—the farmers' interaction with a project representative—marks their first encounter with a particular vision of participation. No doubt farmers have their own perspectives on what it means for them to play a role in water management. Indeed they are already participating, channeling water from mesqas to irrigate their fields and protesting or taking matters into their own hands when that water is lacking (see chapter 2). But in this meeting, the farmers hear about a new type of community—the water user association—that is to both facilitate and moderate their agency over water flows. The WUA is to be the vehicle of their participation.

When the project staff conduct these initial meetings, which the project terms "awareness meetings," they narrate a vision of participation and participant. The first element in the narrative is an explanation of what a water user association—a rabita—is. Community organizers often use the root of the word, rabata, which means to connect, bind, tie, unite, to communicate an understanding of this term. They talk about how farmers are connected by their shared need to access water. They say a WUA is like a family.

Frequently, the organizers explain that a WUA is a type of cooperative, like the agricultural cooperatives but "belonging to The Irrigation." Since the cooperatives are essentially run by employees of the Ministry of Agriculture, even though they have some farmer representatives, the comparison reveals how little autonomy the community organizers see the WUAS as actually holding. But the reference to agricultural cooperatives still has positive connotations for most farmers. Cooperatives supply farm inputs at subsidized prices; they also convey farmers' requests for canal dredging and other services to the ministry.[6]

The next element that the community organizers stress is that the establishment of WUAS is ministry policy. Their message is that farmer participation is not something that the donors have instigated but a commitment of the ministry. This is not necessarily what the community organizers believe. They are proud to work on a foreign project. They know that they receive substantially higher monthly wages than they would if they worked for the ministry, and they enjoy being based in the project offices, which stand apart from the rest of the ministry in their cleanliness, plastic plants, computers, and air-conditioning. But Sarah has told the community organizers not to mention either the word "project" or international funding when they talk to farmers. The WUAs are more likely to be sustainable, she thinks, if the farmers see them as ministry policy rather than as the initiative of a foreign donor project. Projects come to an end. If the WUAs are to continue playing a role, they must be linked to the ministry's day-to-day activities.

Finally, the community organizers explain why the WUAS are important and what they will accomplish in practice. In Mohamed's speech to the farmers in the mosque, his explanation centers on how difficult the ministry's job is, given the number of farmers it has to deal with. He draws figures of the large area of land served by the canals and the multitude of farmers farming that land into contrast with the figure of the solitary district engineer. Through this narrative, he also accomplishes a deft transferal of blame. If water problems are not being addressed, it is not because of bad ministry policies or poor managers, but simply because it is not possible for a limited number of engineers to get around all those canals.

The role of the WUA, the community organizers tell the farmers, is therefore one of communication. Participation is about talking about problems, setting priorities, and then communicating those priorities to the authorities. The water users are to be problem identifiers. If farmers face water scarcity, the WUAS will help convey this information and its causes to the ministry so that officials can take action. Based on an assumption of a dichotomy between farmers and the ministry (a simplification, since many ministry officials and community organizers also own and farm land), the organizers say that the WUAS will bring these two sides closer. Mohamed talks about the ministry and farmers walking together. Another organizer described this relationship as a marriage, telling a group of women, "I am like the engagement (al-khutba). You, the association, are the bride, and The Irrigation is the groom." The organizers talk about how the association will help take the farmers' voice (their complaints) to the authorities. It will help them solve their problems. It will make their lives easier.

Two months after the meeting with Mohamed, I am standing by a canal. It is the middle of the annual maintenance period and the flow of water into Fayoum has been stopped for two weeks. Garbage-choked mud is piled on the banks as excavators move along the canals, removing sediment from the bed. I am with some engineers from the Fayoum Irrigation Directorate, and we are visiting an offtake that is being reconstructed. A group is gathered around the offtake: an Egyptian consultant to the project, wearing suit pants and a blazer; the district engineer, in a black leather jacket and bright blue construction hat; technicians and engineers from the min-

Figure 3.1. A district engineer oversees maintenance work on a canal.
Photograph by the author.

istry in jeans and shirts; and two presidents and one secretary from local
WUAS, dressed in *galabiyas*. They are watching as laborers empty baskets of
pebbles, sand, and cement into a revolving concrete mixer. As we approach,
the consultant comes toward me, a smile on his face. Shaking my hand, and
gesturing toward the WUA representatives, he says, "You see the participation!" He tells me, with a note of pride in his voice, "The president of the
WUA has been here the whole of the past week [supervising the work], ten
hours a day." Slapping the district engineer on the back and laughing, he
continues, "At first the district engineer wasn't convinced [about the WUAs'
involvement], but then I convinced him!"

To this consultant, participation is about the farmers' presence as the
ministry carries out maintenance work on their branch canal. Rather than
being passive recipients of the services that the ministry provides, these
farmers are taking an active role in overseeing the maintenance work. To
participate is to play a larger role in practices like canal repairs. Hence while
donors advocate education programs to teach farmers how to use water
more wisely (see chapter 2), they also trumpet those farmers' participation
as a means of getting the water to flow more efficiently. The two goals are
not, however, as contradictory as they may seem. Every WUA establishment

project includes a series of training sessions for the farmers that cover the technical aspects of the irrigation system, the operational structure of the WUA, and its mode of interaction with the ministry. Participation is therefore about a particular type of *trained* water user playing a role in water decision making. As the expatriate director of one WUA project once said to me, "Some basic training is needed so they [the farmers] know what they are talking about and so they are not suffocated by technical terms."

Donors and consultants, like the one present in the scene by the canal, talk in terms of levels of participation, ranging from farmers merely being informed of ministry actions, through to being consulted, negotiating decisions, and ultimately controlling decision making. This rhetoric mirrors the typologies of participation that have been developed by a number of academics (e.g., Pretty 1995; Agarwal 2001; Drydyk 2005), many of them drawing on Arnstein's (1969) notion of a "ladder of participation" spanning from nominal to very active participation. The ultimate goal is that one day farmers will be able to take on the day-to-day operation of the branch canals, leaving the ministry to focus on managing water in the main canals and making strategic decisions. This is a way of freeing ministry engineers from "the nitty gritty," to use one international consultant's words, so that they can focus on bigger issues. Thus participation is about much more than farmers just communicating their problems to the ministry in an effective manner. The water user is to be a decision maker, not just a complainer.

This same vision of participation as a gradual transfer of roles to the WUA is reflected in the ministry's policy statements. The Institutional Reform Vision, for example, asserts that "the process of building participation is best designed as a series of agreements between the government agency and the WUO [water user organization], in which increasing rights are transferred as the WUO demonstrates it is capable of discharging increasing levels of responsibility" (MWRI 2005b, 23). Since this report was developed through a donor project, though, it is difficult to ascertain the degree to which it truly reflects opinions within the ministry.[7] Within the ministry, there are a range of different perspectives. Many of the high-level officials support the suggestion of the foreign project managers and donors that there should be a fundamental shift in how the ministry operates in order to incorporate farmers in the management structures. As one senior official said to me in an interview, "The participation of the users should be there and they should be completely entitled. I think my [i.e., the ministry's] future role should be focused on planning and monitoring performance, not on water distribution." For officials in these positions, the transferal of various decisions to the farmers does not pose any threat. They envision farmers taking responsibility for routine operations, which are far removed from the tasks that constitute the basis of their authority.

There is also a financial rationale behind senior officials' supporting a shift in the mode of governance. Daily management of the irrigation network is very expensive. If the ministry could transfer some of those tasks to the WUAS, it would cut costs. In addition, these officials know that donors are keen to support participatory projects and that aligning with the donors' vision will ensure the continual flow of donor funds into the ministry. "Some engineers see the WUAS as an investment opportunity," one Egyptian manager of a donor project admitted. He pointed out the number of outside agencies currently funding WUA projects. "If they [high-level officials in the ministry] say that they are not working with WUAS, maybe they won't get that funding."

In contrast, those at the implementation level—the ministry officials in provincial offices and district engineers—are in a different political position. They are not so concerned with balancing the central ministry's budget. An ability to make decisions about the water within their jurisdiction is a marker of their power. Any transfer of water decision-making tasks to the farmers would constitute a direct erosion of their authority. It is not surprising, therefore, that they do not share this vision of participation as farmers taking on more responsibility. They are also skeptical that the farmers have the technical expertise to play a greater role in operation tasks (even though many engineers are themselves farmers and come from the communities where the WUAS are being established). So more in line with how the community organizers explain participation to the farmers, these low-level officials continue to see participation—and the participants—in more limited terms. The water users will help identify problems, but they will still be the ones to make the decisions that they deem best. The words of the director general of irrigation in one meeting in Fayoum were revealing: "We will use water users just to inform us and give us data." Clearly in these officials' minds, there will be no shift in how decisions are made.

Hence whereas leading policy makers see water users as decision makers, those at the implementation level see them merely as problem identifiers. Between those talking about WUAS in Cairo and those involved in WUA establishment in the field, there is also a middle group of officials in the ministry who are not really involved at all. For many of these officials, WUAS remain a project-based initiative that has nothing to do with them. As Sarah acknowledged to me, "The water users are a relatively small issue in the central concerns of the ministry. Many in the ministry are old and nearing re-tirement and so aren't bothered about altering the status quo."

Sitting in the cool foyer of USAID's offices in Cairo in June 2008, having passed through three security gates, I hear another perspective on what participation means. "Our job is to empower people," Frank tells me. "This is a democracy exercise." Frank is a water specialist at USAID, and he for-merly worked on a project to establish WUAs in the Nile valley and delta. "Now some of the farmers can see that they can do things," he continues. "It's like opening Pandora's Box, and it won't be easy to close the lid." At the time of this conversation, two and a half years before the 2011 revolu-tion, democracy was not a feature of the political regime. In many donors' minds, the WUAs held the potential for a more participatory form of gover-nance. "We don't say the word 'democracy' in our project," Sarah remarked during one conversation, "but that's what it's about, good governance." In this vision, participation is about more than just farmers playing a role in shaping where the water flows. It is about democracy building. It is about forging water users as citizens.

"The WUAs are an interesting phenomenon in Egypt," one consultant commented, "because they are one of the few grassroots democratic orga-nizations that the government permits." The elections for WUA representa-tives held on front porches, in farmers' sitting rooms, mosques, and village halls contrast with the municipal and national elections, which up until 2011 were carefully staged and manipulated. The WUAs are, in the words of one consultant, "playing parliament at a local level," and it is a type of par-liament that meets the ideals of the international donor community. Even though the election procedure for WUA representatives is far from perfect, the fact that the elections take place at all, that the representatives are not selected by elites or ministry officials, and that there is some turnover in the representative body is sufficient grounds for democracy building claims.

Not surprisingly, this rhetoric of democracy building is not found in the ministry's documents on the WUAs, and I have never heard a ministry offi-cial refer to WUAs in these terms. Instead, it is a rhetoric that finds support in international policy discussions around water. At the Fifth World Water Forum, where participation was a central theme, the panels on this topic fo-cused heavily on concepts of citizenship, rights, and democracy. This vision of the WUAs aligns the goal of promoting "democratic governance" in the Middle East, which has been pursued by many donors over the past decade (Heydemann 2007). Although the WUA projects generally fall within the donors' agricultural or natural resource programs, rather than their programs on governance, the underlying rationale driving the WUAS is a similar one of trying to foster a more participatory form of decision making.

But what do the participants themselves think participation means? What kind of water user do they see themselves as being? Perhaps most significantly, a national survey found that only 6 percent of farmers know about the WUAS (El-Zanaty 2001, 40). While at the time of my fieldwork the project had yet to start working in all parts of Fayoum, even in areas where there were WUAS, awareness of them was limited. In the survey of fifty farmers that I conducted, only 32 percent had heard of the WUAS. Evidently the WUAS are not something that the broader farming community is discussing.

In fact, even among those who do attend the meetings and become members of WUAS, many still do not understand what a WUA is or does. One day I talked with a WUA representative called Om Zainab. I asked her, "So have you heard of the association (rabita)?" Om Zainab looked puzzled. "They say 'the association,' but I want to know what it is," she replied, unsure of herself. "You are part of it!" I responded, surprised that the term rabita failed to resonate. Om Zainab finally caught on. "Oh," she said, "the cooperative (gama'iya) on water, the meetings?" Clearly the WUAS are not the vehicle through which farmers generally envision their role in decision making around water. As Glynn Williams (2004, 565) acknowledges, "While participatory development projects can seem all-consuming to practitioners and academics evaluating them, they may play a relatively small part in their intended beneficiaries' lives."

Of those who have heard of the WUAS, they tend to see them in terms of meeting with other farmers, talking about their problems, and campaigning to the ministry for those problems to be solved. They are happy to play the role of the problem identifier. There does not seem to be a sense among farmers that acting together, through the institution of the WUA, they can take power into their hands and effect change on their own terms. In all the farmers' meetings I attended, the interactions between farmers and ministry officials I observed, and the conversations I had with farmers in the fields, I saw no indication that farmers are eager to assume more responsibility for running the irrigation system. To farmers, it is the ministry's duty to provide them with water. They are not keen to shoulder the labor and financial burden that would come with helping operate and maintain the irrigation network.

Hence there are multiple definitions of participation and water user. The donors driving these projects have a certain vision of participation that to a certain extent is adopted by high-level officials within the ministry. This is a vision that draws legitimacy from international fora of discussion, from what some academics describe as a "global consensus on participatory irrigation management" (Groenfeldt 2000). It is a vision that transcends national boundaries, as not only the ideas but also the consultants and donor staff who promote these ideas move from place to place. On a number of occasions, for instance, consultants related to me their experience working on projects in other countries and drew comparisons between the WUAs in Egypt and elsewhere. But as this vision is translated into everyday practice, different notions of participation emerge. Participation morphs and contracts. It becomes no longer about democracy and role change but about communication with existing power nodes. It becomes not about decision making from below but about problem solving from above. The significance of these multiple meanings lies in the contrasting expectations they generate about how, when, and where different parties are able to shape the quantity and quality of water that an area receives.

Thus participation is not an object of mutual understanding but rather a process fraught with ambiguity or, as Anna Tsing (2005, xi) writes, one of the "zones of awkward engagement, where words mean something different across a divide even as people agree to speak." Andrea Cornwall (2002) charts the "tracks and traces" in academic discussions of participation, highlighting a shift from participation as meaning a need to include the poor to participation as meaning that the poor are empowered to take control. Where participation is implemented in the field, however, a variety of conceptualizations actually exist side-by-side, often contradicting one another in their implications, yet shrouded by the ambiguities of the term. While other discussions of participatory water management have highlighted the diverse goals linked to WUA establishment (e.g., Harris 2005), this analysis shows how those goals are variously prioritized and promoted by differently positioned actors. I also see these goals not just as different visions of participation but, more fundamentally, as attempts to build different types of participants—people who will act in a particular way to help shape what Egypt's water comes to be.

While participation and participant are multiple in their meanings, the goal of the participatory project is clear: to establish water user associations. In the next section, I look at the practices through which the project creates these communities of what are variously perceived to be problem identifiers, decision makers, and citizens.

Fifteen community organizers are crammed into one small room at the project office. The room has four desks, eight chairs, and one computer. People stand, sit, perch, chat, drink tea, read the newspaper, and listen to recitations of the Quran on their cell phones. The air-conditioning unit is not working; the office is sweltering. A group is clustered around one of the desks, poring over a large sheet of white paper. One man draws while the others comment. In a thick marker he sketches one section of the irrigation system: a long sinuous line of the branch canal, with mesqas branching off on both sides. He marks the villages with red squares. This man is a community organizer, and he and his teammates are writing up the results of the previous day's field visit. Next to the map is a pile of loose papers, containing the information that one of them will type later on the aging computer—the position and size of each offtake along the branch canal, the name and area served by each mesqa, the water level in each section of the canal, and the name of each settlement.

This scene reveals some of the work that goes into constructing a community of water users. This is the work that must be done to convert an array of elements—the canals that wind across the landscape, the water that flows through them, the large farmer cultivating 100 feddan of grapes for export, the small farmer cultivating a few qirat of wheat to make bread— into a bounded arena of action. Through the sketch and the lists, the project team maps a community of water users in space, words, and numbers. In doing so, the team determines who is to participate, by delineating a group of water users, and sets each community's remit, by defining the WUA's boundaries. Unlike other forms of community-based resource management, participatory water management in Egypt is not based on an assumption that a distinct community of water users already exists. The establishment of WUAs is merely predicated on a belief that farmers will come together to identify as a community because they share the common goal of accessing water for their fields.

Several months later, I am sitting on a threadbare armchair in the reception room of an elderly farmer's house. Three community organizers explain the WUA that they are establishing on this farmer's branch canal. The man seems confused, and his son, who is sitting with us, does most of the talking. Before we leave, the community organizers need data. They ask the farmer for the names of the other people who draw from the same mesqa. The son stays silent as his father wrinkles his forehead in concentration and starts relaying a stream of names. Without a pause, he gives the names of thirty-one farmers and their precise areas of agricultural land, down to the qirat. As we drive away, I express my wonder at the ease with which this elderly man reeled off the names of each farmer and his landholding. The community organizers look at me in surprise. "But this is his life. He lives it every day," one of them says to me.

This moment demonstrates how water builds community. The elderly farmer knows everyone who draws from the same mesqa as he does and each farmer's exact landholding, because this is a group that he is integrally tied to through the flow of water. While the ministry controls how water passes into each mesqa, it is up to the farmers along the mesqa to divide this water between them according to a rotation system. The farmers build up and break down earthen dams across the irrigation ditch to manipulate the flow of water between them, in turn stopping it, so that it can be diverted onto the first farmer's land during his turn, then releasing it, so it can flow on down to the next farmer's land. When the mesqa needs maintenance, the farmers work together to do the maintenance work themselves or contribute the money necessary to pay laborers to do that work, their contribution proportional to the size of their landholding. This is not a perfect form of community. Often there are disagreements, and sometimes there are serious conflicts. But nonetheless, it is the community that makes the water flow; a community that is generated not by turning up at a meeting but by everyday practices of blocking, unblocking, digging, and weeding an irrigation ditch. It is a community generated not through a collective imagination (Anderson 1991) but through the shared work of maintaining the flow of water.[8] In Fayoum, the space of water community is one of the mesqa; in other parts of Egypt, where due to the topography farmers must lift water from the irrigation canals, farmer communities have emerged around the use of a water wheel (saqia) (Attia 2005) or communal irrigation pump (Hopkins 1999, 2005).[9]

The project to establish WUAs introduces a new community, which adds not only to the water-linked communities of the mesqas but also to the multiple, dynamic, and intersecting communities of extended families, friendship, and neighborhood that characterize the Egyptian countryside (Bach 2004; Hopkins and Saad 2004). The WUA, structured around clusters of branch canals rather than the mesqas, is not a community of everyday practice, at least not in its initial stages of foundation. It is a community crafted in the office of the ministry, overseen by international consultants, coordinated by project staff, and funded by a donor. Tracking this one particular form of community reveals some of the tensions that are manifest when an attempt is made to construct a community around a resource that flows.

Defining Participants

To build a community of water users, it is necessary first to define who the water users are. Given that everyone uses water, in some ways the term is a meaningless descriptor. Use of water is not a primary form of identification. During my time in Egypt, I never heard anyone describe themselves as a water user (muntafi' al-mai or mustakhdimi al-mai). In the rural community where I lived, when I asked people where they were from, they might reply with their village of birth, or their family name, but never with the branch canal or mesqa that they use. Thus although people in this area have always used water for various purposes, "water users" per se are something new. In the scene in the project office, it is in the lists of names and figures stacked on the desk that the process of water user creation is underway.

The project defines two types of water user: agricultural and residential. The distinction is driven by the donors, who argue that since the canals pass through towns and villages, any organization designed to help manage the canals has to take into account what happens to the water in urban areas as well as how farmers use the water to irrigate their fields. This concern is primarily one of water quality, since in terms of quantity, irrigated agriculture consumes a much higher volume of water than domestic usage. The discharge of household waste into the canals is a significant source of pollution, which impacts the health of people living near the canals and the agricultural produce irrigated with that water. The project defines agricultural water users as those who own land that draws water legally from a branch canal. Residential water users are those who live in villages located directly on a branch canal, who use canal water daily (generally to wash dishes, clothes, or livestock and dispose of waste, but also on occasions when they do not have access to tap water, to drink or cook). The former is the user type of most concern to the ministry. Indeed often in conversations about the WUAs, people use the term for farmer (fellah) interchangeably with that of water user, effectively erasing those who use water for nonagricultural purposes.

The categories of water user are implicitly defined along gender lines by project staff (Barnes 2013a). The agricultural water users are male farmers; the residential water users are female housewives. At the start of the project, Sarah tried to break down this gender dichotomy. A fifth of Fayoum's land is owned by women, and many women help their husbands in the fields or farm the land of husbands who are working overseas.[10] But when Sarah suggested that women are agricultural water users, too, she faced resistance from the project team and ministry engineers. Women in Fayoum do not irrigate, they said.[11] Lacking evidence to counter this, she asked me to conduct a study in collaboration with the female community organizers. We surveyed twenty-five male and twenty-five female farmers from around the province. Almost half of the women we spoke to said that they irrigate the land themselves. This number is most likely an underestimate, since women often play down their own contributions to irrigation because they regard it as just "helping out" (Radwan 2007). However, even this data, garnered from the fields of Fayoum, was not enough to convince the project team. When I presented the report to the team, many of the men were skeptical. These cases where women irrigate are very rare, they insisted. Even some of the female community organizers, who helped me conduct the study and heard the stories of the women we surveyed, maintained that women play little role in irrigation. This perspective may have partly reflected the fact that the female community organizers were all social work graduates from Fayoum City and not all that familiar with agriculture, but it may also have reflected their unwillingness to challenge the status quo. In the end, despite her convictions to the contrary, Sarah gave up trying to challenge the exclusion of women from the agricultural water user category.

Based on these two user types, the first step in forming a WUA is to create a list of water users from whom the representatives will be elected. During the awareness meetings, such as the one with Mohamed that I described earlier, the male community organizers record the names of all the farmers alongside each mesqa and their landholdings. This list is important so that the community organizers can ensure that the elections are representative. The female community organizers make a similar list, except that rather than creating a comprehensive register of residential water users, they just record the women who attend the awareness meeting. This is not a representative sample, since attendees are generally the friends, relatives, or neighbors of the woman hosting the meeting in her home, but the project team does not perceive this to be a problem. "Women's problems are all the same," a female community organizer said to me. "One woman can represent all the women from their area."

At the outset of the process of WUA establishment, therefore, in the definition of water users and determination of who are the individuals that will be associating, certain exclusions are set. These exclusions are partly gender oriented—male/agricultural, female/residential—but they go beyond this. The category of agricultural water user does not include the landless, who either rent or sharecrop other people's land. Nor does it include those who draw water without an official permit, either from pumps directly on the main canal or through illegal mesqas (see chapter 4). The residential water user category only includes those who live in villages directly on a branch canal. When talking with rural women, the community organizers abruptly cut off their conversations if they find out that someone is from a village that is not on a branch canal. This distinction is largely for logistical reasons; given the limited project staff, it is simply not feasible for the female community organizers to visit every village in Fayoum. The distinction is justified by an assumption that those living in villages on the branch canals will use the canal water the most. What this assumption ignores, though, is the fact that women from other villages may also make extensive use of canal water, depending on whether or not they have other sources of water in their villages.

Drawing Boundaries

The next step in community formation is to draw boundaries around the community. While various forms of cooperation and community identification are already present along the mesqas, the donors are not organizing WUAs around the mesqas. The first pilot programs in the 1980s did establish some mesqa-level WUAs, but as the donors started to promote participatory management on a wider scale, they shifted to establishing WUAs on the branch canals. These WUAs draw no claims of legitimacy from a longer tradition of community identification.[12] The decision to organize water users at the level of the branch canal rather than the mesqa came about through dialogue between the donors and senior policy makers in the ministry. Expatriate advisors argued, first, that it would be unfeasible for the ministry to interact with associations from every small mesqa. Second, they reasoned that bringing together the head and the tail ends of a branch canal would help WUAs to address water distribution issues. Indeed, the quantity and quality of water that any farmer receives is closely tied to the actions of his or her upstream neighbors. One consultant told me that they also chose this policy direction because it was in line with the "internationally accepted" procedures for WUA establishment.

The project initially planned to form a WUA for each of the 150 branch canals in Fayoum. As project implementation began, however, project staff began to realize that the situation was more complicated. Some of the branch canals only serve quite small areas, maybe as little as 500 feddan. Other branch canals have different names, but are essentially just continuations of each other. Thus the project team decided that it made more sense to form WUAS for clusters of branch canals, as these larger WUAS would have "economies of scale and more workable decision-making structures" (FaWUOP 2007, 1).

The community organizers decide which branch canals should be clustered together to form each WUA in consultation with officials from the Irrigation Advisory Service. The WUAS that result from this boundary drawing process include two to seven branch canal sections and up to 145 mesqas (the average is 35). In planning how the representatives will be elected from each of those canal sections, the community organizers draw a sketch map of the WUA community space. There is no comprehensive diagram that maps the WUAS' boundaries and their spheres of influence, though. "We can't make such a map," explained one organizer, "because there are not clear hydrologic or geographic boundaries between the WUAS. There is no clear line on the ground that marks the difference between the areas of the different WUAS." This indicates one of the difficulties of creating a community space around a fluid substance that evades borders. While the project team seeks to set a new realm for community formation by recasting the branch canal network from a line of continuous flow into a series of clusters, even to the project staff these realms are not all that clear.

The process of bounding water into distinct spaces of use generates various tensions. First, the project tries to bring together people from different branch canals who have no reason to identify with each other. Frequently farmers do not know those who draw water from the other end of a branch canal, which may be over 10km away. Although people do not have to know each other to identify as a community, the kind of shared collective imagination that Benedict Anderson (1991) writes about as the binding force of communities is also not present in the water user associations. They are communities imagined by their architects rather than by their members. Most water users have never heard of the associations that they are part of by virtue of their geographical location. The cluster of canals that constitutes the WUA community space means little to a farmer. That scale of interaction is not part of their everyday water practices. Unlike along the mesqas where it is the farmers who make the water flow, farmers from one mesqa on a branch canal have no need to cooperate with farmers from another. As a result, when the community organizers meet with the farmers to introduce the idea of the WUA, they have to explain multiple times what canal sections each association will include. In explaining over and over, the organizers seek to reify the new community's boundaries.

Second, while the project's rationale is that bringing together the head and tail ends of a canal will lead to more equitable water decision making, farmers are not always happy with this. Along canals where the tail end receives very little water, in part due to the excessive use of those upstream, bitter animosities have often developed between the farmers. Those at the tail end do not necessarily want to be clustered with the more fortunate head enders; they are skeptical that their needs would be met in such an organization. They would prefer an individual WUA that could represent their specific interests. At one awareness meeting in a village at the end of a branch canal, for example, the community organizer's suggestion that this branch canal would be clustered with ten others into a WUA met with great resistance. The farmers started shouting out that they needed their own WUA. The community organizer tried to explain that grouping this branch canal with upstream canals would allow the farmers to talk together and solve their problems. But the farmers were adamant. "Daquf [the name of their village and branch canal] has been oppressed for a long time," one said. "It won't do (ma yanfash) to put us in an association with anyone else." Another man concurred, "For twenty years we've been trying to solve the problems together, with no result." Despite the community organizer's pleas, the farmers were resolute. "We're agreeing to the idea of the association," one asserted, "but we're all agreeing that we want to be on our own."

Another tension generated in the process of community construction stems from the way in which the communities of water users transcend village community boundaries. Villages are one of many forms of collective identification that structure rural life in Egypt. Yet the bounds of the water user associations ignore these social communities. On average, each WUA contains seven villages, but some include as many as forty-seven. Farmers from any one village may belong to different water user associations, depending on the way the water flows to their fields. In fact, a farmer may be part of more than one water user association if his or her land draws from branch canals that have been clustered into different WUAs.

The project's visualization of the branch canals rather than the villages as the basis of community identification does not necessarily match the farmers' view. In one meeting run by a community organizer, a man in the group told her, "You should work with other villages as well, not just with this village." The community organizer's response was revealing: "Well, I'm working all along the canal." These comments encapsulate two contrasting forms of spatial identification. The man sees an enlarged view of the world incorporating multiple social relations with other villages. The community organizer, in contrast, structures her identification along the course of the water (up to the point where the water flows out of the ministry's hands), reducing the complex and messy relationships of life into a simple linear community. Rather than looking at the map of neighboring settlements, as the man implicitly does, she uses the branch canal as her starting point and then sees which villages lie along it. Those are the only villages she is going to work in to organize female representatives for this new association.

Selecting Representatives

The third step in the process of WUA formation is for the water users within the set boundaries to select their representatives to the WUA's representative assembly. In the project office, the community organizers and Irrigation Advisory Service managers determine how the representatives should be elected, based on criteria set by an international consultant. The size of a WUA depends on its command area, ranging from fifteen members for a WUA covering less than 2,000 feddan to seventy members for a WUA covering over 5,000 feddan. Each mesqa that draws from the branch canal has a male agricultural representative in the WUA, except where there are too many mesqas, in which case the mesqas are grouped together for the purpose of representative selection. Each village along the branch canal has a female representative in the WUA, up to the project's limit that there be 10–30 percent as many (female) residential representatives as there are (male) agricultural representatives. Once the male and female members of the representative assembly are elected, the community organizers bring them together to elect a management committee, proportional in size to that of the assembly.

This is the procedure, as set out in the project documents, but how do the elections play out in practice? While this is a process of community formation that is driven by an outside donor and expatriate consultants, once the project team sets the boundaries and parameters of each WUA, the process for electing members of the community to the WUA is led by the community organizers.[13] The election meetings, organized separately for men and women, generally start like Mohamed's, with an explanation about participation and the role of the WUA. The election itself begins when the community organizer asks who would like to nominate themselves or someone else to represent the group in the WUA. Occasionally the community organizers suggest people who they think would be most appropriate participants. Often only one name comes up, and the organizer will ask the group, or whoever within the group is listening, if they agree with this person representing them. There are normally a few nods and comments of affirmation and equally as many blank looks. If more than one individual is nominated, the organizer asks the assembled to vote by a show of hands.

In some meetings that I observed, it seemed to me that most of those in the room did not understand what was going on or who had been elected and for what purpose. This misunderstanding comes from the community organizers' limited ability to explain the novel concept of a WUA or, sometimes, from people not really listening. In other cases, though, particularly in the men's meetings, people took the elections quite seriously. When the farmers from Daquf were told that the project was going to cluster them into a WUA with other branch canals (despite their opposition), they were very concerned that someone from their village should at least be head of the organization. A group of them came together to take charge of the situation. Three days before the election, they met with leaders from the communities that draw from the different branch canals to discuss who should be in the WUA management committee. When the community organizers and I arrived for the election meeting around midday, we discovered that some farmers had been there since the early morning, negotiating who should take the presidential role.

Not everyone participates in this community defined by type (water user) and space (branch canal cluster). Lines of difference within communities strongly impact on who plays a role in the WUAs. These structures of power, in turn, are reworked as the WUAS open up new possibilities for political alliances and action. It is often the wealthier and more powerful individuals who are elected to the WUAS. When community organizers arrive in a village, the first people they seek are the *omda* or *sheikh al-balad* (community leaders appointed and paid by the Ministry of the Interior). These powerful figures (or, in the case of the residential user meetings, women whom the omda or sheikh al-balad recommend) tend to dominate the awareness and election meetings. Frequently the community organizers direct their comments specifically to them. There is a bias, especially among the female community organizers, for working with more educated people—women who, they say, are "active" (*nashita*), have a "love for awareness work" (*hub shughl al-tawa'i*), or "can speak" (*ta'rif tahki*). In fact, this bias is also prevalent among rural men and women, who often say that they would like an educated person to represent their interests in the WUA. Given the public setting of the elections, in cases where less influential members of the community want to put their name forward for election or to reject someone else's nomination, it is difficult for them to do so.

The participation of women in the WUAs is minimal. This is partly linked to the fact that they are incorporated as residential representatives in an institution that is focused on irrigation and improving cooperation with the Ministry of Irrigation. From the outset, therefore, the priorities that are branded as female concerns (improved drinking water quality, garbage collection, and connections to the sewage system) tend to be ignored and female members lose interest in participating in the organizations. The lack of female participation is also related to the fact that the WUA meetings are often organized at times and in spaces where it is difficult for women to attend.[14] Furthermore, the ministry staff continue to see female WUA members as insignificant. During the celebratory registration of the WUA described at the opening of this chapter, the ministry official did not even read out the names of the female members of the representative assembly.

These axes of social difference interact to determine who is included and who is excluded from the WUAs. It is not just wealth, power, or gender alone, but their combination with respect, knowledge, education, connections, family, and enthusiasm that play into the dynamics of the representative selection process. There are different types of exclusion (Peterson 2010). Some people are never invited to attend the meetings in the first place and thus have no voice in deciding who should represent them in the WUA. Other forms of exclusion operate during the WUA meetings, effectively precluding certain people's participation in the discussion. The fact that many people do not participate in participatory institutions has been widely identified in the literature (Meinzen-Dick and Zwarteveen 1998; Leach et al. 1999; Mosse 2003; Harris 2005; Pellissery and Bergh 2007; Peterson et al. 2010; Zwarteveen et al. 2010). Such patchy participation is not surprising, given that WUAs are not established within a vacuum but within a context already heavily laden with power relations.

Perhaps more interesting, though, is to consider how the excluded perceive their exclusion. Much of the literature on community resource management seems to start with an assumption that all community members would like to participate. If participation is viewed as a fundamentally good thing, then those who are excluded are disadvantaged. This understanding of participation as being desirable is, however, called into question by Callon and Rabeharisoa's (2004) study of a muscular dystrophy patient who refuses to join a patient association, to accept treatment, and to undergo medical testing. Callon and Rabeharisoa argue that the refusal to participate is not a rejection of agency but a choice to opt for a different form of agency. In refusing to join the patient association, the patient is opposing a reconfiguration of his identity—an identity that is being constructed through certain kinds of procedures, such as the testing and treatment. He is rejecting a network of attachments that would cause him to behave differently. In a similar way, in refusing to actively participate in a wua, the male farmer is refusing to be recast as a form of participant water user who will interact with the ministry in particular ways. He is refusing to be a user who will attend meetings, who will only voice his complaints to the ministry through a formalized process, and who will take on more responsibilities. The Fayoumi housewife, in refusing to join a wua, is refusing to be recast as a residential water user who will spend time attending meetings with men from different areas and use this institution to address her water-related concerns. Both male and female nonparticipants are rejecting entry into an uncertain territory, dominated by terms and conditions that they do not control and are not familiar with.

Some farmers feel that they have no need for the specific form of agency encapsulated in the wua. When one community organizer explained to a farmer that the wua would help farmers realize their rights, the farmer responded, "We know our rights." When another organizer explained to a farmer that the wua would offer a forum for the farmers to talk about their problems, the farmer responded, "We haven't been talking about the problems for one year, but for ten years. We're tired from how much we've talked about it!" When a community organizer explained to some farmers that the wua would help them communicate problems to the authorities, one farmer responded, "We have complained and complained about our situation and still have no water. We have been to The Irrigation three times, but it's no use, there is no benefit!"

Nonparticipation in a wua may also be a deliberate strategy to choose a different method of action. Farmers already have everyday practices for getting the water that they want. Many women are skeptical that their concerns about the quality and quantity of water flowing through their villages and into their homes will be addressed by this irrigation-focused organization. Many men are skeptical that the ministry will listen to the wuas' requests. These women and men are not silenced by their nonparticipation. Rather, instead of attending meetings organized by a community organizer, nominating himself or herself to be a wua representative, and attending committee meetings, the nonparticipant water user chooses another strategy.

He or she meets with others to discuss water-related issues in the field, on the road, at the market, or in the home, in the way that he or she is accustomed. When facing a critical water problem, the nonparticipant takes the bus to Fayoum, either alone or with a group of users who face a similar issue, and knocks on the door of a senior irrigation official or municipal manager rather than reporting the problem to the local WUA. Many of the farmers whom I described in chapter 2, waiting in the hallways to meet with officials to complain about their lack of water, are there of their own accord, not as representatives of WUAS. Alternatively, the nonparticipant may call by the house of one of the more influential large landowners in the village, who may or may not be part of a WUA, to ask for his or her help. Others, especially women, may find that they are better positioned to influence decision making in the WUA from outside the organization, through relatives who are members. Thus WUAS are only one of a number of ways in which farmers can work to shape Egypt's water in their interests. Frequently farmers may prefer to utilize social connections that either precede or exceed those forged through the WUAS to access water. The individual who chooses not to participate is not opting for a status of non-agency but for a different form of participation.

Fluid Communities

Through the steps of member definition, boundary delineation, and representative selection, the multiple visions of participation are translated into an output: the water user association. The water user association is what Tania Li (2007) calls an assemblage, bringing together things (water, branch canals, offtakes, mesqas, rotation systems, lists of names and landholdings, registration documents), socially situated subjects (farmers, district engineers, community organizers, donors, consultants, policy makers, international conference attendees), objectives (communication, efficiency, democracy), and an array of knowledge and regulatory regimes. These elements are drawn together under a label that resonates in itself—that of the water user association. The process of forming the assemblage is an incomplete one in which only some choose to participate, while others choose alternative strategies to meet their water requirements. The "community" of water users is not a given but requires extensive work from project organizers, ministry officials, and donors to build, craft, and solidify its boundaries and contours.[15]

But looking closely at the process of the WUA foundation reveals, also, that just as the community cannot be taken for granted, neither can the resource on which that community is based. To form a community space of management, the project team must rework the irrigation canals into a series of clusters. Participatory management is based on a notion that those who live close to a resource and whose livelihoods depend on it have the most interest in the sustainable use and management of that resource. Participatory projects therefore tend to define community geographically, as those who occupy a particular space, in close proximity to the resource. This geographical definition of community ignores the fact that community is also generated through economic, political, cultural, and social relations (Gauld 2000). Furthermore, it gives an impression of geographic isolation, erasing a community's position within a larger cultural, economic, and political context, which can prove problematic. Just because people live near a resource does not mean that they identify as a bounded group, that they are dependent on the resource, or that they have a long tradition of interaction with that resource (Li 2002).

In the case of water, its liquid properties pose additional challenges for a geographically defined community. Water can be bounded in a canal, and this, in effect, is what the project does when it establishes communities around branch canals. But the physical structure of the canal is only one part of the resource, the integral technology for transferring water from place to place. The other part of the resource is the water flowing through that canal: a resource that is always moving. Not only is the WUA not a space of economic, political, cultural, and social interactions, but it is not a tangible water domain. Farmers do not identify with the WUA as a community space. They are skeptical about the ability of the WUA to effect change, perceiving that the problems come from outside that realm—a belief that chapter 2's discussion of the multiscaled drivers of scarcity shows can often be valid. It is therefore not surprising that the WUAs evolve after their point of creation into something that is not necessarily what the donors had in mind. Rather than the WUAs emerging as key participants in the making of Egypt's water, the next section reveals the multiple interests, strategies, and social relations that actually shape how different groups exert influence over where the water flows.

REEDS IN A STORM: PARTICIPATION IN PRACTICE

It is January 2008 and midway through the two-week annual maintenance period. I am sitting in a meeting with the district engineer and a group of representatives from different WUAS. The farmers are livid. It turns out that even though the WUAS submitted their lists of priorities for maintenance work, the district engineer changed them. None of the farmers' priorities have been implemented. The president of one of the WUAs protests, "The idea is that we set priorities and The Irrigation respects them. You have your technical opinion and we respect it. You must respect ours! But you changed the positions of the works!" The district engineer responds that he took their priorities into consideration, but ultimately decided that other works were more important. Everyone becomes more and more incensed, until finally the district engineer silences the group, shouting, "Is it because I'm short?" (He is indeed much smaller than the farmers.) "You must respect me!"

This interaction between the engineer and the WUA representatives reveals some of the tensions manifest as the WUAs seek to influence water management. Once the WUAs are released from the hands of those who managed their establishment—the community organizers—they evolve. Regular meetings of the representative assemblies, which sometimes comprise over 50 members, are not feasible. Thus the WUAs generally become embodied in their management committees or in certain members of those committees. The very premise of the WUA—that it will provide a vehicle for farmers' participation—is undermined as the WUA shifts from a collective to a single person or small clique. These individuals tend to be the more influential members of the committee, who often knew each other previously, coming from the same families, villages, or mesqas. They are the farmers who feel comfortable in the power-laden meetings with ministry officials. They are proud of their leadership role and enjoy the prestige it gives them. I was struck by this when a man came up to me at the end of one meeting with ministry officials and gave me his shiny business card. The card stated his name and that he was *Boss of Water Councils Union*. On the other side of the card, written in Arabic, the card stated his title as president of a water user organization management committee. The business card, which the farmer designed and paid for, signifies his attempt to consolidate the idea of community, to reinforce the idea that the group of water users within his area is a unity, and to demonstrate his authority as the group's representative.[16]

Where the WUAs carry out work on the canals, local people often associate this work with the efforts of these charismatic individuals rather than their WUA. When I asked one woman who was responsible for cleaning out her branch canal, for instance, she replied, "Ahmed Saleh, he stands by the excavator." Another woman in the same village said, "There is a group with Ahmed Saleh. They clean it." Neither woman identified this prominent member of the community with a WUA, even though he was on the WUA management committee. They attributed the maintenance work to Ahmed and his "group," not to a formal institution of which they were part.

The future of each WUA as an entity depends to a great deal on who ends up speaking for that association. Where those individuals are well connected, the WUA tends to be active; where they are disengaged, the WUA becomes, in the words of one of the project team, "sleeping and lazy." When I asked one WUA president if he knew officials in the ministry, he responded, "My personal relations with these people are *mumtaz*, excellent! I know the undersecretary, the director general, the inspector." He mentioned each by name. "This helps my work. If a WUA didn't have these relations, it would find things difficult."

But even with strong leadership, what can the WUAs do? To what extent can they intervene in the processes that produce scarcity (see chapter 2), to ensure that their constituent farmers receive the water that they need? The legal status of the branch canal WUAs remains tenuous. Under the current legislative framework of Irrigation and Drainage Law No. 12, WUAs are not permitted, for example, to raise funds or contract out maintenance works. Thus even if members of a WUA identify a problem on one of the branch canals, which is impeding the flow to certain areas, they are reliant on the ministry to bring the necessary equipment and materials to address that problem. For a number of years, donors have been pushing the government to change this law. The ministry drafted an amendment, but it is still under review by the parliament and has yet to be approved. Many in the donor community hoped that the regime change in 2011 could provide the necessary impetus for parliament to finalize the amendment and give the WUAs the legitimacy that they need. "We thought the revolution would solve things," one international consultant commented to me in November 2011. "But," she added ruefully, "it hasn't." The WUAs therefore lack legitimacy. If the law amendment is not finalized before all the donor projects come to an end, this raises significant questions about the sustainability of these institutions, which remain constrained in their mode of operation and lack a legally grounded position within the irrigation bureaucracy. The possibility that the WUAs will become key players in determining where Egypt's water flows and what it becomes seems remote.

Among farmers, there is a great deal of skepticism about the ability of the WUAs to effect change. There is a prevalent sense that the source of the problems lies outside the boundaries of the WUAs and thus beyond the power of the WUAs to address. This judgment is not unfounded, for water scarcity—which comprises probably the most significant problem that farmers face—is produced by actions that take place on multiple scales (see chapter 2). Farmers often make explicit reference to how their sphere of influence is limited to particular scales, saying that the problems come "from above" (min fowq), meaning both from above them in terms of the hierarchical irrigation system (from the main canal or an upstream branch canal), and above them in terms of the ministry's hierarchical power structures (from the director of irrigation or district engineer). "There are some things in my hand, but there are things in the hand of The Responsible (al-mas'ul, i.e., the authorities)," said one farmer. Another commented, "We don't have enough power (sulta) like The Irrigation to solve the problems." To most farmers, the solution to their problem of insufficient water lies in increasing the amount of water flowing into Fayoum. This is something that they are not able to control. The farmers do not believe that the ministry will keep its side of the contract and make the changes that they request. As one farmer said when I asked his opinion on the WUA for his area, "It won't do anything. They'll demand their things, but it requires follow-up, and they [the ministry officials] won't follow up. Those are good people [the WUA representatives], but the problem is with The Irrigation. The problem is in the implementation (tanfiz)."

From the interactions I observed between the ministry and the WUAS, it seemed that the farmers' concerns were warranted. I was struck by the wide circulation of water-related problems and yet the elusiveness of their solutions. At every opportunity, farmers explain to ministry officials the problems they face. Lists of problems are pinned to the wall of WUA offices. At donor-coordinated workshops, farmers gather in breakout sessions to discuss their problems. Yet nothing seems to happen beyond this. After one workshop, I saw the president from one WUA give the consultant who facilitated the workshop the list of problems his group had written, neatly recorded on sheets torn from his notepad. The consultant thanked him, then passed the sheets on to one of the community organizers, who put them in his pocket. "What will you do with this list?" I asked the community organizer. "Nothing," he replied, looking surprised at the question.

In the absence of an amended law, the donors have decided to focus on one limited area in which the WUAS may play a role—canal maintenance—to provide evidence that participation is valuable. Under the donors' encouragement, the minister issued Ministerial Decree No. 10, in November 2008, which states that the WUAS should help identify what maintenance works the ministry should conduct during the annual maintenance period. In theory, maintenance priorities are to be decided by all the water users in a WUA. In practice, it is generally the people who attend WUA meetings and are engaged in this particular process of participation who write the lists of priorities.

In some cases the WUAS are successful in determining the work that the ministry carries out on their branch canals. In one irrigation district, the maintenance period of 2008 was considered by the ministry to be a great triumph. The project staff organized a party to celebrate the success of involving the WUAS in identifying and implementing the maintenance works. Over a rousing pop song, a ministry engineer presented a slideshow. The presentation started by introducing the key players: officials from the irrigation directorate, the district engineer, the project staff, and representatives from three WUAS. Photographs and names flashed up against a backdrop of sparkling roses, red hearts, and fluttering butterflies. In bright green, pink, yellow, and white lettering, the slides then listed the achievements of the recent maintenance work: offtakes mended, canals cleared, bridges repaired, lining inserted, walls built. The words disappeared too quickly to read them all, but the message was unmistakable. Participation works. Following the words, a stream of photos faded one into the next. Excavators clearing a canal, a newly built offtake, a group of WUA representatives talking to ministry officials, an engineer using a theodolite, dark mud piled up beside a canal. I cringed at my presence in many of the photos, notebook in hand, but the engineers grinned, happy that an international observer had witnessed their success. When the slideshow reached its end, it went on repeat, the bright words and images forming a dynamic backdrop to the dinner and speeches that followed.

I looked around the room and was struck by the fact that most of the WUA representatives were wearing suits rather than the *galabiyas* more commonly worn by farmers. As the evening progressed, I began to realize that these were highly influential individuals—a group that one consultant working in Fayoum described as a "big old boy's circuit." One was a professor in agriculture at Fayoum University. Another was a large landowner with close links to some of the high-level officials in the irrigation directorate. During the dinner, they talked with the ministry officials with an ease and familiarity far from what I saw in the tense interaction between the district engineer and WUA representatives that I described at the start of this section.

Thus where the WUAS are effective in influencing the ministry's work, it is often because of their leaders' personal relationships with ministry officials. In the absence of those relationships, ministry officials are less inclined to listen to the WUAS' opinions. Indeed in an evaluation that a consultant conducted at the end of the project in 2010, he found that 65 percent of the sampled WUAS had not been informed, let alone consulted, by the ministry about the works that it carried out during the annual maintenance period (FaWUOP 2010b). The following year, in 2011, the maintenance period coincided with the revolution. As crowds gathered in Tahrir Square to protest their lack of voice in political decision making, the farmers of Fayoum saw little change in how their voice was incorporated into decision making about maintenance work. In an interview that I conducted in November 2011, an official admitted that that year's closure was "not a success." "The water user associations made their list of priorities, but the engineers didn't listen," she recounted. "If someone is a relative, they will do it (the requested maintenance work), but not for others. It's not fair."

While the power of the WUAS is limited at present, it is possible that as more and more WUAS are formed, their influence will increase. Although it is quite easy for ministry officials to ignore just a handful of WUAS scattered around the landscape of irrigation canals, when there are hundreds of these organizations, one for every canal section, it may be more difficult for them to do so. As one consultant commented, "Whereas I see a single WUA like a single reed in a storm, if it is a cluster of WUAS it is like a field of reeds, all equally weak but they keep each other up."

This is an unsettling prospect for some of those in power. During an interview with a senior official in the agency funding the project in June 2008, he told me how he took a parliamentarian to a workshop that brought together WUAS from Fayoum and from the delta. "There was a moment when this parliamentarian almost fell off his chair," the official recounted. "He said to me, 'I just realized that these water user organizations are going to be strong. They're going to be stronger than us! Oh no no no, they'll be stronger than us!'"

Yet the WUAS do not operate within a sphere that is isolated from government influence. Decentralization of tasks to private or non-state actors does not mean a decline of state control but a transformation of that control, a scattering of control around a network of patronage relations and channels of power (Hibou 2004). The WUAS open up space for new forms of intervention at the local level. Given the various ways in which ministry officials and international donors direct and influence the formation and functioning of the WUAS, one could argue that rather than being a tool of farmer empowerment, participation is a new form of ministry and donor control at the field level.[17] The establishment of WUAs can be seen as an attempt by the ministry, with donor support, to shape the role that farmers play in making Egypt's water, by organizing what famers are doing at the level of the branch canal, structuring the relations between them into hierarchically organized committees and providing guidelines (not that those guidelines are necessarily followed) to govern their interactions. The participatory reforms do not replace central government control over water flow with an empowered local rule, but create new spaces where different forms of control can be organized.[18]

The participation of farmers in WUAs creates novel opportunities for the ministry to exert indirect influence. Indeed over the course of the project, senior officials in the Fayoum Irrigation Directorate tried to intervene in the process of electing representatives to the WUAs or to bypass that process altogether by suggesting certain allies for the position of WUA president. On one occasion, for example, the undersecretary asked the Irrigation Advisory Service to replace the president of one WUA because he was being too demanding. Thus while the WUAs might offer up a new space for agency over Egypt's water, it is a highly controlled one, in which the boundaries of what is acceptable remain closely monitored.

FLUID GOVERNANCE

I returned to Egypt in November 2011 on the eve of the first round of elections for Egypt's new parliament. On the radio, songs lauded the wonders of democracy; conversations returned consistently to the protestors, Mubarak, security, and the elections; television adverts used playful cartoon figures to entreat everyone to get out and vote. There was a palpable sense that Egypt was in a new era in which people could talk freely and in which there was at least a possibility that their voices might be heard.

One morning in Cairo, I met with a ministry official who had been involved in the establishment of the WUAs. I asked her about how the WUAs in Fayoum were faring, eager to hear what had happened in the year since the project came to a close. "Their performance has not been good," she told me, slightly apologetically. "The problem is that the ministry expects them to fix everything. But last year there were many problems in Fayoum. Many, many problems. More complaints from Fayoum than *anywhere* else in the country. People in the ministry say that the water user associations are clearly not doing their job. They aren't improving water management! This even got to His Excellency (the minister), who now says that it seems that the WUAs are not working."

The minister's critical evaluation of the WUAS reflects, at root, a lack of clarity about what exactly the WUAS are meant to be doing. As this chapter's analysis of the multiple understandings of participation has demonstrated, most farmers understand the role of the WUAS to be to identify problems and report them to the ministry. By this metric, the large number of complaints coming from Fayoum could be interpreted as an indicator of the WUAS' success. But to officials in the central offices of the ministry who only have a limited budget to work with, such complaints are not always welcome. They see the role of the WUAS as being to relieve some of this burden, even though they know that the WUAS lack the legal recognition to do many of the things, like collect funds from their members, that would allow them to do so. The WUAS are failing, therefore, because they are not solving these problems.

Thus the donors' efforts to promote WUAS as key actors in water decision making seem to have had a limited impact to date. Ultimately, farmers do not need the WUAS to participate in the making of Egypt's water. They may capitalize on opportunities created through participatory projects, such as the chance to meet with other farmers or ministry officials, but they are not reliant on such projects to form social connections. Farmers have been interacting with other farmers and with ministry officials to try and ensure that their water needs are met since well before the participatory projects arrived on the scene. These everyday interactions, which persist today despite donors' visions of the most efficacious way for farmers to participate, are fundamental to shaping what Egypt's water comes to be.

CHAPTER 4

Irrigating the Desert, Deserting the Irrigated
LAND RECLAMATION AT THE MARGINS

We head south, away from Warda in the direction of the main canal, toward the desert hills (*gabl*) that border the agricultural land.[1] We walk through what are now fields of tall maize and dark green onion seedlings, threaded with earthen irrigation ditches, and small fields of olive and pear trees, interspersed with fodder grasses. The land is gently sloping upward, although you would not know it except for the water running through the ditches in the opposite direction. We pass by scattered houses; ducks and chickens run around outside, and lines of clean laundry dry in the sun.

As we walk, Abu Khaled tells me what the land used to be like. "It was just desert (*gabl*)," he says. "There was *nothing* here, it was scary, terrible (*kan mukhif, mukhif*)! There were no houses, no electricity, nothing!" He paints a picture of a lawless wilderness, telling me that when he and his family first started to reclaim the land, someone would sleep with their water pump because they were worried it would be stolen. We walk further, crossing some land that has not yet been brought into cultivation. The barren land is rocky, with sparse, scrubby vegetation. We reach the main canal. A diesel pump sits on the far bank, chugging as its belt rotates and lifts water through a plastic pipe, spurting it into a ditch that runs into the higher ground on the far side. The strip of cultivated land on the other side of the canal is only two fields wide. Beyond that, the sandy plain rolls into the distance and a string of electricity pylons leads to a row of trees on the horizon.

In this western corner of Fayoum Province, the desert and the sown meet along a border that is constantly moving in space and time through the process of land reclamation.[2] The pump on the far bank of the canal lifts water and channels it into a sandy field, as one of the steps through which a farmer converts this patch of desert into a field of onions that he will plant next year. The trees on the horizon mark the new reclamation area and town of Yusuf Siddique, which local people call The Graduates (al-kharigin) because the land is farmed by recipients of the government's program to allocate reclaimed land to college graduates. A short distance downstream lie the lands reclaimed through an American-funded project in the 1950s, now mostly uncultivated due to a lack of water.

These are some of the spaces through which water moves. Up through a pump. Along a ditch. Over the desert. While chapter 3 examined the governance structures through which the water flows, in this chapter I look at the land over which that water flows. I focus, in particular, on how water's material characteristics enable the transformation of desert to field. Water is the limiting factor for agricultural expansion into the desert, for unlike the other inputs required to reclaim land, such as fertilizers and soil treatments, it cannot be easily purchased. As farmers channel water from the canal network to the fields, they shape that water's quantity and quality characteristics. What Egypt's water comes to be is, in part, an outcome of these everyday acts of lifting and diverting water to new desert lands.

Egypt has a long history of land reclamation. For centuries, government agencies, private companies, and farmers have worked to channel the waters of the Nile over a larger and larger area (see figure 4.1).[3] Since independence, however, successive governments have taken up "horizontal expansion" through desert reclamation as a central policy objective (table 4.1). Expansion has been fueled by the greater volume of water available throughout the country since completion of the Aswan High Dam. Unlike the case of participatory water management discussed in chapter 3, this is a program driven by Egyptian policy makers rather than by international donors.[4] In August 2012, the agricultural minister announced a target of reclaiming one million feddan over the next five years (Hussein 2012). This reclamation will, the government hopes, create more land for settlement, boost agricultural production, and generate new jobs.[5]

To accomplish this expansion, the government has launched a series of grandiose schemes over the last couple of decades. Targeting large tracts of land far out in the desert, these projects are ambitious in scale and hugely expensive. The Toshka Project, for example, taps the Nile at the start of its journey through Egypt and transfers water 50km through the Sheikh Zayed Canal from Lake Nasser into the Western Desert to cultivate what the gov-

Figure 4.1. Agricultural expansion in Egypt. Source: Data prior to 1960 derived from
A. Nyberg et al., *Arab Republic of Egypt Land Reclamation Subsector Review*, February 1, 1990,
57; data for 1960–2007 from CAPMAS, "Agriculture Statistics, Planted Area, 1960–
2007," *Egypt in Figures 2009*, 71.

ernment plans to eventually be over half a million feddan. Toward the end of
the Nile, the El-Salam Canal diverts water from the river's Damietta branch
to the northern part of the Sinai Peninsula, mixing it with drainage water,
with the aim of ultimately reclaiming 620,000 feddan[6] (see map 1.2). If
these projects are completed, they will rework the geography of Nile flows.
A fully developed Toshka Project, for instance, would consume nine billion
cubic meters of Nile water, 16 percent of the country's annual water allocation. Many scholars, politicians, and media commentators have raised
questions about the potential costs of diverting so much water out of the
Nile Basin.[7] Indeed, even within the water ministry, many are dubious.

Up until now, though, concerns about water diversions to the government's large-scale reclamation projects have remained largely hypotheti-
cal. For like so many other state-led modernist interventions, these projects
have failed to meet their ambitious targets.[8] By 2012, for example, agricultural investors had reclaimed only 50,000 feddan in Toshka—less than 10
percent of the planned area.[9] The straight lines of the irrigation network
mark out the territory—the fields of the future—but the investors have yet
to come. Rather than telling the story of the government's failed schemes,

therefore, this chapter focuses on the area where landscape transformation is actually taking place. The place where water is flowing over new land. The place where pumps are active, not silent, irrigation canals full, not empty. The place where new fields are emerging in the desert. This is the margins of the agricultural zone.

. All along the boundaries of the Nile valley and delta, the jagged edge of the cultivated zone is testament to the piecemeal addition of blocks of land to farms: a gradual accretion of agricultural space. This is where the most active and effective reclamation is taking place.[10] The government is responsible for some of this reclamation. It is in this zone, for instance, that the Project for Developing and Serving the Land Allocated to Youth Graduates (hereafter, "the Graduate Scheme") is developing land to allocate in five feddan parcels to college graduates, veterans, and farmers who lost their land in the 1992 land reform law.[11] The government has also recently issued a number of large land concessions on the borders of the valley and delta for investors to reclaim. Most of the marginal reclamation, however, has been initiated not by the government but independently by farmers like Abu Khaled. Due to its informal nature, it does not figure in official accounts of Egypt's expansion program. It does figure, though, in the patterns of water flow. Marginal reclamation is having a profound impact on where and how the waters of the Nile move through the landscape.

Water is what makes the desert bloom. As farmers employ a range of everyday practices to access water to reclaim new land, they direct water away from existing land. That water may still reach the old land through a circuitous route. Water that is not evapotranspired by the new land crop infiltrates and flows back into drainage ditches, irrigation canals, or the Nile channel, to be used again by other farmers. But on its way, it dissolves salts and agricultural chemicals from the soil; some molecules percolate into deep bedrock, and others evaporate from the soil. So the diversion of water to new lands fundamentally means less water and water that is more saline for other agricultural lands. The quantity and quality of water each farmer receives is linked to the land which that water has passed over and through. The making of Egypt's water is integrally tied to the making of Egypt's land.

I use a theoretical lens of what David Harvey (2003) terms "accumulation by dispossession" to explore the shifting dynamics of access to water that are generated by agricultural expansion into the desert. Harvey builds on the notion of primitive accumulation, which Marx used to describe how

TABLE 4.1 Land Reclamation since the 1950s

1950s	1953–1967	Egyptian-American Rural Improvement Services Project	Reclaimed 37,100 feddan in Abis (near Alexandria) and in Kom Oshim and Quta in Fayoum.	• Reclaimed land distributed to landless farmers.
	1953–	Tahrir Project	Planned to reclaim 600,000 feddan west of the delta. By 1980 had reclaimed 122,000 feddan.	
	1956	Suez crisis stalled progress.		
1960s	1960–1965	First Five-Year Plan	Government reclaimed 306,500 feddan along the borders of the valley and delta and 83,500 feddan in the Western Desert.	• Private land reclamation companies nationalized. • Creation of state farms in the reclamation areas. • Cooperatives as the principal mode of production.
	1966–1970	Second Five-Year Plan	Reclaimed around 300,000 feddan (only one-third of the planned area).	
	1967	1967 war hampered progress.		
1970s	1970–1978	Low rates of growth	Less than 50,000 feddan reclaimed.	• Progress slow due to other budgetary priorities.
	1971	Completion of the Aswan High Dam	Increased the amount of water available in the Nile valley and delta, facilitating further reclamation.	
	1978	President Anwar al-Sadat launched a "Green Revolution," with the goal of developing 2.9 million feddan of new agricultural land before the end of the century.		

Decade	Years	Policy/Project	Description	Key developments
1980s	1980–1991	New Land Development Project	World Bank–funded project reclaimed 24,000 feddan west of the delta.	• Shift toward the private sector. • Sale of state land to private investors for reclamation. • Privatization of the state farms. • Increasing donor skepticism about the economic viability of reclamation after studies suggested that the productivity of the reclaimed land is too low to warrant the large investment.
	1981	Public Law No. 143	Removed public sector's legal monopoly on reclamation, opening up reclamation to the private sector.	
	1983–1988	Third Five-Year Plan	Reclaimed 189,000 feddan (half in the west delta).	
	1987–	Mubarak Project for Developing and Serving the Land Allocated to Youth Graduates	Started to distribute land in five feddan parcels to college graduates, veterans, and farmers who lost their land in the 1992 land reform law.	
	1988–1992	Fourth Five-Year Plan	Reclaimed 656,000 feddan.	
1990s	1993–1997	Fifth Five-Year Plan	Reclaimed 469,000 feddan.	• Increasing private sector involvement (from one-third of the reclaimed area in 1987–92 to more than two-thirds of the total reclaimed area in 1993–97). • Government started to sell land in mega projects to large investors and companies. • Government encouraged Arab and other foreign investors.
	1997–2017	20 Year Strategy	3.4 million feddan to be reclaimed by 2017.	
2000s	2009–	Agricultural Strategy toward 2030	1.25 million feddan to be reclaimed by 2017 and 3.1 million feddan by 2030.	• Continuing private sector involvement. • Public-private partnerships in the new lands.

Source: Data derived from Springborg (1979); Voll (1980); Johnson et al. (1983); Nyberg et al. (1990); Meyer (1998); Hussein et al. (1990); Zalla et al. (2000); Alterman (2002).

the state in England employed violence and forced dispossession to create the conditions necessary for capitalist production. Where Marx saw this process as a historical precondition for capitalist production—an "original sin" that got the capitalist system going—Harvey, drawing on the work of Rosa Luxemburg and Hannah Arendt, argues that it is a constant process, central to the ongoing ability of capitalism to reproduce itself. The key problem of capitalism, Harvey contends, is one of overaccumulation. To overcome this problem, capitalists are always looking for new places to invest, where they can open up new spaces of demand or new sites for production using cheaper inputs. As they exploit these new sites, the process of accumulation goes hand-in-hand with the dispossession of others of their assets. Harvey argues that the state plays a central role in facilitating this process; other scholars have highlighted the significance of non-state actors, also, such as multinational organizations, international funding institutions, and nongovernmental organizations (Elyachar 2005; Swyngedouw 2005).

Accumulation by dispossession offers a valuable framework for thinking about what happens to the flow of water as farmers reclaim the desert. The desert offers a new site for capital accumulation. It is an untapped asset. Since the land being reclaimed is state land, which was formerly put to little use, reclamation is not contingent upon a process of land dispossession.[12] It is, however, contingent upon a process of water dispossession. As some divert irrigation water to the desert to reclaim land and generate new profits, they dispossess others of the resource necessary to cultivate their existing land. In its use of this theoretical framework, though, my work departs from Harvey's in two respects.

First, I do not see the process of accumulation through desert reclamation as one that is necessarily tied to the grand logic of capitalism. While in some cases, reclamation is driven by farmers' desire to fix a problem of overaccumulation by finding new sites for agricultural investment, in many instances those carrying out reclamation are smallholder farmers, operating on a feddan by feddan basis. As they reclaim land, these farmers are also accumulating profits and dispossessing other farmers of irrigation water. Yet their reclamation activities are driven not so much by the fact that they have overaccumulated capital that they need to invest somewhere new, but by a desire to expand their landholdings so they have land to leave to their children, are able to produce more food for the household, and can increase their income from crop sales. Thus the impetus behind accumulation can be as much the socially defined needs of individual households as it is the larger dynamics of capital expansion.

Second, I pay particular attention to the material basis of capital accumulation, which in this case comprises both desert land (widely available) and irrigation water (much more limited in availability). Chris Sneddon (2007) has critiqued the literature on accumulation by dispossession for failing to attend to the nature of the resource being dispossessed and to how the different materialities of nature condition the accumulation process. Given that water is the limiting factor for desert reclamation, my analysis therefore focuses on the flow of water, the canals that channel that water, and the pumps that lift it up to the desert lands. It is these flows and technologies that are at stake in how different forms of dispossession transpire.

I start by describing what it means to reclaim land and how water plays into this process. I then introduce two cases of land reclamation to explore how reclamation is shaping what Egypt's water comes to be. The first is the reclamation that is taking place on the borders of Fayoum Province, through the efforts of individual farmers, small investors, and graduates. The second case is the reclamation of land west of the delta, which is taking place on a much larger scale as investors develop vast export-oriented farms in the desert. What links these two cases is that those involved are all trying to tap into the same source—the Nile. In doing so, they help mold its contours.

MAKING LAND NEW

As a process that may take up to four years, it is difficult to observe reclamation in action. Instead, the process is revealed through a kaleidoscope of refracted moments. Farmers take buckets of fertile Nile sediment from the banks of a canal to spread on the fields they are reclaiming; ridges in the sand demarcate the main lines of a future drip irrigation system; a tractor sprays fertilizer over a patch of green in the desert; a pump lifts water from a canal; two large gates in the desert mark an investor's first footprint on the sand; a graduate digs a shallow reservoir to store irrigation water; the canals of a government reclamation scheme, excavated before the water is sourced to fill them, lie empty; a young man stoops low, removing stones from the soil.

These moments feature the key (and in many ways overlapping) groups of actors involved in making new land in the desert margins.[13] First, there are the male and female smallholder farmers (*fellahin*). Working independently, these farmers seek to expand their landholdings into the desert, one feddan at a time. Second, there are the capital-rich agriculturalists, whom policy makers term "investors" (mustathmirin). Seen by policy makers as being distinct from farmers in their larger scale of production, investors sometimes work to develop lands on their own initiative; at other times, they develop reclamation concessions granted by the government. Third, there are the men and women who have received land through the Graduate Scheme and are known collectively as the "graduates" (kharigin). In addition, government agents enter the story in various ways. While the government is committed to expanding Egypt's cultivated area, it envisages doing so through a government-led, not farmer-led process. Engineers from the Ministry of Water Resources and Irrigation are therefore tasked with limiting informal reclamation, by ensuring that only government-authorized new land receives water.

But what does it really mean to transform the desert into a field? Over a cup of tea in Abu Khaled's house some months after our walk together, he explained the steps of reclaiming his land, narrating a process that is similar to what also goes on in the Graduate Scheme, except that in those areas it is the government authorities that carry out the initial steps. "I took the land when it was tired," he told me.[14] "Its top layer was not good (kan wisho mish kwais). First we made drainage ditches. We took out the big stones, but the small stones are good, as they allow the soil to breathe. Then I brought in sand, manure, and dry clay (raqash). We built up at least 50cm of soil on the surface. For 2.5 feddan we brought 400 tractor loads of sand!"

The process that Abu Khaled described to me is one of creating a new topsoil. His vision of reclamation is to develop a soil with certain quality characteristics in the desert. Whereas the soils of the old lands are rich in clay (tin), dark (aswad), and have a dense texture (shadid, masika), those of the desert borders are light and sandy (rimle), of aeolian rather than alluvial origin, lying beyond the bounds of where sediment was formerly deposited during the Nile flood.[15] In Abu Khaled's mind, for those sandy soils to bring a good yield, they need fertility and texture development. This is why he adds sand, manure, and dry clay, choosing the particular inputs according to the soil type in the field that he is reclaiming. The common feature for all soils, though, is the necessity of water to render them productive. To access water, Abu Khaled bought a pump to lift water from a branch canal. He dug ditches to channel that water into his new fields. He leveled the ground, then flooded the fields several times before planting, so as to

Figure 4.2. Unreclaimed land. Photograph by the author.

Figure 4.3. Reclaimed land in the first year of cultivation. Photograph by the author.
Note: Photograph taken in the same location as fig. 4.2, looking in the opposite direction.

leach the salts out of the soil. Following two irrigations, he planted wheat, with great success. "We were threshing from morning to night!" his wife reported happily.

Agricultural investors, on the other hand, go about reclamation in a different way. In April 2009, I went with a group of investors to visit the American University of Cairo's Desert Development Center in the delta. The men were young, in their late 20s and early 30s. They were wearing designer jeans. One had an Armani belt, another Prada sunglasses, a third was carrying an iPhone. The government had just given them concessions of new land to reclaim west of the Nile valley, ranging in size from 500 to 10,000 feddan and they wanted to learn about the best way to reclaim the land. One of the managers at the center gave us a presentation about the research center's key findings. "A desert should be treated as a desert," he proclaimed. "This means that you don't bring soil from the old lands and put it here. You can't treat this soil like the old lands. . . . You can't grow the same crops, use the same methods." The approach that he advocated, and which the investors follow, is to use specific chemical inputs to meet crops' fertility requirements within the sandy desert soil. Yet despite this difference in approach, water is just as critical to investors as it is to farmers. With more funds at their disposal, investors use drip and sprinkler irrigation systems to apply the exact amount of water that a crop needs. They also buy bigger pumps, allowing them to look deeper into the soil or further afield for their water supply.

A couple of days later, I spent the day with one of these investors, Waseem. Waseem has been working for his family's agro-processing company for ten years. They have a 1,000 feddan farm on reclaimed land east of the delta, an onion processing factory, a 50 feddan farm in Fayoum, and a new 10,000 feddan concession west of Minya. They plan to reclaim this 10,000 feddan piece of land to grow fodder for a large beef farm. The Nile will provide the water they need for reclamation. They will access this water, though, not by extending the canal system but by digging down into the Nile aquifer. This is the store of water in the alluvial sands below the valley and delta that is interconnected to the river channel. They have the money to buy the powerful pumps necessary to lift water from about 50m below the surface. He showed me a video on his iPhone of the moment they found water. A large yellow drilling rig stands in the middle of the desert, sand on every side as far as the eye can see, marked only with the tire tracks of four-wheel-drive vehicles. A large green pump sits at the top of the well shaft. Water starts gushing out of a pipe eight inches in diameter. Two men look

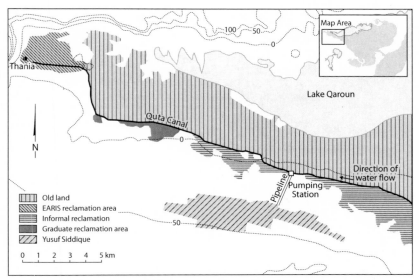

Map 4.1. Agricultural expansion in Quta, Fayoum

on, taking photographs on their cell phones; another man reaches out with a cup to taste the water. They are all smiling. After a week of drilling, they have found the water required to transform this desert into fields of fodder grasses.

In these different ways, therefore, farmers and investors work to reclaim the desert. They employ pumps, operating either directly on canals or over groundwater wells, to tap the water they need to develop the new land. To see how this process both shapes and is shaped by the flow of water, I turn now to the two contrasting cases of marginal reclamation.

FARMING FAYOUM'S BORDERS

The village of Warda, where I lived during my fieldwork, lies in the western part of Fayoum Province. The cultivated zone here is only a few kilometers wide. On the southern side of the village, the land rises slowly toward the Quta Canal (see map 4.1). As I saw in my walk with Abu Khaled, the land gradually transitions from green fields through land under reclamation to the bare desert plateau. To the north, the land drops down sharply to the shores of Lake Qaroun. On summer evenings, I would sit on the roof of my house, in the shade of an awning made of palm fronds, hoping to catch a breeze coming up from the lake. Looking north the view was divided into three contrasting bands. In front of me, the green of lush irrigated fields sloping downward, textured with the spiky crowns of palm trees. Be-

Figure 4.4. Lake Qaroun. Photograph by the author.

hind the green, the blue salty waters of the lake, clear and still now that the fishermen had returned home for the night. Behind the blue, the yellow of the desert escarpment, apparently empty, with the intermittent cars of the archaeologists, tourists, and oil company personnel passing by largely out of sight. From my roof, the bowl-shaped topography of Fayoum was tangible. The sandy cliffs behind the lake were a constant reminder of the desert that surrounds the depression on every side.

In Fayoum, it is this topography that marks the distinction between old and new. The lands at the base of the depression, like those that I looked down on from my house, have been cultivated for thousands of years. In the nineteenth century, some of the large landowning families of the province made use of Fayoum's sloping topography and extended the canal system, expanding the zone of gravity irrigation and bringing more land into cultivation. The irrigation administration completed further extensions to the canal system in the early years of the twentieth century. This was when the land immediately surrounding Warda started to be cultivated. In the 1950s, the first donor-funded project of reclamation (the Egyptian-American Rural Improvement Service project) chose western Fayoum as one of its target areas.[16] By the late 1980s, almost all the land within the depression that could be irrigated by gravity had been brought into cultivation.

The next target for reclamation was the desert slopes (al-gabl) that rise up gradually on the southern and eastern sides of the depression.[17] Whereas the old lands are irrigated by gravity, pumps are required to irrigate these new lands. The government plans to develop 14,000 feddan of land in this marginal zone through its Graduate Scheme.[18] It is also in these desert hills that individual farmers, like Abu Khaled, are working to expand their land holdings, as are small investors, like the high-level politician who owns a 75 feddan farm on reclaimed land downstream of Abu Khaled, where he grows grapes for export using drip irrigation. Although the scale of their cultivation is different, graduates, farmers, and investors share a common goal: to access the limited volume of Nile water that enters Fayoum.

The Pump Mafia

As water flows to the desert to help create new land, it moves out of the ministry's control at the point of offtake from the branch canal. For the Graduate Scheme reclamation areas, the ministry provides the infrastructure necessary for farmers to access water. Where the new lands are immediately next to an irrigation canal, clusters of electric pumps lift water up to that land. Where reclamation areas are some distance from the canal, large pumping stations divert water through pipelines and concrete channels to the new lands.

For the 80 percent of land reclamation taking place informally, though, the farmers have to find their own means of accessing water.[19] Given the elevation of the desert land, pumps are central to farmers' ability to get water to flow to these sites. There are other mechanisms that farmers can use to lift water, such as water wheels or the lever system for lifting buckets of water on the end of a pole, known as the shaduf, but these technologies do not have the efficiency required to lift water high enough to reclaim new border lands. Most farmers therefore use the widely available mobile diesel pumps (makina). These pumps are relatively inexpensive to buy (in 2010 a pump cost about LE3,000) or rent (at a rate of around LE10 an hour). Those who have sufficient capital use electric pumps, which are more expensive (up to LE15,000) but easier to operate and maintain.

Whatever the type of pump a farmer uses, the positioning of the pump is critical to determining how much water it will deliver. Just as farmers have a variety of techniques for accessing more water from the irrigation system in times of scarcity (chapter 2), they employ similar techniques to access additional water for agricultural expansion. When pumping water from an official point of offtake, they remodel the offtake in the canal bank, reshaping

Figure 4.5. Diesel pump. Photograph by the author.

the technology of water access. If an offtake is enlarged, more water flows through it from the canal and into the collecting pool where the pump operates. At an authorized point of access, therefore, farmers can obtain an unauthorized amount of water. In other cases, they bypass the ministry's system of control and dangle the long plastic pipes of their pumps directly into a branch or main canal, from which they can draw as much water as they need. Alternatively, they take a more subtle approach and install hidden pipes in the bank, below the water, which lead directly into the field. The pipes surface in a ditch at some distance from the canal, where farmers can pump the water up to the new land.

The making of Egypt's water lies in these everyday practices of lifting and diverting water. The ministry seeks to control these practices. In theory, farmers are meant to have licenses for their pumps, which specify the area the pump can irrigate, the size of the offtake on which it is located, and the pump's capacity. But the reality is quite different, as I saw in my trip around Quta irrigation district with the former district engineer, Hassan, in March 2008.

We drive along the canal that skirts the perimeter of the depression. Gesturing toward the narrow band of fields on the outer edge of the canal, backed by the desert, Hassan tells me that most of that land has been reclaimed illegally.[20] The government has not authorized the expansion, and the ministry has not authorized the water use. Hassan points out one illegal pump, then another, then another, then another. One pump has little impact on the flow of water through a canal; numerous pumps have a considerable impact. There are so many pumps that at one point Hassan jokes of a "pump mafia" (mafia al-makina), conjuring up the impression of a pervasive illegality that is deeply embedded within the system of water distribution. The black metal of the pumps punctuates the landscape, the hum of their motors accompanying our journey. Throughout the day, Hassan recounts tale after tale of the various ways in which farmers use pumps to access water to reclaim land. He tells me that farmers are constantly increasing their cultivated area, pushing out the boundaries, using pumps to bring in water and reclaim the land. In some cases, a farmer may have a permit to irrigate twenty feddan but actually irrigates more than a hundred. Not only are farmers stealing water, Hassan explains, but in the process they are also altering the infrastructure of the irrigation system, damaging the banks of the canal, and installing illegal pipes. To Hassan, the illegal accessing of water is three violations in one, a bit like "owning a gun, pointing it at someone as a threat, and then pulling the trigger."

When he was the district engineer, he tells me, Hassan would fine farmers for these violations (mukhalafat). He would carefully calculate the fines, which would typically amount to around LE160. If the farmer had installed an illegal pipe, Hassan would bring an excavator to remove it. If the farmer was using an illegal pump, he would come with a police officer to confiscate it or, if he was on his own, he would bring a knife and slit the pipe leading to the pump.

But these penalties only have a limited effect. Repeat violations are very common. Often when Hassan removed illegal pipes from an offtake, he would return some weeks later and find that the farmers had replaced them. When he confiscated pumps, he would take them a short distance in the car, but then, he says, "the farmers would come running after us and apologize and promise to change their ways and stop using the pumps illegally." Hassan knew such assurances meant little, but he had no choice. Pumps are expensive; there was no way he could have permanently confiscated them, nor would the farmers have let him.

Even to my untrained eye, the illegal pumps are easy to spot. Not only do the penalties have little impact but, according to Hassan, "Some of the district engineers are lazy." Every time there is a new engineer, which is quite often, he does not know where the violations are. Although the engineer could look at the records of his predecessor, often he does not. The bahhars spend more time by the canal and so are well aware of the violations, but tend not to report them to the district engineers as they get paid by the farmers for not doing so. The result is that many district engineers do not see what is going on along the canals because, as Hassan confides, "Beini wa beinik (between you and me), they sit in their houses the whole time." Hassan, he insists, was different. "I was present, day and night, alhamdulallah."

Yet although Hassan has represented the ministry as an agent of policy enforcement and uses the metaphor of an illegal mafia in his description of the pump users, he can empathize with the farmers' position. As someone from a rural area who has neighbors, friends, and family members who farm, it is not difficult for Hassan to see the farmers' perspective. He remarks to me, "Anyone would want to expand their agricultural land if they found water in front of them. . . . If we were in their place, we would also take water. Is there anyone who wouldn't drink if they were thirsty and there was water in front of them?"

The problem is that one person drinking impacts others. Pumps make reclamation possible. With a pump, a farmer can access water from the canal. But with a pump, a farmer also diverts the flow of water away from a downstream farmer. The pump is thus at once a technology of accumulation and dispossession. However this dispossession does not take place without resistance.

Pumping Poverty

One day in the ministry offices I talk with Ghalib, a tall and statuesque farmer in a blue and white striped galabiya with a brown scarf around his neck. Ghalib is from the village of Thania, which lies west of Abu Khaled's land, at the far corner of Fayoum (map 4.1). This village was one of two new villages—imaginatively named The First (al-oula) and The Second (al-thania)—created by the Egyptian-American Rural Improvement Service project. "We came from Beni Suef in 1961. I was sixteen at that time," he tells me. A project report describes the crowd of "thousands of cheering well-wishers" who watched the settlers' transfer, quoting an observer as saying, "It was as if they were moving to a foreign country. They were pioneers!" (Johnson et al. 1983, 10). Ghalib can remember the day well. "We came on the twentieth of July 1961. We found the land all planted with cotton, peanuts, maize, and sorghum." His face lights up. "We began cultivating in the 1961–62 season and grew cotton for seven years. We had the highest production in all the province!" His expression changes. "Then, in 1970, the water started to decline."

If you drive out to the western edge of Fayoum today, the Quta Canal comes to an abrupt end. Palm trees dot the view, and a narrow mesqa leads off into a field of onions and a small grove of olive trees, backed just a short distance away by bare desert cliffs. Another mesqa leads west toward Thania, a remote outpost of sand-blown streets, laid out in a grid, bordered by a few fields of olives and surrounded by the desert on all sides. Nobody grows cotton here today. In fact, even the considerably less water-needy onions struggle to survive. Ghalib tells me that of the 2,000 feddan in the Quta agricultural cooperative, 800 feddan cannot be cultivated because of the lack of water. Many people from the village have left to seek a better livelihood elsewhere.

The reason for this dramatic shift in fortunes lies in what has happened upstream. Reclamation in other parts of Fayoum over the past five decades has diverted water away from this western region. Considerable amounts of land on the south side of the Quta Canal have been developed by small-holders, working independently, using precisely the kinds of everyday practices of accessing water that I discussed above. In 1993, the government allocated a tract of land on the south bank of the canal for reclamation through the Graduate Scheme. Since then, the graduates have enlarged their offtakes and installed electric pumps to draw as much water as possible from the canal. Finally, in 2001 the ministry constructed an offtake further upstream to divert water from the main canal to a large pumping station, which lifts and pumps the water through an underground pipeline to the graduate reclamation area of Yusuf Siddique (map 4.1). The pumping station is meant to function only seventeen hours a day, but Hassan told me that the graduates sometimes bribe the operators to run it longer. As a result of all this pumping, very little water flows on to the tail end of the canal. New government-sponsored reclamation is taking water from land that the government developed previously.

Some of those who farm land in the Graduate Scheme areas are actually from Thania. No longer able to cultivate their own fields near the village due to insufficient water, they rent land upstream. I talked with one man who rents four feddan in the Graduate Scheme on the south bank of the Quta Canal. He also has five feddan in Thania, but is only able to cultivate two of them. The other three feddan are left barren (bur). "It used to be the best land," he told me sadly, "when we arrived in the 1960s in the Nasser program. Nasser, God rest his soul!"[21] Today things are different. "We are at the end. We are tired. The problem is the projects upstream that take all the water. Like the new pumping station at Yusuf Siddique, which runs on electricity and takes so much water from the canal." Ironically, by renting and farming the land where he does now, this man also becomes one of those upstream who are taking Thania's water. Everyone wants to be what they call *fowq*, "above," meaning upstream.

Each phase of reclamation reorients the flow of water through the landscape, reworking patterns of access to good quality water. This often exacerbates the head-tail distinction that has been well documented in the irrigation literature, with those at the downstream end of the canal typically disadvantaged (Boelens and Davila 1998; Price 1995). The ministry seeks to minimize the impact of upstream diversions by requiring farmers to use what it calls "modern irrigation" (*al-rai al-hadith*) in reclaimed lands. Sprinkler and drip irrigation technologies are, in theory, more efficient than flood irrigation, since the farmer is able to tailor the water application more precisely to the crop's needs.[22] The ministry therefore thinks that mandating their use in the new lands will minimize the additional water demand generated by agricultural expansion. It can only attempt to enforce this policy, however, in reclamation zones that the government officially recognizes. Thus it is not surprising that very few farmers of reclaimed lands in Fayoum actually use such technologies, which are more expensive and often not feasible given the rotation system of water delivery.[23]

Hence in diverting water to cultivate one piece of land, other land is left with insufficient water. As the desert is irrigated, the land downstream reverts to a hard, parched surface, sprinkled with a layer of salt crystals, or shifts from a field of cotton to a grove of hardy olive trees. Pumping in one place generates poverty in another.

Ghalib is measured in his critique. He has amassed thirty-five feddan in addition to the five feddan that the initial reclamation program allocated to his family. His sons cultivate ten feddan of land in the Yusuf Siddique graduate reclamation area. Even though he is unable to cultivate twenty feddan of his land in Thania because of a lack of water, he can still make ends meet. But many farmers are not so lucky. The diversion of water to new lands is a source of considerable tension and anger among farmers, particularly during the hotter summer months of heightened demand when scarcity is more pronounced. Many of those who farm older lands have a sense of historical water rights, or legitimacy of presence, which is confounded when their water is diverted elsewhere. In one meeting I attended between farmers and ministry officials, the discussion turned quickly to the lack of water. One farmer stood up, saying angrily, "The problem is the new lands. They take a lot of the water."[24] Another man joined him, "The solution is that the water should go to us and not to the new lands." The undersecretary nodded, acknowledging that there has been 20,000 feddan of new land development in this area. Another farmer shouted, "The problem is The Irrigation (the ministry). There is enough water, but it's just a question of unfair distribution!" A senior official responded, "It is true, there is enough water for Fayoum, but [and here his reasoning differed from the farmer's] some people act illegally and take other people's water. We have to find those people!"

On the regional scale of Fayoum Province, therefore, the expansion of agricultural land through land reclamation can be seen as a process of accumulation by dispossession. As some farmers accumulate irrigation water—a resource that allows them to grow their agricultural land and profits—they deprive others of this means of production. Yet this process is complicated in two ways.

First, the actors are not fixed in space. Both the farmers and the means of tapping into the resource—the diesel pumps—are mobile. Consequently, some farmers are able to elude the dispossession process. The farmers from Thania who are able to use land in the Graduate Scheme areas upstream of their village can escape the impact of this water diversion. Although their land around Thania may be uncultivable, they can tap into the resource at another point and therefore maintain their agricultural production. While most farmers can afford to buy or rent a pump, the key factor determining their ability to use that pump is whether they can access land in a location favorable to the water supply.

Second, while the literature on accumulation assumes a process of appropriating noncapitalist or subsistence forms of production so as to stimulate more "advanced" forms of capital accumulation, the processes at work in Fayoum do not necessarily fit this formulation. There are farmers in the old lands who grow wheat for household bread making, just as there are investors in the new lands who grow grapes for export. But the categories of production also overlap. There is no purely subsistence category; old land farmers also sell produce to local or national markets. At the same time, some of those diverting water for land reclamation use that new land to expand their household production. Thus accumulation by dispossession may not necessarily mean a shift from one mode of production to another.

TRANSFORMATIONS IN THE WEST DELTA

The desert road leads out of Cairo from behind the pyramids, cutting through the desert west of the delta toward the city of Alexandria on the Mediterranean coast. The villas and mango orchards give way to rocky hills

Figure 4.6. Center pivot irrigation in the west delta. Photograph by the author.

as the road winds steadily up the desert escarpment. Over the crest of the hill, past the Pyramids Heights resort and a cell phone tower disguised as a palm tree, the road starts to descend to a sandy plain. Billboards adorn the side of the road, advertising sushi restaurants, luxury cars, and prospective shopping malls ("Park Avenue on the Cairo-Alex desert road"). We pass by a series of nascent housing developments. "Breathe, Play, Relax" entreat the advertisements. Bright photographs evoke the promise of the future: a space of luxury and clean air where residents will sit in gardens, swim in pools, and play golf on lush turf. A green space. And all in the desert. So far, the small olive trees in the highway median are the only sign of greenery.

After about 30km, a line of tall trees in the distance signifies the start of agricultural development. This stretch of the desert road is no longer the desert that it was thirty or so years ago. As one agronomist working for a UN agency commented to me in amazement, "The entire ecosystem is changing. You don't see the desert now. There are foxes and birds. It really is a case of greening the desert!" On both sides of the road there are farms, the fields demarcated by windbreaks of trees. Each farm has large gates flanked by high walls with ornate signs stating the name of the owner. Some farms have villas, fronted by pillars spanning three floors. Others have private mosques. Orchards of mangoes, oranges, lemons, peaches, bananas, and

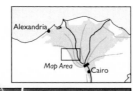

Map 4.2. Cultivation in the west delta

grapevines, rooted in a sandy soil, linked by the snaking line of black drip irrigation tubes, stretch into the distance. Plastic greenhouses nurture young seedlings. We pass by one farm called "The European Countryside." Further along the road, the arched beam of a center pivot irrigation scheme rotates slowly through a huge circular field of onions, spraying water in all directions.

This is quite a different type of agriculture from that taking place in the reclaimed lands around Fayoum (and also from that of the land lying immediately to the east, which was reclaimed in an earlier phase through the government's Graduate Scheme) (see map 4.2). The farms are large, generally over 100 feddan and many over 1,000 feddan, the levels of investment are huge, the irrigation technology is expensive, and the production is export-oriented. One single field in a center pivot system may be ten times the size of Abu Khaled's land and fifty times the size of an average Egyptian farm.

The ministry car reaches Helwa Farm, where I have an appointment scheduled with the farm manager. I meet Engineer Yasser in his large office. He tells me that they grow fodder crops, grains, vegetables, and fruits on this 10,000 feddan piece of land, which they have reclaimed in phases over the last twenty years. The farm exports fruit and vegetables to Europe and the Gulf; it has a herd of 8,000 dairy cows and the first and only milk powder plant in the Middle East. He presses a button by his desk and barks, "Paper!" at his office assistant. The paper duly delivered, he starts drawing a cross-section through the Nile delta. He tells me that whereas on the eastern side of the delta there is a steep desert escarpment, on the western side the incline is much more gentle, reaching only 30 or 40m above the level of the floodplain. Elevation is critical when considering the costs of lifting water for irrigation; each meter matters. The western side of the delta is also rich in groundwater, he says.

The water that Helwa Farm taps comes from 200m below the surface. Electric pumps lift the water through deep wells. Yasser is vague on the details. Scientists' accounts of the hydrogeology of the region suggest that the aquifer they draw from is either the Quaternary Nile aquifer, comprising a band of sands and gravels deposited over the last 1.8 million years, with a thickness ranging from 50m to over 1,000m in the north, or the interconnected 50–250m thick Moghra aquifer, made up of older sand, gravel, and sandstone deposits (Dawoud, Darwish, and El-Kady. 2005). Both these aquifers are recharged by infiltration from irrigated fields. They are also both hydrologically linked with the Nile channel, although hydrologists understand little about the nature of the subterranean flow regime (NWRP 2001). When I ask Yasser if the groundwater that they tap is linked to the Nile, he replies that he does not know. To the new land investor irrigating with groundwater, the key factor is whether a borehole of a particular depth will yield water. It is not so important to him (and they seem to be primarily men) exactly where this water is coming from or how the extraction might affect underground flow patterns.

Up until now, reclamation of this marginal desert has had little impact on the old lands of the delta lying to the east, which have been cultivated for thousands of years. Even though the groundwater that these farms use is hydrologically linked to the Nile system, there is no indication that extraction from the aquifer has affected river discharge. It has, however, affected the aquifer. With only limited recharge from the surface, the high rate of pumping has depleted the groundwater store. In the early 2000s, investors in the west delta started noticing that the water table was dropping at a rate of about a meter a year. Each year they have had to lift water one meter more. Each year, the salinity of the groundwater has increased, impacting yields. So the investors turned their sights to the waters of the Nile 30km

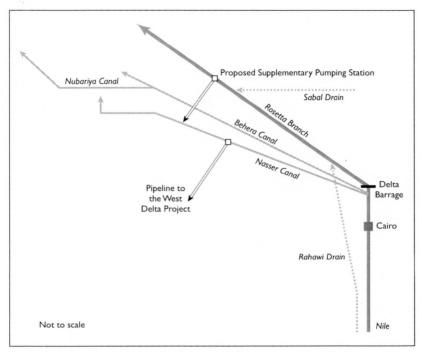

Figure 4.7. Water flow to the proposed west delta project. *Source:* Data from
J. Hoevenaars et al., *Environmental and Social Impacts Assessment and Framework
Management Plan*, 33.

to the east. For these powerful individuals, their acts of the everyday can
include phone calls with key officials in the water ministry or lunch meetings to lobby influential politicians. This is how they make their claims on
Nile water.

The ministry has been receptive to their concerns. Officials are eager to
curry favor with the influential investors, and they recognize that it is in the
government's interests to maintain these profitable forms of agricultural
production. As one senior engineer in the ministry explained, "If the government leaves them [the investors] using saline water then in the future
they will all be destroyed. The government wants to keep the farms working." In 2004, in response to the investors' demands, the ministry launched
a project to pump Nile water from the Nasser Canal through a pipeline to
the newly reclaimed land of the west delta (see figure 4.7). The World Bank
and French Development Agency approved loans to help fund the project,
and the embassy of the Netherlands provided a grant. The donors laud the
project as a promising example of the potential for public-private partner-

ships in irrigation development. Private firms will be involved in the design, construction, and operation of the new irrigation system and the investors will have to pay to connect to the system and benefit from the water that it delivers. The ministry plans to give the private company that will manage the conveyance system a formal right to a particular volume of water, thereby granting it a legally backed water right that almost no other water user in the country has.

In his office, Ahmed shows me a large map of the project area. The fields are outlined in black and the farms shaded in various colors. Helwa Farm is one of the biggest in the area. Ahmed points on the map to the Nasser Canal, which draws from the Nile. This stretch of the canal is at an elevation of 15m above sea level, whereas the project land in the west delta lies at around 85m, so the water will have to be lifted 70m. Through the project, a high pressure pump will propel water from the canal along an underground pipeline at a rate of 22 cubic meters a second (see figure 4.7). From a distribution point on higher ground, the water will then flow by gravity through four distribution pipes. Along those pipes, booster pumps will distribute water over 2,000 feddan parcels, at a pressure sufficient for sprinkler or drip irrigation (Attia et al. 2007; Hoevenaars et al. 2007).

These pumps and pipelines will redirect the flow of the Nile. The government has authorized the extraction of water sufficient to irrigate 190,000 feddan. Siphoned off to the west, this water will no longer continue its journey down the Nasser Canal to feed the fields of downstream farmers. The project will deliver sufficient water to allow the farmers in the target area to irrigate with Nile water alone. Only in particular times of need will they need to tap groundwater through their wells. Ahmed reassures me that they will only use the groundwater pumps at the recovery rate; they will conserve water. The new land investors will, in essence, safeguard their groundwater resources by taking other farmers' surface water resources.

In recognition that this diversion will impact on farmers downstream along the Nasser Canal, the ministry has agreed to construct a new supplementary pumping station on the Nile to replenish the canal downstream of the point of extraction (figure 4.7). This station will pump water from the Nile's Rosetta Branch to the Nasser Canal. In theory, the new station will maintain the downstream farmers' irrigation supply. However, the environmental impact assessment report tellingly gives no indication of when the pumping station will be constructed, raising the question of whether it actually will be (Hoevenaars et al. 2007). Nor does the report address whether the quality and quantity of water available in this stretch of the

Nile is sufficient. This is a particularly important consideration given that the proposed location of the supplementary station is downstream of the outlet of a main drainage canal. Instead, the report underplays the potential significance of the water diversion. It suggests that the demand for water is actually decreasing within the delta, due to improvements in irrigation efficiency and the encroachment of urban development onto agricultural land. Although it is unclear how widespread these processes are and what exact impact they have on water use, they provide a convenient justification for the diversion of water elsewhere.[25]

Shortly after the plans for the project became public, downstream farmers began to express concern about how it would affect their long-cultivated land. In September 2009 the Land Center for Human Rights, an Egyptian nongovernmental organization, filed an appeal in the Egyptian courts on behalf of a group of delta farmers. Instead of the project diverting Nile water to the west delta, they proposed that the ministry construct a treatment plant on one of the main drainage canals and then pump that treated drainage water to the investors' farms (LCHR 2009). Another civil society organization sent letters of protest to the World Bank and ministry in February 2010, urging them to consider different water sources (BIC 2010). Not surprisingly, though, under pressure from investors determined to access the best water they can, the project management rejected these alternatives. As one foreign consultant commented to me, "Investors are independent thinkers, they have good ideas, and they are also very influential. Not only do they have the money but they have the connections. If they say they want a project, they'll get it. If the minister doesn't want to do it, they'll sack the minister!"

At the time of writing, in the spring of 2013, construction on the project has yet to begin. Progress has been stalled by delays in the government's selection of a contractor to design, build, and operate the infrastructure. Following the revolution in early 2011, two consortia withdrew from the bidding process, further delaying progress. In June 2011 the World Bank closed its project, due to the government's failure to spend any of its approved loan, rating the project as "unsatisfactory" (World Bank 2011). But despite the delays, the ministry still plans to move ahead with the project and officials are hopeful that the World Bank will consider financing it again in the future. In November 2011, a ministry official posted an entry about the project on a web-based platform designed to showcase innovative "solutions for water," as part of the preparations for the Sixth World Water Forum. The entry describes the project as a "new vision promoting water conservation," although it notes that work "is on hold until the political situation in Egypt stabilizes" (Anwar 2011).

While Nile water is not yet flowing to the west delta, this case demonstrates how closely the distribution of water is tied to technologies of access and access to technologies. Investors were able to start reclaiming the desert land west of the delta because they had the money to buy powerful electric pumps to lift water from the underlying aquifer. Now that this groundwater supply is declining, they are drawing on another source of power—their relations of influence with government officials—and a different set of technologies—a pumping station, pipeline, and booster bumps—to tap into the water of the Nile. Thus where the Nile flows and what it comes to be is intimately linked to the technologies of lifting and diverting water on a day-to-day basis and to the sociopolitical relations that both shape and are shaped by the use of those technologies.

Pumping the Future

This project is only one component of the government's strategy, begun by Mubarak's administration and continued by the authorities since the revolution, to foster the development of desert agriculture along the margins of the valley and delta. While the government continues to invest in developing its mega projects far out in the desert, it is also interested in building on the investors' independent initiatives to promote further large-scale reclamation on the margins of the cultivated zone. Instead of trying to improve agricultural production in the old lands, many policy makers think that it is better to invest in these new lands, where yields and profits can be greater.[26] According to an agricultural specialist from the UN, "The commercial sector says, 'Let the delta disappear and let's move to the desert!' Desert agriculture is the future." The government's attempts to court investors to develop land along the agricultural borders have been more successful than its efforts to attract investors to the mega projects. Investors see the potential in this marginal land, which is conveniently located for transportation networks and access to markets. Driving through the desert just west of the Nile valley with one investor, he explained to me this land's appeal. "It's close to Cairo. It's good land. It just needs clean water."

As the investor said, all the desert needs is water. The government's goal to promote desert agriculture is contingent on a redirection of Nile waters. The strategy for a future transfer of water to the desert margins is laid out in a brightly colored printed booklet, developed by the Ministry of Agriculture and Land Reclamation and designed to elicit international funding. Based on the premise that the efficiency of water use in the old lands can be improved, the plan states a goal to transfer that "saved water" to the borders of the delta for large-scale land reclamation. The plan presents a simple mathematical calculation. The irrigation efficiency of traditional surface irrigation is only 45 percent whereas that of sprinkler irrigation is 75 percent, drip irrigation 85 percent. Convert 5 million feddan to modern irrigation and 13.1 million cubic meters will be saved to be used for land reclamation. Some scenarios follow. Assume that each reclaimed feddan with a modern irrigation system requires 4,000m³/year, then 3.2 million feddan can be reclaimed with this water; assume that each reclaimed feddan needs 5,000m³/year, then 2.6 million feddan can be reclaimed with this water (Al-Bultagi and Abu Hadeed 2008, 25).

The Ministry of Agriculture's calculations are underpinned by certain assumptions about the efficiency of modern irrigation techniques, which are probably overly optimistic (Perry et al. 2009). They are also based on the premise that it would be possible to accomplish such a huge transformation of on-field water management practices. Such a premise fails to take into consideration whether farmers will be receptive to new irrigation methods.

If the efficiency increases are not realized, will water transfers still take place? The fact that the investors in Helwa Farm and its surroundings have managed to persuade the government to divert Nile water to their land suggests that further diversions might well take place. This diversion of water from farmers in the old lands to investors in the reclaimed lands is a clear case of dispossession—a dispossession rooted in pumps, pipelines, and the material flow of water. As large investors use water to develop new lands and accrue great profits, accumulating water to accumulate capital, other farmers who have been using that water for many years find their supply declining.

This process of dispossession is not only one of economic and political marginalization but one that may challenge historically constituted forms of collective identity (Elyachar 2005). When I asked policy makers what would happen to old land farmers downstream if they no longer had the water necessary to cultivate their fields, they told me that those farmers could take on jobs as laborers in the new farms. They presented this as an option that would be equally appealing to those farmers. Yet there is a fundamental difference between farming your own land and farming someone else's. Owning land enables farmers to produce food and fodder for the household and to capitalize on market opportunities through crop choice, in a way that is not available to agricultural laborers. Farmers are integrated in networks of family, friends, and neighbors. If farmers are forced—by a lack of water—to leave their villages and the land that their families have farmed for generations to go and work as laborers on someone else's desert farm, it will disrupt the very fabric of their social, cultural, and economic identity. It seems unlikely that they will go easily.

PUMPING DISPOSSESSION

When I returned to Cairo after one of my visits to the west delta, the word GREENERY flashed in front of me, high above the urban sprawl, in huge green neon letters. In the dark of the evening, I could not see the screen on the hilltop on which the words were projected, nor could I see the residential development that the advertisement was promoting. It was as though the words were suspended in midair, a visual imprint of the impetus toward changing Egypt's landscape that has deep political and cultural roots.[27]

Land reclamation is achieving this vision. Reclamation along the margins is transforming the Nile's watershed, pushing out the boundaries of the area that is irrigated and drained by this long river. All along the borders of the cultivated zone, individual farmers and investors are taking the opportunity to expand their landholdings. The government continues to pursue its mega projects far out into the desert, but it is also starting to encourage investment in these marginal zones. In the two cases I have discussed in this chapter, smallholder farmers of Fayoum and investors of the west delta exhibit contrasting forms of agency in their efforts to tap into the Nile to reclaim the desert. They employ different technologies to divert and lift water. They draw on different networks of social and political connections to enable them to use those technologies, either by evading government regulations or by getting the government to change those regulations.

As some farmers accumulate profits from agricultural development in the desert—be it strawberry cultivation for export or wheat production for household consumption and national markets—they dispossess others of the resource necessary to make their land produce. But this is not a clear-cut process of the dispossessors versus the dispossessed. It is a complex, shifting landscape of multiple actors seeking to access Nile water in any way possible to cultivate land. Hence some of the farmers from the village of Thania, for example, who find their reclaimed land from the 1950s uncultivable due to subsequent diversions, start renting land in more recently reclaimed areas upstream. In doing so, the dispossessed also become the dispossessors.

Ministry officials justify the diversion of water to the desert by the savings that water users can make elsewhere. If farmers in one place use less water, then it is not problematic to redirect some water to another place, assuming that the former do not seek to capitalize on those water savings themselves. In Fayoum, the use of modern irrigation methods in the new lands is the ministry's mechanism for achieving these water savings, but most farmers ignore this policy. In the west delta, the ministry hopes to save water not only through the use of modern irrigation technologies on the desert farms but also through shifting to the use of those technologies in the old lands. However, the fact that a project is underway to divert Nile water to the west delta, even though those irrigation improvements have yet to be realized, raises questions about whether these neat calculations of diversions equaling savings will be met.

Following Sneddon's (2007) call to focus on the "things" being accumulated, I identify two main ways in which the nature of water as a resource complicates the patterns of accumulation and dispossession. First, the diversion of water to desert lands does not mean a straightforward dispossession of downstream farmers, because much of that diverted water infiltrates into the soil to be used again. As a fluid, water slips between realms, from channel to soil matrix and back again, multiple times. As water passes through the system, it becomes increasingly saline and polluted. Thus in some cases farmers at the ends of canals receive water, but that water is not good enough for them to use to irrigate their crops. In other words, dispossession can take place not only through changing the quantity of a resource available for use but also through changing its quality.

Second, when the resource being dispossessed is irrigation water, the process of dispossession is refracted into degrees. Unlike dispossession through land appropriation—if a farmer's land is taken away, then he or she has no means of production—dispossession through water diversions operates more through shifting the terms of production. The channeling of water to the desert does not necessarily mean that downstream farmers are unable to farm their fields at all. Maybe they are just not able to grow the number or type of crops that they would like to in a year. Irrigation water diversion is therefore a much more subtle and gradual process of dispossession than, for example, when a government appropriates land to flood a reservoir. It is this lack of visibility, perhaps, that allows the authorities to largely overlook the dispossession that is taking place.

Hence desert reclamation simultaneously opens up and closes down spaces of agricultural opportunity. Scarcity in one place, as I argue in chapter 2, is produced by the constellation of politically mediated technologies and decision-making processes that divert water away from a particular location and toward another. The development of agricultural production in one area means the depletion of production in another, as that land faces a lack of water or water of insufficient quality to sustain production. This illustrates the profound social, political, and economic consequences that accompany the making of Egypt's water. Given the government's future vision of a shift in production focus from the old lands to desert agriculture on the margins, there is considerable potential for future conflicts as some farmers see their water declining. As the desert is irrigated, downstream, the irrigated is deserted: deserted of particularly water-needy crops, or of any crops at all, and ultimately, perhaps, deserted of those who used to farm it.

CHAPTER 5

Flows of Drainage THE POLITICS OF EXCESS

Lutfi and I drive through the Fayoum countryside in a battered white pickup truck. It is April 2009 and Lutfi, a drainage engineer, is giving me a tour around his drainage district. He stops the vehicle and we get out to look at a field planted with fodder maize and small cucumber plants. The green of the field is broken only by the cylindrical shape of manholes jutting above the surface every 100 meters or so. Lutfi removes the heavy cover on one of the manholes with some effort. We peer down the concrete cylinder at the water pooled below. On one side of the manhole, water trickles into the pool from a narrow pipe about 1.5 meters below the surface. Around the other side of the manhole, water flows steadily out into a lower pipe, slightly larger in diameter and partially visible above the water surface. I am captivated. Two trickles of water through the soil might appear mundane, but not when you know they are part of one of the largest water management interventions in the world.

Beneath the green fields of Egypt's agricultural land lies a hidden grid of 450,000km of pipes. Laid end to end, these pipes would wrap around the world eleven times. This is Egypt's subsurface drainage system. The pipes channel excess water from the soil into 18,000km of open drainage canals, known as "drains," which cut across the landscape.[1] Not only the scale but the costs of this system are staggering. Egypt has spent an estimated US$1.47 billion on its drainage program since the Aswan High Dam. This is almost half a billion more dollars than it spent on the dam itself.[2]

The network of pipes and drains is responsible for maintaining the productivity of Egypt's agricultural land. Without a means of channeling away the water that is not taken up by plants, soils become waterlogged, saline, and uncultivable. Throughout Egypt's fields, the occurrence of a crust of white salt is a marker of the poverty of what lies below, an indicator of the drainage system's failure to channel away the water that the crops do not need. In the absence of a good drainage system, the hot sun overhead and excess water in the soil combine to generate saline soils. In the presence of a good drainage system, crop yields can increase by over 40 percent.[3]

Despite the integral significance of drainage, it has received little coverage in international water management discussions.[4] Support from international donors for drainage has been much lower than that for irrigation-related projects and has declined in recent decades.[5] Within academic scholarship, too, while there has been a rich tradition of social science engagement with irrigation, this literature has largely neglected to address the question of where the water goes after it is applied to the fields.[6] Irrigation is alluring; drainage is not.

In this chapter, I take this largely hidden flow and make it visible. I continue the journey started in the previous chapter, following the water after it has moved across the surface, from canal to field, tracking it as it moves down and through the soil. I trace the different forms of human and non-human agency that control the subsurface realm. I argue that practices of managing these underground flows play a central role in shaping what Egypt's water comes to be.

This analysis speaks to the everyday politics that emerge in and around the issue of too much water. As Samer Alatout (2009) has argued, water abundance requires just as much attention as water scarcity. His analysis of narratives of water abundance in early twentieth-century Palestine offers a powerful example of how abundance, like scarcity, can be made into a strategic resource to serve political ends. My approach differs from Alatout's, however, in the way in which I develop my theorization of abundance. My interest is not in social constructions of abundance but, rather, in the places within Egypt's irrigation system where water is abundant (or, more precisely, overly abundant). The significance of abundance in this case lies not in its employment as a political tool in discourse but for what it means in terms of the productivity of the land. While many discussions of scarcity imply that the problem would be solved if only the resource were more plentiful, this analysis illustrates that abundance, too, can be problematic.

The focus of this chapter, therefore, is on the points within the Egyptian irrigation network where supply exceeds demand. These are the places where water in the soil matrix underlies a crop that has already taken up all the water that it needs, or where water gushes out of the end of a drain. Since the localized buildup of water in these locations has problematic ramifications, causing salinization and generating a flow of poor quality water, I use the term *excess*, which lacks the positive connotations of the word *abundance*.[7] Focusing on the material dimensions of water in excess, I draw attention to the technologies used to manage abundance, revealing not only the social and political dynamics that influence the use of those technologies but also the inequalities generated by unequal access to them.

I start the chapter by elaborating on drainage as a process. I then trace the historical trajectory of Egypt's drainage program to examine how drainage has come to be seen as something that requires management. I analyze the everyday politics that both shape and are shaped by a partially implemented network of subsurface drainage pipes. Then I look at the management of drainage outlets to illustrate how agricultural development is limited not only by the amount of water available for irrigation but also by the ability to dispose of the drainage water generated by that irrigation. Finally, I explore how drainage water can be recycled back into the system for reuse in irrigation, changing the nature of the water, with profound consequences for those who rely on that water for their livelihoods. I argue that this analysis of drainage as a process, project, waste product, and supplement highlights a vertical dimension to the making of Egypt's water. The vertical movement of water molecules down and up through the soil, dissolving and precipitating salts along the way, helps constitute the quality and quantity parameters of the resource.

WHERE DOES THE WATER GO?

It is a warm day at the end of November 2007, and I am with Abu Khaled in his fields. Today is a big day in the agricultural calendar: the day of the onion transplant. Mahmud, Abu Khaled's brother-in-law, has been here since before sunrise when he opened the mesqa to start flooding the fields in preparation for planting. Neat ridges of earth line the fields, regularly spaced between troughs of water. Open drainage ditches border the fields. Piles of onion seedlings lie along the top of the ridges. Laborers, calf-deep in water, pull individual seedlings from bunches that they hold under their arms and plant them in the soaked earth, just above the water level. Every so often, Abu Khaled or Mahmud take up their *fass* (a tool with a wooden handle and perpendicular metal blade) and open a gap in one of the earth bunds that divide the fields into rectangular basins, redirecting water into

Figure 5.1.
Transplanting
onion seedlings.
Photograph by
the author.

a part of a field that needs more and away from a part of a field that has
too much.

At 11:30, four hours after the laborers started work, the half feddan of
land is fully planted with onion seedlings. Mahmud blocks off the flow of
water from the mesqa onto the land, using a few big rocks and mud to
form a dam. We move to the edge of the fields, where we sit in the shade
of a shelter made from date palm fronds. Mahmud's daughter makes tea
on a fire, and we eat roasted corn-on-the-cob, which she has picked from
a neighbor's fields. Alongside us, the drainage process continues. Water
seeps slowly into the ground, some of it evaporating before it has a chance
to work its way down into the soil. As the top layer of the soil becomes saturated, some of the water moves across the surface to the drainage ditches
that border each field. Of the water that infiltrates the soil, much is taken
up through the roots of the onion seedlings to pass through the plant and
be transpired back into the atmosphere. The rest of it moves through the

Figure 5.2. Salt crust on the soil surface. Photograph by the author.

soil, dissolving salts along the way. Since the government's program to install subsurface drainage has yet to reach Abu Khaled's land, the water that remains in the soil does not pass into a pipe but, instead, through the pores between soil particles. Some molecules percolate down beyond the reach of the plant roots; others move laterally until their path is intercepted by a drainage ditch.[8]

We spend the heat of the day in the shade, then gather our things and head home. The late afternoon sun casts a warm glow over the fields. As the surface dries, it sets up a pressure gradient within the soil profile. This draws water up through the soil via capillary action—the process through which water moves upward, against gravity, due to the cohesion of the water molecules to each other and adhesive attraction between the water and the soil particles that it moves between. At the surface, the water evaporates into the atmosphere, leaving behind the salts that it has picked up on its journey through the soil.

Drainage is the technique through which farmers remove both the excess water pooled on the surface and the water that has penetrated down below the level of the roots or remains in soil pores.[9] In managing these surface and subsurface flows, farmers aim for a critical balance. Enough water must remain in the soil to provide sufficient moisture for the growing crop. At the same time, they must channel away surplus water to pre-

TABLE 5.1 Impact of Soil Salinity on Crop Yields

	Salinity thresholds (dS/m) for different yield potentials				
Crop	No impact on yield	10% yield loss	25% yield loss	50% yield loss	No crop growth
Clover (birsim)	≤1.5	3.2	5.9	10	≥19.0
Corn (maize)	≤1.7	2.5	3.8	5.9	≥10.0
Cotton	≤7.7	9.6	13.0	17.0	≥27.0
Faba beans	≤1.5	2.6	4.2	6.8	≥12.0
Fodder maize (garawa)	≤1.8	3.2	5.2	8.6	≥15.0
Onions	≤1.2	1.8	2.8	4.3	≥7.4
Rice (paddy)	≤3.0	3.8	5.1	7.2	≥11.0
Sugar beets	≤7.0	8.7	11.0	15.0	≥24.0
Sorghum	≤6.8	7.4	8.4	9.9	≥13.0
Tomatoes	≤2.5	3.5	5.0	7.6	≥13.0
Wheat	≤6.0	7.4	9.5	13.0	≥20.0

Source: Figures from Ayers and Westcot (1994).

vent the soil from becoming saturated.[10] Soil saturation deprives crops of the oxygen that their roots need to draw from pore spaces and limits the movement of water down through the soil, which is vital to leach away any salts that have accumulated. Furthermore, if excess water remains in the soil, it will be drawn to the surface and evaporate, contributing to the process of salinization.

Traveling through Egypt's agricultural land, the serious effects of salinization are evident. Dotted within the green are the fields left barren as a thin crust of salt granules renders the land uncultivable. Among the tall healthy crops are the patches of stunted crops, floundering in soils that are too saline for them to thrive. In a country as hot and sunny as Egypt, evaporation rates are high, between 1.5mm and 8mm a day, which means that at the peak, a depth of 8mm water is lost to the atmosphere from the surface each day. Salinization is thus a huge problem. An estimated 35 percent of the agricultural lands are saline (with an electrical conductivity over 4dS/m) and the proportion is as high as 60 percent in northern parts of the delta (Kotb et al. 2000, 248).[11] Salinity adversely impacts crop growth, reducing yields by over 25 percent in the case of some of the crops commonly grown in Egypt (table 5.1).

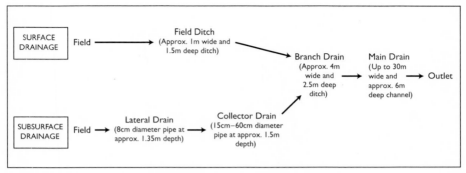

Figure 5.3. Flow of water through the drainage system.

The main problem of salinity is that it limits the amount of water that a crop is able to extract from the soil.[12] To demonstrate, I will zoom in for a moment to focus on the point of water uptake—the crop's roots in the soil. At the interface between the crop and its growing medium, the key factor determining water movement is the relative concentrations of the liquids within and outside the plant root. It is this concentration gradient that causes water to move into the plant through the wall of the root through the process of osmosis. Water enters the root when the soil water has a lower concentration of solutes (i.e., dissolved salts) than the solution inside the root. When, however, the soil becomes saline, the concentration of solute in the soil water increases and alters that concentration gradient. This means that water no longer moves from the soil into the plant root. Herein lies the irony. Application of too much water to the soil leads to salinization, which ends up limiting the amount of water the crop is able to absorb. When crops are unable to take up water from a salinized soil, they experience molecular damage, growth arrest, and may die (Umali 1993). It is not long before it is no longer possible to plant a crop in a salinized field. Obviously this is of critical concern both to the farmers, who do not want to see their land rendered uncultivable, and to the government, which does not want to see an erosion of the country's cultivable land.

To prevent salinization, drainage is vital. In the next section I trace the emergence of two different technologies for facilitating drainage flows. The older surface system, like that which I saw in Abu Khaled's fields, involves a series of open drainage ditches and serves 40 percent of Egypt's agricultural lands. The subsurface system, like that which I saw with Lutfi, is made up of a network of pipes and serves approximately 60 percent of Egypt's land. Both systems discharge into the branch and main drains, which transport the drainage water to an outlet (see figure 5.3).

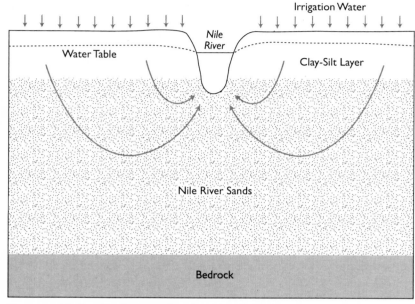

Figure 5.4. The interface between the Nile River and aquifer.

A GENEALOGY OF DRAINAGE

Natural Drainage: No Drainage

Prior to the introduction of perennial irrigation in the mid-nineteenth century, drainage was not a critical concern for the Egyptian authorities. That is, there was still drainage—excess water had to drain off the fields—but because the flow was only of a limited volume, there was no need for special technologies to manage that flow. Some farmers dug drainage ditches on their land to channel away excess water, but many did not, and there was no integrated state-run system.

Each year in early August, the Nile flooded and farmers opened cuts in the high banks along the river, allowing the rising floodwaters to flow into the valley. They channeled water across the floodplain, through a series of basins demarcated by dykes. Farmers would flood each basin up to a depth of 1.5 meters and leave the water at this depth for 40 days before opening the dyke and draining the water on to the next basin.[13] Water that infiltrated the soil percolated down into the underlying body of coarse sand, joining the aquifer that is dynamically linked with the river channel (see figure 5.4). Although the water moved slowly through the soil, since most of the alluvial soils of the Nile valley and delta have a relatively low permeability, the inputs of water were not sufficient for this to be a problem. When the water level in the river declined after the flood, pressure gradients within the groundwater allowed water from the aquifer to move back through the earthen layers of the bank into the Nile channel, where it flowed away to the Mediterranean. As one drainage engineer explained to me, "The Nile itself acted as a drain." Most of the salts that built up as water evaporated from the surface were dissolved and washed down through the soil the following year when the floodwaters flowed over the floodplain once again. The layer of sediment deposited by the floodwaters also helped keep soil salinity levels in check.

Hydrologists and engineers refer to this system as "natural drainage." Water drained down through the soil and, stimulated by pressure gradients within the groundwater, entered the river channel to be transported away. The way in which farmers and local authorities tightly controlled the floodwaters' progression across the floodplain and the draining of surface water from one basin to the next was far from natural. But the authorities did not at this stage see drainage, specifically, as something that required bureaucratic control. They could rely on the Nile to do the work.

Open Drainage: Drainage as Ditches

The situation changed over the course of the nineteenth century, however, as agricultural expansion and intensification led to increased water use.[14] Irrigation water applications escalated, filling the soil at a rate faster than it could drain away. The water table rose, bringing the soil water closer to the surface from where it could evaporate. With this evaporation, more and more salts started to accumulate. This was exacerbated in those parts of the delta affected by the Delta Barrages, where the Nile no longer flooded annually and thus did not wash away the salts.

Colonial administrators within the Public Works Department began to voice their concerns.[15] In 1884, a senior irrigation engineer wrote that he did "not think the importance of this drainage question can be over-rated."[16] An agricultural expert on a tour of Egypt's irrigation system in 1890 stated that of all the water management schemes in Egypt, nothing was as urgent as drainage. He observed, "It may be safely assumed that any . . . addition to the amount of water without extensive drainage works would probably be more of a curse than a blessing to the country."[17] There was a sense among the department officials that drainage needed state intervention. So in the last decades of the nineteenth century, the Public Works Department started to dig drains.

By 1892 the department had excavated more than 1,600km of open drains (Hollings 1917, 205). In his annual report of 1898 the British Consul General in Egypt, Lord Cromer, concluded that "every landowner in the country understands the advantage of a drain."[18] Most of these early drains, though, were just converted from irrigation canals, as the government did not have sufficient funds to dig new drains of sufficient depth and capacity (Elgood 1928, 201). This technology of channeling drainage water into converted canals was not very successful. As Sir William Willcocks, a leading engineer in the department, wrote in 1899, "Time . . . has brought out all the faults of the system, and now that the Caisse of Public Debt is giving hundreds of thousands of pounds per annum for drainage it would be statesmanlike to return to the best and most scientific method" (Willcocks 1899, 235). The way in which Willcocks drew on nationalist tropes, referring to what behavior would be "statesmanlike," illustrates the shift from the authorities seeing drainage as a management-less sphere to being something that required state intervention. Willcocks's vision for the best scientific method of drainage was to establish a system of main and branch drains at the lowest elevations, which would be able to capture more of the drainage flows moving downward through gravity than the previous drains, not located in the lowest areas, were able to. "This method is natural, is healthy, and should, in my opinion, be followed everywhere," he stated definitively in the second edition of his book *Egyptian Irrigation* (1899, 233).

The Public Works Department's plans to construct an open drainage network were given further impetus in 1909 when a particularly high Nile flood led to a disastrous failure of the cotton crop, with devastating economic and social consequences. The commission established to look into the causes of the crop failure determined that the primary problem had been one of inadequate drainage.[19] Large landowners in the northern delta, who grew cotton and rice and were particularly affected by the problem of poor drainage, lent strong support to the government's drainage program. Also influential were the politically connected construction magnates who were eager to make profits through government contracts to build the drainage system.[20] By 1938, the system of open drains covered 35–40 percent of the agricultural land and the minister of public works announced a need to further extend this drainage system, saying, "Our aim is to produce real drainage in the land for every plot in Egypt from Aswan to the sea."[21]

In these early decades of the twentieth century, government officials saw drainage as an intervention to guard against waterlogging and salinization. The open drains were designed to intercept excess water passing over or through the soil and channel it away from the fields. Initially, the ministry assumed that farmers would dig their own field ditches to conduct drainage to the branch drains. The premise was that drainage would be a joint responsibility. The government would provide the drains to remove drainage water to an outlet; the farmers would provide the means of channeling excess water from the fields to those drains. But officials soon found that only large landowners and farmers with land directly abutting drains were willing to dig ditches through their fields. The historical accounts contain no indication of the reasons behind this reluctance, so it is not clear if farmers did not judge the ditches to be necessary, did not want to lose some of their cultivable land, lacked the time to dig them, or just assumed that the government would do it. Whatever the reason, from the 1920s onward, the Ministry of Public Works took charge of the whole process, from the field to outlet, excavating not only branch and main drains but also field ditches.

Thus through the first half of the twentieth century, the government put a drainage system in place. By the late 1960s, the Ministry of Public Works (which became the Ministry of Irrigation in 1964) had dug more than 16,200km of open drains. In addition, it had installed over fifty pumping stations to maintain a gradient in water levels between drain sections and hence the flow of water through the system. This system served nearly seven million feddan and has not been modified much since. However, while this system was nearly complete, the whole notion of what a drainage system entailed was soon to change.

Subsurface Drainage: Drainage as Pipes

The Aswan High Dam fundamentally altered the parameters of what water needed to be drained from the fields. As more farmers started to multicrop their fields, grow water-intensive summer crops, and expand their land into the desert margins, drainage discharge increased significantly. Below the surface, less visibly, the dam altered the relationship between the Nile and the alluvial aquifer underlying the floodplain. With water levels no longer falling as they used to after the flood, there was no pressure gradient to cause water to drain naturally from the aquifer back into the river channel (Amer et al. 1989). The High Dam made water a possibility, but at the same time, it also made water a problem.

Long before the dam was complete, government officials had anticipated that the existing drainage system would not be able to cope with such a marked increase in drainage flows. Back in the 1930s and 1940s, the Ministry of Public Works had conducted field trials of subsurface drainage (which is known in Arabic by its other name, covered drainage, *al-sirf*

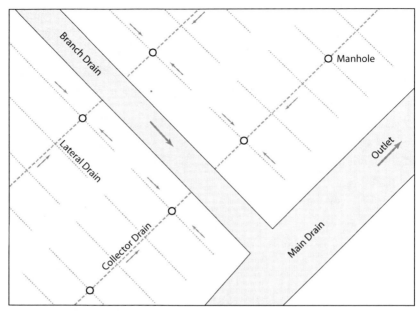

Figure 5.5. The subsurface drainage system.

al-mughati).[22] In this system, excess water in the soil passes into perforated lateral pipes, which channel it to nonporous collector pipes, to be transported to open branch drains (see figure 5.5). The trials had proven the system to be more efficient than surface drainage, since the water can move through the pipes freely, unimpeded by the weeds and debris that often block open field ditches. Installation remained limited, however, to a few small areas (despite the government passing Law No. 35 in 1949, which said that it would implement subsurface drainage on all agricultural lands). As part of its preparations for the High Dam, therefore, in 1960 the ministry initiated a series of five-year plans to install subsurface drainage throughout the country.

By the time the dam was complete, though, only half a million feddan had subsurface drainage. The government turned to international donors for assistance. In 1970, the World Bank approved an interest-free loan of US$26 million to help fund a subsurface drainage project in the Nile delta. A series of internationally financed projects followed as the drainage program, in the words of one donor, "took on a life of its own" (table 5.2). By the late 2000s, just over 4.5 million feddan—57 percent of Egypt's total cultivated area—had subsurface drainage (Abdel-Dayem, Abdel-Gawad,

TABLE 5.2 Subsurface Drainage Projects in Egypt

Project (Donor)	Dates	Total area (thousands of feddan)	
		Remodeled open drains	Subsurface drains
Government of Egypt	1930s–	3,473	1,478
Nile Delta Drainage Project I (World Bank)	1971–80	950	959
Upper Egypt Drainage Project I (World Bank)	1974–79	300	300
East Bahr Saft (Netherlands)	Late 1970s	—	41
Upper Egypt Drainage Project II (World Bank and USAID)	1980–85	500	463
Nile Delta Drainage Project II (World Bank and KfW)	1981–85	815	400
Integrated Soil and Water Improvement Project (CIDA)	1987–92	84	60
Drainage Project V (World Bank and African Development Bank)	1983–94	256	87
Islamic Development Bank	Early 1990s	—	75
Hamoul (European Economic Commission)	Early 1990s	—	35
National Drainage Project I (World Bank, KfW, the Netherlands, and JICA)	1992–2000	398	331
National Drainage Project II (World Bank, European Investment Bank, KfW, and the Netherlands)	2001–2008	365	423
TOTAL		7,141	4,652

Source: El-Kadi et al. (1995, 369–83), ADB (2000), Fathi and Hamza (2000: 29), and Ali, van Leeuwen, and Koopmans (2001). In the case of some projects, there is variation in the figures quoted by the different sources. The total area of subsurface drainage calculated here slightly exceeds the total of 4.52 million feddan cited by Abdel-Dayem et al. (2007, 104). However, this data still gives an indication of which donors have been involved, where they have worked, and the extent of their involvement.

and Fahmy 2007, 104). In addition, the ministry had remodeled many of its open branch and main drains to make them deep enough to receive water from pipe outlets. Expansion of this program continues today as the ministry plans to increase the coverage of subsurface drainage to 6.4 million feddan by 2017 (MWRI 2005a, 5–10).

Farmers' response to this new technology initially was mixed. One senior official in the ministry recounted his experience in the early years of the program. "When I started work in this field in 1965, we were not mature. We just went to the field as a group of engineers. . . . We didn't tell the farmers what we were doing. . . . They saw us destroying their crops by digging up their fields, and they were very angry. They tried to stop the machines. But we were the authority. We brought the police and just continued our work." As farmers began to see the benefits, though, their attitudes changed. The official explained, "They saw how production can increase by 30 percent or as much as infinity on particularly problematic land that was not in cultivation before. They saw how there were now no ditches to disturb their work in the fields, which is now mostly mechanized rather than by hand. Also their land increased, because they could plant where the drains had been. It's also more healthy [because open drainage ditches often become very polluted]."

From the official's description of the benefits that farmers have come to see in subsurface drainage, it is clear that drainage is now about more than just managing waterlogging and salinization. It is, instead, a management intervention that has a range of economic, social, and environmental benefits (van Steenbergen and Abdel-Dayem 2007).[23] Indeed many of the farmers who I talked with in Warda who do not have subsurface drainage say that their primary reason for wanting it is to free up the land currently given over to ditches for more cultivation, rather than to improve drainage from their fields.

Hence over the years, the notion of what it means to manage Egypt's excess water has shifted. As it has done so, the types of knowledge, expertise, materials, and funds that the government has mobilized to support its drainage program have changed. These practices are critical to shaping where water flows below the surface and how that affects the quantity and quality of water in Egypt's irrigation system. In the next section, I explore how the current focus on implementation of a national subsurface drainage network plays into the everyday politics of water in Egypt.

SUBSURFACE POLITICS

With subsurface drainage now serving more than half of Egypt's agricultural lands, part of what Egypt's water now is is a stream flowing through pipes under the fields. In these fields, rather than water molecules pooling in soil pores, causing waterlogging, or moving up to the surface to evaporate, causing salinization, the molecules make their way through gaps in the edge of lateral pipes and then are whisked away, down a lateral pipe, into a collector pipe, and out into a drain. By reworking flows of water below the surface, subsurface drainage creates new landscapes of agricultural possibility on the surface.

"We Don't Have Drainage"

The installation of subsurface drainage in some areas and not in others generates new lines of inequality. Nowadays, when farmers and officials refer to drainage (*sirf*) they generally mean subsurface drainage. Farmers without a subsurface system will often say, "We don't have drainage (*ma 'andnash sirf*)." The network of drainage ditches does not seem to count as drainage any more. Drainage has come to mean a series of pipes, producing a new sense of marginality for those who lack this grid beneath their fields. The subsurface space of where there are and are not pipes reflects an overlying inequality in access to the most efficient means of removing excess water from the system. This is an inequality structured not according to who has enough water (see chapter 2) but according to who has too much. When it comes to the water below a farmer's fields, more is not necessarily better.

The significance of uneven access to subsurface drainage lies in the positive influence that this technology has on agricultural production. One of the donor-funded projects in the delta recorded a notable increase in crop yields over a five-year period after it installed subsurface drains, due to the increased efficiency of evacuating excess water. Yield increases averaged 326kg/feddan (15%) for wheat, 1,260kg/feddan (41%) for maize, 126kg/feddan (13%) for cotton, and 399kg/feddan (14%) for rice.[24] This yield increase, in addition to the ability to cultivate the land that was formerly taken up by drainage ditches, has a marked economic impact. Annual farm incomes in the project site increased by 33 percent and land prices also increased disproportionally (Ali, van Leeuwen, and Koopmans 2001). People whom I spoke to in Fayoum told a similar story. One drainage engineer told me that crop production in fields with subsurface drainage has increased by 50 percent. "*Alhamdulallah*, Thanks be to God!" replied a farmer when I asked him about the new drainage system. "It has increased our production and solved our problems."

Thus the decision about which areas receive subsurface drainage and reap the benefits of increased production carries with it important political implications. To understand how this decision is made requires a closer look at the process of designing and installing the network of subsurface pipes. This work lies with officials within the Egyptian Public Authority for Drainage Projects, a department of the ministry that was established in 1973 to manage the country's subsurface drainage program.

One day in November 2011 I visited the drainage authority in Cairo, which occupies the top three floors of a building on one side of a busy roundabout in Giza, opposite the zoo. I met with Ayman, an engineer from the authority, who explained to me the process of designing and installing subsurface drainage. A natural teacher, he was excited to share some of his long experience. As he talked, he showed me a PowerPoint presentation on his laptop, which he had prepared for a lecture to students in an on-farm water management course for African water management professionals.

The first step, Ayman explained, is to conduct a field survey. They drill auger holes at regular intervals to determine the type of soil and its hydraulic conductivity—a critical factor for drainage planning. In Egypt's heavier soils, water may move less than 10cm in a day; in lighter soils, it can move over half a meter. His PowerPoint slide showed a group of people standing around an auger hole. Ayman pointed to a man standing with the group. "This is a Dutch expert," he said, explaining that the Dutch have played an important role in helping Egypt develop its drainage program. But, he emphasized, the drainage authority has tailored the design and installation process to the Egyptian context.

After the samples have been gathered and analyzed, engineers input the results into a computer program. The computer program helps design the subsurface system, specifying the number of lateral and collector pipes that will be needed for each area and their diameter, slope, length, and spacing. Officials put together a large album, with maps depicting the baseline data on subsurface characteristics, the proposed layout of the pipes and manholes, longitudinal sections, and tables listing all the materials that will be required. When the plans are complete, the authority contracts out the work of installing the system to specialized contractors, who have the machines required to install the pipes.[25]

The implementation of subsurface drainage is therefore dependent on particular kinds of specialized knowledge: the knowledge of how to collect and interpret data on soil quality characteristics; the knowledge of how to use a computer design program to map the subsurface space and determine what pipes should go where; the knowledge of how to read technical drawings and operate a pipe-installation machine. So whereas any farmer can dig an open drainage ditch along one side of a field if he or she chooses to, the work of installing subsurface drainage pipes lies primarily with ministry engineers and specialized contractors. Farmers cover the infrastructure costs, but the ministry is responsible for all the design and implementation work.[26]

Given that the drainage authority only has the resources to work on installing subsurface drainage on about 150,000 to 200,000 feddan a year, it has to prioritize. The first areas to receive subsurface drainage were the parts of the delta where heavy clay soils make drainage particularly problematic. Once those areas were complete, the authority turned its attention to the whole country. It now ranks areas according to two criteria: soil salinity and waterlogging. For the ministry to proceed with subsurface drainage installation in a given location, over half the auger holes in the preliminary field survey must indicate either that the water table lies within a meter of the surface or that the soil has a salinity of more than 4dS/m.

The decision about which areas should receive subsurface drainage is not, however, just a matter of meeting technical criteria. One senior official in the ministry told me about how farmers actively campaign for their land to be prioritized. He recalled his time working for the drainage authority. Gesturing with his hand about 30cm above the table in front of him he said, "I had a pile this high on my desk of requests from people who wanted drainage—from farmers and also from parliamentarians who wanted to raise their region up in the priority list." The degree to which the ministry officials take the farmers' requests into consideration, though, no doubt depends on who those farmers are. The requests from the parliamentarians are likely to hold more weight than those of small farmers. As powerful individuals lobby for the government to prioritize their lands, using their position of influence to get the ministry to install piped drains, they alter the flow of water beneath their fields and bolster their crop yields, thereby casting new relations of privilege and influence.

But farmers do not always wait for the drainage authority to act. When I returned to Fayoum in 2011, I spent a morning with Abu Khaled back in the same fields where I had watched him plant onions four years previously. As we walked through the fields between rows of maize that were nearing harvest, he said, "If I had the money, I would install subsurface drainage."

Assuming I would not know what this was, he explained, "This is pipes with holes in them that you put where? Under the ground!" I responded that I had read about the government's program to install subsurface drainage throughout the country. He looked confused. "The government is not involved," he said. He had not heard of the ministry's work to install subsurface drainage, perhaps in part because up until this time it had only been working in the eastern part of Fayoum.[27] His knowledge of this technology came, instead, from a few other farmers in the village who have worked independently to install subsurface drains under their fields.

More farmers are taking the initiative to install their own subsurface drainage systems. As most are not familiar with the design and installation process, they generally contract people with specialized knowledge of this technology. Often they hire ministry engineers as private consultants to help them design the system outside of office hours. Wealth is the critical determinant of whether or not a farmer is able to pursue subsurface drainage independently. Abu Khaled told me that it would cost around 5,000LE for him to install subsurface drains on his 5¼ feddan plot of land—a considerable expense, currently out of his reach.

Controlling the Subsurface

The fact that drainage pipes lie below the surface has important political implications for different actors' ability to control the flow of water away from the fields. Take, for example, the case of maintenance. Maintenance is vital for ensuring the steady flow of water through the drainage system, just as it is through the surface irrigation system (see chapter 2). If a field ditch becomes blocked with weeds or sediment, it is easy for a farmer to clear it out. If, however, an underground pipe becomes misaligned, damaged, or blocked, a farmer can do little other than lodge a complaint to the ministry and then wait for the ministry to bring its high-pressure flushing machine to clean out the pipe or special materials to reconstruct the pipe. One official admitted that they are not able to keep up with the maintenance work, due to a lack of laborers and limited funds. Hence in many places, the flow of water through the drainage system is interrupted due to disrepair of the pipe network. In these cases, a view inside a manhole reveals a stagnant pool, the water not moving, unable to continue its piped journey to an outlet.

Yet despite the importance of keeping soils well drained, there are some circumstances in which this kind of interruption to the flow can be in the farmers' interests. If, for instance, the supply of water in the irrigation canals is insufficient, limiting drainage outflow means that farmers can access that drainage water to supplement their irrigation supply (I discuss this further later in the chapter). In other cases, where farmers grow water-intensive crops like rice, they need to maintain a high level of water in the root zone. Within a surface drainage system, it is easy to manipulate drainage flows. By building earth dams across the field drainage ditches, farmers can prevent the drainage water from leaving their fields. In a subsurface drainage system, however, controlling these flows away from the fields is much more difficult, although not impossible. In some rice-growing areas, the ministry has installed metal gates on the collector drain pipes (this is known as "controlled drainage"). By opening and closing these gates, farmers are able to control the flows of drainage underground. In most areas, though, farmers have to employ different mechanisms to exert their control. If they do not want the excess water to drain away, they plug the end of the pipe outlets or manholes with straw, leaves, and mud. If they wish to access drainage water in times of irrigation water shortage, they remove manhole covers and use pumps to lift water from the piped drains.

These are some of the everyday practices that farmers use to assert their control over flows through a subsurface drainage system, much as they do over flows through the surface irrigation system (chapters 2 and 4). From the ministry's point of view, such actions compromise the efficiency of its drainage network. A poster on the wall of Lutfi's office, produced by the Water Communication Unit, indicates the ministry's position. "Subsurface drainage improves your land and increases your income," the title states. But, the poster demonstrates, for the system to function as intended, farmers must behave in a certain way. Below there are six photos, grouped in pairs. The photo on the left shows the correct behavior, marked with a bold yellow check mark; the photo on the right shows the incorrect behavior, marked with a cross. One set of pictures depicts the outlet of a pipe into a drain. In the photo on the left, the pipe is securely surrounded by stones; in the other, the bank is eroding around the pipe. In the next row of photos, the left-hand picture shows a farmer clearing sediment from a manhole; the picture on the right shows a farmer emptying crop remains into a manhole. In the final set of pictures, one photo shows a manhole with its cover firmly intact; the other shows a farmer smashing the cover. The message is clear: in order for the drainage system to function properly, farmers must not block the pipe outlet or manhole.

To try and enforce these regulations and maintain its control over subsurface flows, the ministry issues fines to farmers who disrupt the system.

On the day that I visited the drainage district with Lutfi, for example, he noticed that the cover to one of the manholes in a field was broken. "This is a violation," he explained to me. The ministry's concern is that if the manhole covers are removed, farmers will start pumping water from the manholes for irrigation or use the manholes for waste disposal. He called out to an old man who was passing by. "Who owns this land? He has done a violation by breaking the cover!" he shouted. The man replied with the landowner's name, but said that it was not his fault that the cover was broken. It was the ministry's excavator that had bumped into the manhole and cracked the cover when cleaning the canal, he explained. "It does not matter what happened," Lutfi replied. "The owner of the land is still responsible." He asked the old man to tell the landowner that he would write a report and that if the cover was not fixed within three days, the farmer would be fined. As with the violations within the irrigation system (see chapters 2 and 4), though, these practices tend to persist despite the fines that the ministry levies. Ultimately, the benefits that farmers gain from being able to control subsurface flows to suit their needs, by modifying technologies of drainage water distribution, outweigh the costs of paying a fine.

Visibility and Invisibility

Hence subsurface drainage alters different parties' ability to control water flows at the level of the field. In terms of its impact on political relations at the national and international levels, on the other hand, an interesting comparison can be drawn with the Aswan High Dam, another major state-led and donor-funded intervention in Egypt's water management sector. The two projects share a common goal: improving the management of water in Egypt's agricultural lands to foster agricultural development. Yet while the High Dam has received huge amounts of attention in both the academic and popular literature, the subsurface drainage program has remained almost unknown except to the farmers and experts working in this particular area of water management.[28]

Indeed large-scale dams have been the focus of much of the critical literature on water management.[29] Dams are, in some ways, the antithesis of drainage. Prominent in the landscape, their scale clearly evident, dams are a visible manifestation of states' (or donors') power and engineering skills. They are projects with great iconic and symbolic resonance. As such, they become rallying points for nation-building. Timothy Mitchell writes that the Aswan High Dam "became the centerpiece of postwar nation making in Egypt" (2002, 45). In heroic imagery, drawing a line of continuity between modern and ancient Egypt, President Nasser said of the dam, "In antiquity we built pyramids for the dead. Now we build pyramids for the living."[30] The High Dam is a marker to the world of Egypt's technological expertise and its mastery over the Nile. This is reinforced today each time one of the many tourist buses stops off at the dam on its way back to Aswan from Abu Simbel, the magnificent temples dismantled and reconstructed at a higher location as the waters of Lake Nasser began to rise. Tourists get out of their tour bus and peer over the edge at the long concrete structure of the dam. While they may be disappointed by the dam's underwhelming height, they still snap photos of the national landmark. Drains, a matter of the everyday rather than grand rhetoric, do not build nations in the same way.[31] The sub-surface drainage project, lying under the ground, does not hold such symbolic valence. I may have been fascinated to look in a manhole, but buses will never stop so that tourists can marvel at the pipes that channel water through the soil.

If governments and donors invest in dams, in part, to make a statement of their power and expertise, what motivates them to invest in a drainage project? While the white, lotus flower–shaped monument to Soviet-Egyptian cooperation stands tall by the High Dam as a symbol of the Soviet Union's role in funding the dam, there is no such marker of the Dutch, German, Canadian, and Japanese dollars that have gone into the network of subsurface pipes. When I talked to international donors, they narrated their involvement in drainage as a simple matter of expertise transfer. "The Dutch are known to be experts on water management," the director of development in the Netherlands embassy commented to me. "Who lives under the sea? Who has been able to defend themselves?" It was hardly surprising, in his view, that when the Egyptians started to work on land drainage, they turned to the "masters of drainage."

Yet as James Ferguson's (1994) seminal work, The Anti-Politics Machine, demonstrates, development interventions are never purely technical in motivation. This raises the question of what different types of politics drive the government's and donors' willingness to invest so much in Egypt's drainage program. No doubt donors are keen to maintain good relations with an important partner in a geopolitically significant region. They have a reason, therefore, to offer funding for projects that the government wishes to pursue. The government, on the other hand, has an interest in ensuring that the productivity of its lands is maintained. It would reflect badly on the government if its grand achievement—the High Dam—resulted in the fields, no longer washed by the flood, becoming increasingly saline.

The unrest within the farming population that would accompany a deterioration in land quality would also not be politically desirable. In addition, agricultural production is a cornerstone of the government's food security strategy and provides a valuable source of foreign exchange from exports. Thus it is in the government's strategic interests to invest in a subsurface drainage system if that system will help maintain a certain level of agricultural production.

A second point of contrast between a drainage system and a large dam is the power dynamics that surround these technologies of water manipulation. Mitchell argues that part of the significance of the Aswan High Dam lies in the ways in which it brings together circuits of power into one central nexus of control (2002, 35). The power of the dam, therefore, stems from the concentration in space of the technologies for managing the flow of water through the country. While there are multiple points within the irrigation network where people can intervene and exert agency over water, the High Dam is the ultimate control point. In contrast, while the subsurface drainage program has made Egypt's subterranean flow controllable, it is a diffuse network of control. There are nodal points—the manholes for inspection, the joints between different pipes—but there is no one site where this flow can be turned on and off. Thus different types of power operate through a drainage scheme: a power that comes not from being able to dictate flow from one location but from facilitating subsurface flows to make the fields more productive; a power held by the engineers who understand the computer program that designs the layout of the pipe network; a power wielded by the contractors who own and operate pipe installation machines; a power held by farmers who have subsurface drainage to use as much water as they choose without worrying about waterlogging or salinization.

Drainage is not, however, just a matter of channeling water from the fields. When water flows into the branch and main drains, this is not the end of its journey. Drains need an outlet. Hence water managers have to deal not only with collecting drainage water but also disposing of it.

THE END OF THE DRAINS

All along the Nile valley, the drains discharge back into the Nile. As the river winds its way northward, water that is not lost by evapotranspiration cycles from river to canal to field to drain and then back into the river again. By the northern delta, the drains are wide and full of water, sometimes black and with a strong odor from the wastewater and refuse that people have disposed in the drains en route. The ends of the main drains are low, their depth necessary to stimulate gravity flow through the drainage system. Hence pumps are required to lift the drainage to a point of outlet: a final exertion of energy to remove the excess water and salts from the system. Pumping stations discharge about 12.5bcm of water a year, either directly into the Mediterranean Sea or into the northern lakes of Mariut, Edku, Burullus, and Manzala (which, except for Lake Mariut, are connected to the sea) (Zhu et al. 1998, ch. 1, 5). So approximately a fifth of the water that enters Egypt leaves via the sea; the rest leaves via evapotranspiration.

The province of Fayoum is an exception. Lying in a depression west of the Nile valley, Fayoum is one of only a few places where water flows from, but never returns to, the Nile (see map 1.3).[32] Fayoum therefore offers a valuable example of how excess water may be manifest as a problem on a regional level at the same time that water is scarce. In Pharaonic times, much of the Fayoum depression was flooded, forming a large reservoir known as Lake Moeris. The surface of the lake lay at around 20m above sea level. This meant that as the Nile floodwaters receded, water would return to the Nile valley, helping replenish the river's discharge during the drier months (Brown 1892). In the Ptolemaic period (beginning 323 BC), however, lake levels declined dramatically, most likely as a result of water diversions for agricultural development (Flower et al. 2006). Today the shrunken remnant of Lake Moeris, Lake Qaroun, lies far below sea level. Once water drains down to the lake at the base of the depression, it cannot return to the Nile valley. Water flow into Fayoum is now only one way. The water flows in; it never flows back out.

Disposal of the unusable excess—the saline drainage water—poses a significant challenge to ministry officials. When I returned to Fayoum in April 2009 after some months away, Lake Qaroun was a common topic of conversation. The lake was overflowing, its waters lapping at the wall that borders the main tourist road which runs along the southern shore of the lake. The small beach resorts were closed, and picnic tables and chairs were stacked on the narrow strip of beach that remained, their feet in the waves. In places, the rock wall that protects the road had crumbled into the water. On windy days, salty spray blew over the road, causing havoc to drivers not used to driving under wet conditions. Many of the fields near the lake were flooded, their cultivation not an option this year. The drains were completely full, relentlessly channeling large amounts of water down to the lake. The local government had started to invest in shore protection measures, and laborers were working to construct new walls and piers. Many people were

Figure 5.6. High water levels in Lake Qaroun. Photograph by the author.

talking about how the bottom floor of what had once been a hunting lodge for King Farouk on the lakeshore, now a five-star hotel owned by a Scandinavian hotel chain, flooded completely a few weeks previously.

The level of water in Lake Qaroun has never been static. It varies from year to year depending on the balance between drainage inflows and evaporative losses (Boak 1926; Flower et al. 2006). But over the course of the twentieth century, lake levels rose markedly. Between 1900 and the early 1970s, the lake surface rose by more than a meter, from 45m below sea level to 43.7m below sea level (FWMP 2006a, 1). The increase in drainage inflows that caused this rise in lake levels was linked to agricultural expansion (see chapter 4) and to the proliferation of multicropping after completion of the High Dam. As the lake level rose, it started to flood the adjacent road, fields, and shoreline settlements.

A point was reached when the local authorities decided they could not allow the lake to rise any further. Without some means of disposing of the excess, they would not be able to let more water enter Fayoum. Further agricultural expansion was placed in question due to the additional drainage water it would generate. This was a critical situation in a province where the vast majority of the population is reliant on agriculture for at least part of its income. The irrigation directorate turned for a solution to the open space that borders the province on all sides. It drew up plans to divert some of the drainage water to an expanse of desert, Wadi Rayan, on the south-western edge of the province.[33] To divert water from its gravity-led course required construction of an 8km tunnel, excavation of a 9km open channel, and installation of a large pumping station. Construction work began. The ministry completed the infrastructure in 1973 and lakes of drainage water started to grow in the desert. Nowadays, if you turn south from the western edge of Lake Qaroun, you find two large lakes shimmering in the desert like a mirage, linked by a smaller lake and Egypt's one and only waterfall, where many Fayoumis flock to bathe on a sunny day. These are the lakes of Wadi Rayan (see map 1.3). By redirecting the flow of drainage water using pumping power, the ministry solved the problem of excess.

However, this solution did not last. While the diversion of about 30 percent of the drainage water to Wadi Rayan led to a temporary reduction of the water level in Lake Qaroun in the late 1970s, from that time on, lake levels have been rising. Given the infrastructure located along the shoreline, this has generated considerable concern among local populations and ministry officials. Since 2000, both the maximum and minimum annual lake levels have risen by about half a meter (FWMP 2006a, 18). The increase in drainage flows is partly due to the expansion of rice cultivation, since rice requires about double the amount of water as other major crops. It is also a result of mismatches in the timing of water release and water requirements, due to lack of communication between ministry officials and farmers, which means that water in the canals sometimes flows unused into the drains (see chapter 2).

In light of the recent high water levels, ministry officials have started to explore a new potential solution: pumping some of the water from Lake Qaroun into the desert north of the lake. Since the northern shore of the lake is bounded by a high desert plateau, such a solution would require either considerable pumping power, to lift the water up to the plateau for disposal, or a huge excavation project, to dig out a lower lying reservoir. The ministry is conducting studies into this plan's feasibility. But one international consultant I spoke to was skeptical. He told me that he did not think it logical to spend thousands correcting a problem that would not exist were it not for the ministry's inability to match water supply with farmer demand. "Mismanagement, mismanagement!" he repeated several times with incredulity.

Thus the solution to excess—finding a drainage outlet in the desert—has not been completely successful. Although almost all farmers in Fayoum feel they have insufficient water, on a provincial level the ministry officials do not know what to do with the water that they have. Farmers and ministry officials alike argue that the problem of water shortages would be solved if only the central ministry would increase the province's water allocation. Yet this is not possible due to the problem of where the excess will drain. Irrigated agriculture development in Fayoum is limited by its sink as well as by its source. The question of where Egypt's water should flow rests not only on considerations of which places need more water but of which places need less.

So while Samer Alatout (2008) looks at abundance and scarcity as distinct phases, in this case these two states exist side-by-side. Water managers — from the ministry through to the field — have to manage a supply of what is at once too much and too little water. In the next section, I consider an alternative technique for dealing with excess water: recycling it for reuse. The determining factor for whether drainage water is disposed or reused is quality. The water at the ultimate point of outlet — in Lake Qaroun, Wadi Rayan, the northern lakes, or Mediterranean — is too saline and polluted to be of use for irrigation; hence the need for its disposal. At points further up the system, however, drainage water can be of good enough quality to be used to irrigate the fields. As different actors utilize pumps to redirect water from drains back into the irrigation network, they rework the nature of Egypt's water, challenging distinctions between fresh and saline, clean and dirty, acceptable and unacceptable.

DRAINAGE WATER AS IRRIGATION WATER

In March 2008 I stayed the night with Nagat, a woman who lives with her husband and three children in Gharaq, on the southern border of Fayoum. After a breakfast of beans, eggs, and toasted bread accompanied by sweet tea, we went for a walk. Nagat wanted to show me something. There was a problem on the branch canal that her water user association had prioritized for ministry action during the next maintenance period. We set out down the road, which was paralleled on one side by a drain. We came to an irrigation canal, running perpendicular to us. Herein lay the problem. A concrete pipe carrying drainage water over the canal was broken, its jagged end jutting out. Drainage water was gushing into the canal instead of continuing its journey along the drain on the far side. The disjointed pipe was a powerful demonstration of the constant work needed to maintain the drainage system — work which, in this case, had not taken place. My initial thought was that Nagat must be upset because the drainage water was polluting her canal. I was wrong. The problem, Nagat said, was that the farmers downstream along the drain did not have enough water. They would like to be able to pump drainage water for irrigation, but due to the broken pipe, their drain was almost dry.

The way in which Nagat pictures drainage is revealing. Rather than seeing drainage water as a waste product, as something that would degrade her water supply, Nagat sees it as a resource. To her and her downstream neighbors, drainage water is an important source in the face of scarcity. Ever since mobile diesel pumps became widely available in the 1970s, farmers have lifted water from the drains to supplement their irrigation supply. The ministry does not strictly condone this practice, since it undermines its ability to control what water is flowing where and the quality of water being used on the fields. But officials make little effort to enforce the ban. They recognize that farmers only use drainage water when the water in their canals is insufficient. It is far easier for them to turn a blind eye to this practice than to try and make up that shortfall themselves. The ministry estimates that farmers reuse between 2bcm and 3bcm of drainage water a year (Ismail 2011); other sources suggest it could be as much as 4bcm (van Achthoven et al. 2004, 38).

At the same time, while the ministry officially prohibits farmers from reusing drainage water in their fields, it has its own program to recycle water from the drains into the irrigation network. The government's first efforts to reuse drainage water date back to the 1870s, when it started to divert two million cubic meters a day from one of the main drains in the delta into a canal to boost irrigation supplies during the period of low water prior to the annual Nile flood (El-Guindy and Amer 1979). It was in the 1970s, though, that the ministry began to actively develop this program and to construct large reuse pumping stations on the main drains of the delta and Fayoum. By 1984, it was pumping 2.9bcm of drainage water back into the main canals and the Nile's branches for reuse. Since then, the ministry has further expanded its network of pumping stations, with support from international donors, and by 2011 official reuse had reached 7.5bcm (Ismail 2011).[34] This reuse program has been facilitated by the installation of subsurface drainage around Egypt, which more efficiently evacuates water from the soil into the open drains from where it can be recycled.

In redirecting water from one place to another, reversing and recycling flows, the everyday work of the ministry's mixing stations and farmers' pumps on the drains help make Egypt's water in both quantity and quality. To take, first, the question of quantity, drainage water offers a valuable supplement to Egypt's water supply, in addition to providing a partial solution to the problem of where to dispose of drainage effluent. Over 10 percent of the country's water needs are now met by drainage water.[35] More than a million feddan in the delta and Fayoum depend either partially or entirely on drainage water for irrigation (NAWQAM 1999, ch. 3, 1). The ministry's target is to increase its reuse program to about 8.9bcm by 2017 (MWRI 2005a, ch. 4, 21).

At a local level, the reuse of drainage water generates new patterns of access to water. In many cases those at the head end of canals are in an advantageous position, being the first to receive and use the water flowing through those canals (Price 1995). But the positioning of a pumping station to lift water out of a drain and divert it into the tail end of the irrigation canal alters those dynamics of access. On some canals in Fayoum it is actually those in the middle of the canal who are most disadvantaged, as not only do they not receive the full inflow of irrigation water like those at the head of the canal, but they do not benefit from the drainage water replenishment at the tail end of the canal. Thus a head-tail dichotomy along canals is not sufficient for understanding access to water. Rather, a patchwork of varying degrees of access is much closer to the reality.

Given the value of this additional source, farmers calling for the ministry to establish new reuse pumping stations, or to complete stations that are under construction but have not been finished, is a recurrent theme in their meetings with ministry officials. In December 2007, I attended a meeting in Fayoum City between farmers and senior officials from the Fayoum Irrigation Directorate. One of the officials started the meeting by asking if the farmers had any issues they would like to address. "We have problems," shouted one, others clamoring to speak at the same time. They explained that they did not have enough water and that some canals were completely empty. They asked about progress on the reuse station that the ministry had promised but which they had heard would not come into operation for five years. They were desperate for it to be completed before then. One farmer complained that the drainage water is just going into Wadi Rayan and Qaroun and nobody is benefiting from it. "Fayoum has all this water," he said. "Where is it?" A number of farmers followed with calls for pumping stations to reuse drainage water that is being "wasted." Eventually the undersecretary of the irrigation directorate said, "If anyone has a drain near an irrigation canal that we could pump and reuse, please tell us." The response of "I have," "I have" rang out around the room.

Yet while drainage water reuse provides an important supplement in

TABLE 5.3 Water Quality in the Nile River and Drains

		Salinity (ppm)	Biological Oxygen Demand (mg/1)	Chemical Oxygen Demand (mg/l)	Fecal Coliform Bacteria Count (MPN/100ml)
Nile River	Range	169–240	1–5	5–24	50–3,000
	Average	203	2	13	608
Drains	Range	200–1,430	1–43	2–144	250–35,000
	Average	565	7	33	8,023
Standard set in Law No. 48 (1982) on the Protection of the Nile		500	6	10	1,000

Source: Data (for the year 2001) from the National Water Research Center (cited in Brown et al. 2003, 11 and 15) and for Upper Egypt (between Aswan and Cairo). Since water quality deteriorates markedly through the delta, were that data to be available, the figures would illustrate an even more pronounced deviation of water quality from the standards.

spaces of scarcity, its impact on water quality is less positive. Drainage water is often polluted with sewage, industrial effluents, and solid refuse. Water quality in the drains is well below the government's regulatory standards (table 5.3). Pollutants found in drainage water can pose serious health risks and environmental hazards. This is a critical issue for the farmers who export their produce and so have to meet stringent international quality standards. It is also a pressing concern for the Egyptian company responsible for providing drinking water, since the drinking water treatment plants draw their water supply from the canals.[36] The reuse of lower quality water has further problematic ramifications on aquatic ecosystems. The northern lakes, for example, have seen increasing eutrophication linked to the high concentration of fertilizer-derived nutrients in the water discharged into them (Rasmussen, et al. 2009), changes in plant morphology and biomass (Eid et al. 2010), and the accumulation of pollutants in fish and bird species (Abbassy et al. 2003).

The quality parameter of most widespread concern to farmers and ministry officials, however, is salinity. Average salinity in the main drains, measured in parts per million (ppm), is 565ppm, but it can reach up 6,000ppm in northern parts of the delta (Brown et al. 2003, 18) (table 5.3).[37] The so-called mixed water (mai khalat) generated when drainage water is added to irrigation water is therefore distinct from, and implicitly inferior to, Nile water, which farmers refer to as "free water" (*mai hurra*).[38]

When using drainage water for irrigation, whoever is responsible—be it a ministry official at a pumping station or a farmer operating a diesel pump—has to make a careful judgment about whether the drainage water is sufficiently low in salinity for reuse. When I asked an official about the ministry's policy on this, he responded that 1,000ppm is the legal threshold but that 1,500ppm is the common practice. He then acknowledged, "Really it's just theoretical. If there's water and it looks good, they [the ministry engineers] use it!" As for farmers, they rely on their taste buds to make this judgment. "How can you tell if water is saline?" I asked one farmer. He looked at me in surprise. "We taste it!" Instead of using units of parts per million to describe salinity, they simply distinguish between good water (*mai hilu*) and salty water (*mai mumilih*).

One day when I was walking in the fields with a Fayoumi farmer, I noticed water pouring out of an already flooded field, straight into the drainage ditch. "Shouldn't the farmers stop the water, so that it's not just lost like that to the drainage ditch?" I asked him. "Oh, the farmers have probably just gone to pray the noon prayer. Then they'll come back and close the water off," he replied. His tone was nonchalant. Clearly he did not think this was a big deal. "And anyway," he added, "the drainage water here is good, so people can reuse it again for irrigation. It's not too salty." To me, the water looked just like water. To the farmer, though, it was a particular kind of water: water with a low concentration of salts, which could therefore be reused. Whereas I saw water being wasted, he saw it merely moving from one storage site to another.

Despite the care taken by ministry officials and farmers to monitor the salinity of drainage water that they reuse, though, the mixing of this water back into the irrigation system affects agricultural production. Research carried out by the ministry found yield decreases of between 7 and 29 percent in cotton, wheat, maize, and rice linked to high salinity levels in mixed water (Abdel-Dayem et al. 2007, S109). In one case from 2005, a large number of trees in orchards in eastern Fayoum died because of excess salinity in the irrigation water. This high salinity was linked to the large volume of drainage water that the ministry had pumped from a main drain into the irrigation canal serving this area. Farmers are well aware that the ministry's reuse program affects the quality of water in their canals. On one occasion when I passed by a reuse station with an agricultural investor, for instance, he said to me, "Here is a very bad thing. Thank God it is after our farm!"

To a person like him, whose privileged position means he is able to access as much irrigation water as he needs, drainage water reuse is not a good practice.

In response to concerns about water quality, some senior officials in the ministry have suggested that the ministry should review its drainage water reuse policy. In 1995, at a meeting between Dutch and Egyptian water management experts, the minister expressed his concerns about reuse in light of the increasing deterioration of drainage water quality. "To develop a strategy for the next 25 years, the present policy that reuse is a must needs re-thinking," he told the assembled group (APP 1995, 58). Yet over a decade later, there is no indication that the ministry has rethought this policy. When I asked a senior official during a November 2011 interview about whether the ministry plans to increase reuse, his answer was simple: "Yes, it's in our strategic plan. We see it as one of our future sources."

So regardless of its problematic impact on water quality, drainage water reuse continues as an important response to scarcity. The most fortunate farmers are those who have no need for drainage water as they have enough good quality irrigation water. Among the vast majority who do not have sufficient water, though, the wealthier, more politically connected farmers are better positioned to campaign for government reuse pumping stations to supplement their canal supply. In addition, any farmer with the money to buy or rent a pump can access drainage water unofficially. Just as social and economic relations shape access to drainage water, so too this access shapes social and economic relations. By influencing the volume and quality of water each farmer receives, everyday practices of drainage water reuse help set the parameters of agricultural potential. The better the quality of water a farmer is able to access for irrigation, the higher the yields and profits he or she will achieve.

The reuse of drainage water for irrigation reveals the heterogeneity of Egypt's water. As the resource comes into being, multiple waters emerge, ranging from good, to mixed, to salty. These qualities are not absolute but socially and culturally moderated.[39] As different people work to determine where drainage water is reused, how much is reused, and who gets to reuse it, they help mold the quantity and quality of Egypt's water across space and time.

MAKING THE VERTICAL VISIBLE

This chapter's discussion of drainage highlights a vertical dimension to Egypt's water. The downward flux of water through the soil and the upward passage of salts are as important to agricultural production as the flow of water across the surface. Water must flow through the system not only to pass into roots and nourish crops but also to flush through salts. The network of drains, ditches, control gates, water quality monitoring stations, pumps, and pipes is as integral as the network of irrigation canals, mesqas, marble gauges, and weirs. Some of these elements are visible, such as the pumps and manholes; others are invisible, like the subsurface pipes. The flows of drainage—and the quotidian practices through which they are controlled and manipulated by farmers, officials within the drainage authority, and international advisors and donors—are as tied into sociopolitical networks of power as the flows of irrigation.

Thus just as studies of irrigation have indicated inequality in access to the fluid inputs of agricultural production, this chapter raises questions about inequality in access to the fluid outputs of agricultural production. The goals are contradictory. On the one hand, farmers call for subsurface drainage to more efficiently channel away excess water and officials search for outlets for drainage disposal. On the other hand, both farmers and officials call for more pumping stations for drainage water reuse. Drainage water is hence a flow that must be managed both as an excess and as a resource.

These ways in which drainage water is channeled from and to the fields, drained downward and pumped upward, discarded and reused, are central to determining where the water of the Nile flows and what it becomes in the process. The contestation over who is able to access the technologies necessary to control these flows and who makes decisions about how these technologies are operated is a valuable example of some of the everyday politics that shape the making of Egypt's water.

CHAPTER 6

Making Egypt's Water

Egypt and the Nile are linked by thousands of years of history. The way in which this river sustains the Egyptian population has become naturalized in the popular imagination. Scholarly and nonscholarly accounts alike often begin with the quote from Herodotus — "Egypt is the gift of the Nile." Schoolchildren around the world learn about the Pharaohnic empires founded at the end of the world's longest river. A cruise along the Nile is a staple of the Egyptian tourist trail, shuttling groups between magnificent ancient sites. There must be few countries for which their source of water is a topic of such widespread general knowledge. The Nile defines Egypt.

Yet not only does the Nile make Egypt, but Egypt makes the Nile. Instead of being a passive recipient of the river's bounty, as Herodotus implied, Egypt — or rather, a range of human and nonhuman actors both within and outside of Egypt — is actively engaged in producing the flow of water that constitutes the Nile. A complex set of social, biophysical, technical, and political processes, operating on a range of scales, mold the course of the river's water. That water can be traced back to a distinct source: rainclouds over the highlands of East Africa. But the way in which the Nile passes through Egypt, making Egypt's portion of the Nile Basin, is integrally tied to a number of technologies, management decisions, and agricultural practices.

This perspective recasts the central problematic of water in Egypt. The question becomes not simply one of how Egypt should manage its water but of what exactly that water is. Rather than taking water as a given, this means looking at the processes through which that

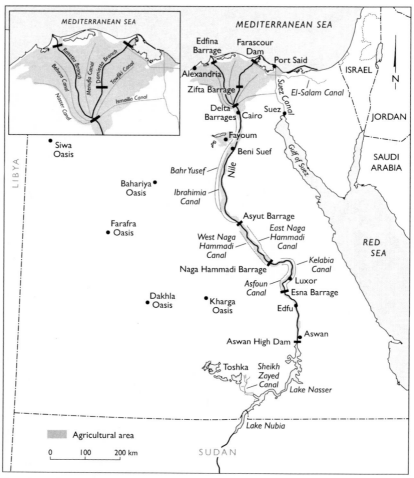

Map 6.1. Egypt's Nile

water comes into being and asking how these processes shape the nature of the water that people are able to access for different purposes.

To illustrate the distinction between water as a given and water as something that is made, I return to the map of Egypt's water that I presented in the first chapter of the book (see map 6.1). The map depicts the line of the Nile snaking its way to the sea and fanning out across the delta. Bold dashes cut across the channel, marking a series of barrages, and thinner lines of the main canals parallel the river. The map orients the reader in the geography of Egypt. Indeed a similar map frames most reports and books on water in Egypt and appears on the opening slide of almost every PowerPoint presentation I have seen given by a water expert in Egypt. The map accompanies a recurrent narrative. As one manager of a donor project commented to me wearily, "In most of the conferences I go to, at least half of the conference is taken up with explaining how Egypt is 95 percent desert and the only source of water is the Nile." Yet in laying out the country's water, a map like this fails to capture the ongoing, day-to-day work that goes into making that water.

First, the color of the river and main canals as they wind upward across the image is constant. There is no shading to demonstrate the places where the water fails to flow; the image does not map the empty channels. At the same time, the line is neat and clearly defined. There are no blurred edges to indicate the places where the channels overflow their borders, where water is in excess to demand. The map is unable to represent the uneven patterning in space and time of Egypt's water.

Second, the map is people-less, as maps often are. It depicts the main dams and canals, which were built by human hands, but not the social processes that animate those technologies for controlling and channeling water. It offers no sense of the communities that emerge around water or of the social networks in which that water is embedded. It provides no hint of the international experts who bring their funds, technologies, and expertise to bear on the water. The map does not reveal, therefore, how the process of making Egypt's water is one that is heavily mediated by many actors, from farmers who use water, to government officials who write and implement water policies, to international donors who fund water projects.

Third, the image is static. The thin shaded band on either side of the river through the valley and the wedge of the delta appears fixed. This is the Nile's watershed: the area of land watered and drained by the river. It is an apparently natural space, united by the flow of water into a single watercourse. Yet as farmers, investors, and government programs extend the canal system into the desert to reclaim marginal lands, they alter this space. They push out the boundaries of the watershed. The border of the map's agricultural area is in fact in a constant state of flux.

Finally, the image is two-dimensional. It is a superficial picture of Egypt's Nile. The river skirts the surface. Missing from the image is the vertical dimension of subsurface flows and the linkages between the river and its alluvial aquifer. The huge network of subsurface drainage pipes, as integral to agricultural production as the canals that the map does depict, are invisible. The map fails to portray how Egypt's water is produced in depth as well as across space.

These lacunae should come as no surprise. A map is, after all, always a simplification, designed to guide rather than replicate a reality. The erasures demonstrate, however, the complexities of the processes at work and the ways in which a straightforward understanding of the resource as an outcome of supply versus demand is unfeasible. What Egypt's water comes to be is the outcome of multiple acts of the everyday.

WHAT IS WATER?

How much water is there? This is one of the most basic questions of water management, a topic of critical concern to policy makers, irrigation engineers, and water users alike. The volume of water that enters Egypt is directly related to the volume of rainfall in the source regions of the Nile. Yet as the Nile progresses through Egypt, the amount of water that arrives in any one place is intricately linked to a complex network of control structures. Over the long course of the river, people work to monitor and manipulate the water so as to determine how much continues along each branch of the distribution network. It is these everyday practices that produce quantity, one of water's key parameters. In a particular time and place, the amount of water available for use reflects much more than a simple summation of sources. It carries with it the imprint of a history of many acts of intervention, some small, like when a farmer builds a dam of earth, some large, like when a ministry official raises the gates on a barrage. Determining what water flows where, and defining the places of scarcity and those of excess, is a central part of the making of Egypt's water.

This process is not, however, only one of determining quantity. It is also one of making quality. It is easy to assume what water is. It is H_2O: molecules of two hydrogen atoms bonded to single oxygen atoms, forming a clear liquid within a specific temperature range. Yet in the move from the laboratory to the real world, water becomes so much more than molecules of three atoms. Water's material properties—an ability to erode, dissolve, transport, and transform—shape what it becomes. As water passes through the environment, it takes on its own characteristics, unique to a given moment.

On its journey northward, the water of the Nile cycles and recycles through the soil, passing from river to canal to field to drain and then back into the river again. Its quality changes progressively along the way as the water picks up salts and agricultural chemicals. Whether farmers are able to irrigate is not only a question of whether they have enough water in their canal but of whether that water is of good enough quality to be used on the fields.

Water quality is not, however, a matter of chance. It is something that is actively managed by both farmers and ministry officials. When they direct water from a drain back into a canal for reuse, they merge different waters, one salty, the other less so, altering water's quality characteristics. Their ability to do this is moderated by access to particular technologies, namely pumps to lift water up from the drains to channel it back into the irrigation network, and the political connections that allow them to employ these technologies. As water users and water managers work to produce a sufficient quantity of water, they constantly challenge what sort of water is acceptable for use.

The process of making Egypt's water, therefore, is not a singular one; rather, it is a making of multiple waters. These differences are captured in the varied terms that farmers employ—"free water" (*mai hurra*), the water of the Nile; "good water" (*mai hilu*) versus "salty water" (*mai mumilih*); and "tired water" (*mai ta'ban*), water that is lacking. To engineers, these distinctions are captured in different kinds of metrics—parts per million, cubic meters per second, and water levels. There are many ways of knowing water.

THE POLITICS OF THE EVERYDAY

The daily practices of blocking, releasing, channeling, and diverting water from the Nile are partly about getting the water to flow, by opening a dam, pumping water up from a canal, or installing a larger diameter offtake pipe in a canal bank. But they are also about stopping the water from flowing. Some mechanisms of obstruction are legal, like a weir. Others are illegal, like the trunk of a palm tree blocking a weir. Still others, like a crop of rice or dam of earth, may be licit or illicit depending on where they are placed, by whom, and at what time.

The politics of water lies in these day-to-day acts that operate on a range of scales. A farmer builds a dam in a mesqa; a bahhar raises the gate of a regulator; a ministry official decides where a pipe installation machine will work; a powerful individual dominates a meeting about canal maintenance; a district engineer turns a blind eye to an illegal pump; an international consultant recommends a change in water policy. This is a politics written not only in the terms of government documents or calculations of hydrologists but in the understandings of those who interact with water on a daily basis. It is a politics that determines who receives water and who does not; who has a say in canal operations and who does not; who is able to expand their land out into the desert and who is not; and who is able to grow crops without worrying about salinization and who is not. It is a politics that revolves around a central question of agency—who is able to shape the nature of Egypt's water?

The tools of political influence are to a certain degree those that are common in the literature on resources. Wealth brings power over water, as do personal relationships with the water management authorities. A farmer with money can buy or rent a pump to supplement her irrigation supply; a landowner with connections can lobby officials to prioritize his land for subsurface drainage; an international donor agency can introduce a new water management technology because it has the funds to do so. But there are other factors at work. A person does not have to be wealthy or well connected to build a dam in an irrigation ditch. He can do it with his own hands, pulling together clumps of mud, stones, sticks, and debris to seal the channel. The farmer's agency in this case derives from his knowledge of how to make an effective dam and of where he can place that dam in order to stop the flow and direct water onto his land. Location also plays into this everyday politics. If a farmer owns land at the head end of a canal, she is implicitly advantaged in terms of being able to access water to meet her needs. But location is not determinative. If the ministry establishes a pump station on a drain to replenish an irrigation canal, it alters the pattern of positional advantage and disadvantage.

Thus in different spaces, different types of politics are at work, rooted in contrasting vocabularies, technical practices, and cultural understandings. In different sites, different assets are a source of power. At a workshop of international donors and senior officials in the ministry, the influence a participant's voice carries depends on his or her ability to speak a particular language of water management. Those who actually use most of the water — farmers — are largely excluded from this realm of knowledge production and expertise development. They are not invited to these workshops; they have little say in where new techniques for channeling water will be installed. In the fields, on the other hand, a person's ability to control water lies in their position within local socioeconomic structures, their understanding of how water moves through the landscape, and their connections to people in the government.

Water's material characteristics moderate the practices required for access and utilization and, consequently, the types of political relationships that evolve around it. As a liquid, water links different spaces. One person's use affects another's. If one farmer decides to grow rice, it decreases the water available for others. If a ministry official diverts drainage water back into a canal, it impacts the quality of water flowing on to downstream farmers. The waterscape is patterned into zones of variable visibility and invisibility, controllability and uncontrollability. Some of the spaces that water moves through are easy to monitor, understand, and manipulate. Others are not. These attributes mediate who is able to exert influence over the flow of water through different sites.

CHARTING NEW WATERS

This, therefore, is the key argument of the book: that Egypt's water is made and not a given and that the politics of water lie in these everyday practices of making the resource in quantity and quality, space and time. But what is the significance of this argument? What are its implications for those who manage, use, and study water around the world? While the Egyptian case may be distinct in the degree of Egypt's reliance on a single source of water, the way in which this source is controlled and manipulated is far from unique. This work hence speaks beyond the particular case in question to broader debates about how we understand water. Rather than offering a set of policy prescriptions for good water management, this book presents a new way of thinking about this substance—a way that may prompt all kinds of people, including policy makers, academics, development practitioners, and water users to think differently about what they do.

The book challenges some of the axioms of the "global water community." Water scarcity is a critical concern, but is it paramount? Participation of water users in management decisions is important, but are water user associations the only or best way to ensure that these opinions are heard? Efficient technologies are valuable, but how are they used and who has access to them? Awareness is critical, but who decides what it means to be aware and what it is important for people to be aware about? The approach presented in this book reveals some of the gaps in these dominant narratives. It demonstrates, for example, the need to manage excess water even in an overarching context of scarcity. It highlights how popular management buzzwords—like participation, integrated water resources management, cost recovery, and water use efficiency—often fail to take into consideration how water is actually produced, distributed, used, and reused. A more complex understanding of water is needed, I suggest, which highlights the multiscaled decision-making processes and technologies that govern where water flows.

This approach to water speaks, also, against a body of scholarship on social constructionism within political ecology. Discourses of and about water are interesting and significant. The way in which water is constructed as a resource and management solutions are framed can have profound political implications. However, the politics of water stems not from the way in which people talk or write about water but from the material ways in which they control, manipulate, access, and consume it.

Thus instead of making policy recommendations, this book raises questions that those involved in water management, whether as analysts or practitioners, might productively ask. Imagine, for example, an international consultant arriving to work on a water project in a new country, a student researching a paper on a dam controversy, a World Bank employee newly assigned to work on a regional water program, or a graduate starting to work for her country's water ministry. A logical place for them to begin would be with a survey of available surface and ground water resources. But if they began, instead, by asking how these resources come into being, this would generate a different set of questions. Rather than looking at datasets of rainfall, river discharge, watershed topography, and aquifer storage, they would focus on the various technologies for controlling the flow of water on and below the surface. Who has access to these technologies, and what criteria determine how they operate? What are some of the ways in which these control structures may be disrupted, evaded, or appropriated? Rather than limiting their scope of analysis to national water policies, they would examine multiple scales. They would ask whether international agencies are involved in funding or managing any of this water production infrastructure. If so, what kinds of technology and expertise do they bring? What are these agencies' interests in this country's water resources? They would look at some of the ways in which farmers and field staff modify the system for their own purposes. What kind of adjustments do they make? How do they elude the central government's network of supervision? In highlighting the various parties involved in producing a particular configuration of water resources, they would ask, whose interests are served by the system functioning efficiently and whose interests are served by blockage, interruption, or disarray? These questions would yield insights into the day-to-day politics surrounding water. The projects and recommendations developed as a consequence would be that bit more likely to achieve their purpose of improved water management.

BY THE CANAL

To end, I return to Fayoum. It is a sunny day early in 2008, and I am visiting a canal with a group of officials from the ministry. The canal has been emptied for maintenance, and laborers dressed in sweat pants, T-shirts, and rubber boots are maneuvering over rickety wooden scaffolding. They are working to rebuild an offtake, which has been widened illegally by local

Figure 6.1. A Fayoum canal. Photograph by the author.

farmers. The district engineer has ordered the replacement of the offtake with a narrower one to limit the volume of water that flows out of the canal. With its new dimensions, the offtake will deliver only the quantity of water that the ministry has calculated to be sufficient for the area cultivated along this mesqa.

A woman wearing a black *galabiya* with small flowers on it approaches us. She is angry. "There is not enough water from the offtake!" she says. "If you are going to remake the offtake here, the important thing is that you do the same along the canal." Clearly other farmers on the canal have also widened their offtakes illegally. "Otherwise," she continues, "those farmers will start withdrawing lots of water and then we won't have enough here." The district engineer reassures her that that is what they plan to do. "I just want us all to have the same amount of water," she reiterates.

The work continues, and I go to speak with this woman, who introduces herself as Om Fatma. She has two feddan of land, which she irrigates with water from this canal. Her husband is dead and her children have left home. She picks a cabbage and cuts out the central stalk for me to eat as we sit together on the edge of her field. "There is not enough water from the offtake," she repeats. "They are making it too narrow." We talk about the past, when the water was good. "But then," she says, "the government cut down the amount of water (*bidaiq 'alena*), causing this crisis (*azme*)." She looks at me earnestly. "Can you tell the government about our lack of water problem?"

Ten days later, I return to the canal with ministry officials to look at the rebuilt offtake. Om Fatma sees our car from a distance and comes to meet us. "The water is not high enough in the canal," she complains to the officials. Her need is simple. "All I want is water," she says. She takes me to one side and asks me, once again, "Could you please tell them about our water situation?"

Encapsulated in this conflict over a canal offtake is some of the work that goes into making Egypt's water. The modified offtake that the ministry is replacing was an effort by farmers to alter the distribution system to access the water that they need, breaking apart the crest in the bank of the canal so that more water would flow into their mesqa. The rebuilt offtake, on the other hand, represents the ministry's reassertion of control; a narrow concrete-lined slit in the bank, designed to limit the flow of water out of the canal to that which ministry officials have calculated to be appropriate.

The result, according to Om Fatma, is that she does not have enough water to irrigate her fields. Her story is one of scarcity. But the offtake is only part of this story. Lying beyond the bounds of the scene by the canal are many other factors at play: the farmers upstream who divert water from the canal into the desert to reclaim new land; the ministry officials who determine that they cannot channel any more water into Fayoum without compromising their ability to dispose of the drainage effluent; the engineers at the Aswan High Dam who limit releases through the dam to prevent erosion of downstream infrastructure. Thus the scarcity that Om Fatma experiences is generated, in part, by the narrowness of her offtake, but it is also generated by excesses at other parts in the system.

Om Fatma is, of course, perfectly able to tell the authorities about her problems herself. Indeed this is precisely what she tries to do on both occasions when she meets the ministry officials. Yet she sees me as a foreigner associated with the ministry and assumes that I have a degree of influence. Sadly for Om Fatma, my voice carries little weight with Egypt's government officials. I can use my voice, though, to talk about her water situation. This book is my attempt to do so. It is the story of how this situation is produced through the work of many people, among them the millions of Egyptians who, like Om Fatma, depend on irrigation water to cultivate their land. These are the people whose livelihoods are ultimately at stake in the struggles over when, where, and how water flows through Egypt's lands and what it becomes in the process.

NOTES

PREFACE

1. Locating the source of a river is a slightly arbitrary process. The Nile has two main tributaries—the Blue Nile and the White Nile. The White Nile is the longer tributary, but the Blue Nile, which flows out of Lake Tana in Ethiopia, contributes the majority (approximately 85 percent) of the discharge. European explorers identified Gish Abay as the source of the Blue Nile in the early seventeenth century, as it is the spring of the longest stream that leads into Lake Tana. On the history of European exploration to discover the source of the Nile, see Bruce (1804); Cheeseman (1936); Moorehead (1960); Moorehead (1962).

CHAPTER 1: THE END OF A RIVER

1. The remaining 4 percent of Egypt's water supply comes from groundwater aquifers underlying the Western Desert and a small amount of rainfall along the north coast. I do not discuss these sources of water in this book.
2. These figures are estimates from MWRI (2005a). Notably, there are considerable uncertainties surrounding both how much water Egypt receives from different sources and the sectoral allocation of that water. Estimating how Egypt's water is used, for example, is complicated by the fact that water can be used more than once (see chapter 5).
3. Figures from MWRI (2005a).
4. For a more detailed account of Nile hydrology, see Said (1993); Howell and Allan (1994); Sutcliffe and Parks (1999). Tvedt (2004a) offers a useful annotated bibliography of geographical references for the river basin.
5. For a more detailed discussion of downstream countries' concerns regarding how the Hidase Dam will affect Nile flows, see Barnes (forthcoming).
6. Ethiopia, Tanzania, Uganda, Rwanda, and Kenya signed the Comprehensive Framework Agreement in May 2010; Burundi in February 2011; and in early

2013 South Sudan declared an intention to sign the agreement. These countries agreed to stall ratification of the treaty after the January 2011 revolution in Egypt, in the hope that Egypt's new regime would be more open to cooperation with its upstream neighbors. The post-Mubarak government made some overtures to upstream neighbors. It sent delegations to Ethiopia, Uganda, and South Sudan and also formed a tripartite technical committee with Ethiopia and Sudan to explore the potential impact of Ethiopia's Hidase Dam. Yet given the political uncertainties in Egypt, whether these efforts at diplomacy will be continued is unclear. In the meantime, the Ethiopian parliament has ratified the Comprehensive Framework Agreement, indicating its determination to move forward with changing the legislative framework of Nile water allocation.

7. For a more detailed account of the negotiations between the states of the Nile Basin over transboundary water sharing agreements, see Waterbury (1979); Collins (1994); Waterbury (2002); Cascão (2008); Cascão (2009); Mekonnen (2010); Nicol and Cascão (2011).

8. To many of the international advisors who work on water management issues in Egypt, the absence of a system of formal property rights for water is at the root of problems of overuse and mismanagement. They have encouraged the government to develop a clearer system of water rights. Discussion of "rights" is very sensitive in Egypt, however, and the government has yet to take up the advisors' recommendation.

9. In the 2007–8 season, at the time when I was conducting my fieldwork, Egypt's top three crops in terms of the harvested area were wheat, clover, and maize (FAOSTAT 2008). Onions were ranked twenty-first, indicating that they are a more significant crop in Fayoum, the province where I lived, than they are in other parts of the country. The only common crop that I did not observe being cultivated in Fayoum was sugarcane, which is widely cultivated in the south of Egypt (and ranked ninth, in 2008, in terms of harvested area). In this description of Egypt's agricultural calendar, I also do not describe fruit production, which is significant in parts of Fayoum and elsewhere around the country.

10. Rainfall in Egypt decreases from north to south, from a maximum of around 200mm a year along the Mediterranean coast to less than 25mm south of Cairo.

11. While the Delta Barrages marked the start of widespread perennial irrigation, there have always been small areas where year-round cultivation has been possible. Farmers who own land right by the Nile, for example, have always been able to draw water from the river during the months of low flow, so as to cultivate a summer crop on the riverbanks.

12. The British-Egyptian irrigation administration completed the first Aswan Dam and the Asyut and Zifta Barrages in 1902, the Esna Barrage in 1908, the Naga Hammadi Barrage in 1930, and the Edfina Barrage in 1951.

13. Some view the neoliberal reforms as a resounding success (Fletcher 1996).

Others criticize the reforms as being inappropriate and poorly sequenced (Abdel-Khalek 2002), providing too many opportunities for crony capitalism (Sadowski 1991), or generating negative social consequences (Bush 2002; Elyachar 2005).

14. The USAID-funded Agriculture Policy Reform Project, which ran from 1997 to 2001, set a series of benchmarks for agricultural reform, most of them focused on market liberalization and privatization. As an incentive mechanism, each time the government met a benchmark, USAID would disburse an additional installment of funds.

15. A number of landowners managed, however, to evade the reform by selling off land or transferring it into the names of relatives before the government had a chance to implement the requisition process (Mitchell 2002, 157–58). As a result, there remain some influential families with very large landholdings.

16. For the economic rationale underlying Law No. 96, see McKinnon (1996). For a critique, see Saad (1999); Bach (2002); Bush (2002); LCHR (2002); Abdel-Aal (2004); Ayeb (2012).

17. Since I focus on the work of this one ministry, I make no claim to an insight into the workings of the Egyptian government as a whole. I therefore avoid use of the term *state*, given that the Ministry of Water Resources and Irrigation is but one of a number of ministries, which along with other agencies, regulatory bodies, and individuals form the Egyptian state.

18. See the ministry's website, www.mwri.gov.eg, last accessed on June 7, 2013.

19. For an analysis of the multiple governmental and nongovernmental actors involved in water management in Egypt and their varied roles, see Luzi (2010).

20. Data from 2008 sourced from Egypt's Central Agency for Public Mobilization and Statistics, www.capmas.gov.eg, last accessed on June 7, 2013.

21. The figure for average annual official development assistance for water includes projects for water resources policy and management, water resources protection, drinking water and sanitation, river development, and water-related education. It excludes, though, assistance for agricultural water resources, hydroelectric power, water transportation, and flood control. The figure is therefore an underestimate (Gleick 2006, 269). Average annual total official development assistance is calculated from the yearly data provided by the World Development Indicators Online Database, accessed from www.worldbank.org on November 23, 2009.

22. The National Water Resources Plan Project, which was funded by the Netherlands Ministry of Foreign Affairs, ran from 1999 to 2005.

23. Egyptian officials and farmers, on the other hand, more commonly talk in terms of "projects" (*mashari'*) than of those who staff and fund those projects. To them, the key thing is the fact that there is a project, rather than who is funding that project per se.

24. Ken Conca (2006, chap. 5) traces the emergence of this transnational network of water policy elites since the 1970s. He links it to the organizations that have

acted as catalysts for networking; a series of global water conferences, world congresses, and international expert meetings; and the foundation of several influential water-focused professional publications. On the history of international water meetings and global water initiatives, and for a critical evaluation of their outcomes, see also Salman (2003, 2004); Gleick and Lane (2005); Varady, Meehan, and McGovern (2009); Biswas and Tortajada (2009).

25. The actual administrative boundaries of Fayoum Province incorporate substantial tracts of desert (making a total size of almost 1.5 million feddan). It is the land within the depression, though, that is the cultivated and settled heart of Fayoum and which is the area that both Fayoumis and non-Fayoumis identify with the province. For the cultivated area of Fayoum, I give an area of 430,000 feddan, but due to the informal land reclamation that is taking place at the province's margins (see chapter 4), this figure is far from precise.

26. On the longer history of irrigation in Fayoum, see Brown (1892); Boak (1926); Ball (1939); Mikhail (2010).

27. In Fayoum, farmers generally refer to mesqas (which means "the places that irrigate") as fathas (which means "openings"). I use the term mesqa, however, as this is the term more commonly used in the literature on water in Egypt.

28. The origin of the rotation system is unclear. Some people told me that the ministry originally organized the rotation; others said that it evolved organically through farmers sitting together and deciding who would take water from the mesqa each day. When I asked about its age, people would generally respond that it began min zaman, a long time ago. The rotation schedules do not exist on paper, nor are they on record in the ministry, but they are well known by farmers. When farmers sell land, the land's allocation of water in the rotation is included as part of the transaction.

29. The edited volume by Goldman, Nadasdy, and Turner (2011) offers another example of an attempt to bring political ecology into conversation with science and technology studies. The focus of these authors is on the production, application, and circulation of environmental knowledge. My interest, though, is not so much in knowledge about water but in the water itself. Thus whereas Goldman and her colleagues draw extensively on the science and technology studies literature on the situated nature of scientific knowledge, production of expertise, and networks of knowledge circulation, I draw more on work within this discipline on technology and the co-production of society and nature, as mediated through technology.

30. For a recent and more detailed account of political ecology's conceptual roots, diverse trajectories, and application to a range of empirical contexts, see Peet, Robbins, and Watts (2011).

31. The ways in which societies mold their environments have been well documented for a range of cases, including forests (Fairhead and Leach 1996; Padoch and Peluso 2003), grasslands (Dove 2004), and river channels (Raffles 2002). In the case of fluvial landscapes, work within environmental history

has also been influential in demonstrating how rivers are shaped by the interplay of social and natural processes (see, for instance, Worster 1992; White 1996; Pritchard 2011).

32. Often when I tell people in both Egypt and the United States about my research, they respond by commenting that the next wars may be fought over water. The widespread popular connection with the idea of a water war is fed by the frequency with which media outlets evoke it. In January 2010, for example, National Public Radio's *All Things Considered* ran a story titled "Will the Next War Be Fought over Water?" Also in 2010, special water issues of the *Economist* and the *National Geographic* included stories on the possibility of water wars (*Economist* 2010; Belt 2010). The Egyptian media, too, has debated the notion (see, for example, Sid-Ahmed 1998; Leila 2008; Bonnardeaux 2009).

33. Sneddon and Fox (2006) provide a similar critique of the international rivers literature for its tendency to focus on the interstate scale at the expense of other scales of analysis.

34. I follow the lead of the farmers, irrigation engineers, and international donors with whom I conducted research in highlighting certain dimensions of water's material nature and not others. For example, since I seldom, if ever, heard people refer to water's capacity to support ecosystems, this is not a theme that features prominently in the book. Thus while the flow of a river could be seen in terms of the flow of fish that inhabit it (e.g., Bull 2011), since my interlocutors did not see the water of the Nile in terms of the food particles, dissolved gases, and plant, algal, and microbial communities that support fish life, this more ecological vision of water is not part of my analysis.

35. In this book I use multiple tenses. This is partly because water itself moves across time. When a farmer irrigates a field, that action engages not only to the present (the work of channeling water onto the field) but also the past (the people and technologies that caused water to flow into that stretch of canal) and the future (the response of farmers downstream to the water withdrawal). By using multiple tenses, I hope to emphasize how both water and the conversations and actions around water cross different temporalities, following the example of West (2006). This is also a way of moving beyond some of the representational problems associated with each tense. As Anna Tsing (1993, xiv–xv) discusses, the ethnographic present extracts ethnographic subjects from history, implying a certain cultural fixity and exoticizing those subjects. Equally problematic, the past tense relegates those subjects to history, implying that those subjects' ways of life are a thing of the past.

36. Warda is a pseudonym. I use pseudonyms to disguise my informants' identity and, where necessary, also for places. In the case of the pseudonyms I give people, my choice reflects the norms of colloquial Arabic. For older members of the community in Warda, whom I would address in reference to their eldest son, for example Abu Khaled or Om Khaled, father or mother of Khaled, this is the type of pseudonym I use. Outside the village when I met people, they would

generally introduce themselves by their first name only, with a title (such as engineer or doctor) if applicable—a format that I also follow in my pseudonyms.

37. This observation may, in part, reflect the types of conversation that I was able to access. The time I spent in farming households was generally in mixed male and female company, often over cups of tea or meals. It may be that the topics of daily conversation among groups of farmers in the fields are quite different and feature water more prominently.

38. The numerous reports written by project staff and consultants over the course of donor projects are an integral part of the production of donor expertise. This gray literature has been very useful in helping me understand how water is distributed and used in Egypt. Since many of these reports are not publicly available, however, I am prudent in my use of these sources and only cite them when I draw on them directly.

CHAPTER 2: THE NILE'S NADIR

1. According to the Falkenmark Water Stress Index, a country faces chronic water scarcity when the per capita annual renewable freshwater is between 500m^3 and 1,000m^3 and absolute water scarcity when it is less than 500m^3. In Egypt, annual water availability per capita is 859m^3 (calculated from FAO figures of water availability and population from the year 2002) (AQUASTAT 2010). This places Egypt in the category of chronic water scarcity.

    Notably, this figure of annual renewable freshwater does not include the volume of rain that falls over a country (it is merely the sum of renewable surface water and groundwater). This is a matter of controversy among water experts in Egypt. At the Second Arab Water Forum, a number of Egyptians argued for "green water" (precipitation that is stored in or on the soil or vegetation) to be taken into account in managing transboundary resources, in addition to "blue water" (fresh surface and groundwater). On the notion of green and blue water, see Falkenmark and Rockström (2006). This argument has significant political implications, since while there is very little precipitation over Egypt, there is considerably more over upstream countries in the Nile Basin. Thus to Egyptian officials, those countries' abundance of green water to some extent undermines their claims to the blue water (the water of the Nile) that they share with Egypt.

2. According to Demeritt's (2002) typology, these two approaches to scarcity could both be seen as a form of social constructionism—the first a construction of ideas about nature, the second a process of constructing nature in a physical and material sense. By using the term production to refer to the latter, however, I seek to avoid some of the ambiguity that Demeritt highlights as being a source of confusion within the literature on the social construction of nature.

3. The literal translation of the colloquial expression *mafish mai* is "there is no water." Here I sometimes abbreviate the expression to "no water," so as to make it fit better within English sentences.

4. The other site where water scarcity is experienced is at the faucet. The ministry claims that 95 percent of the population has access to treated, piped drinking water, either in the home (90 percent) or from standpipes (5 percent) (MWRI 2005a, ch. 2, 36). During my time in Fayoum, however, I heard frequent complaints about there not being enough water of sufficient quality for household use. The fact that some people do not have the water they need to drink, cook, or wash is obviously a critical issue. But since agriculture consumes over 90 percent of Egypt's water (MWRI 2005a, ch. 4, 5), this book focuses on irrigation as the most significant sector in determining what happens to the water that flows into the country. Given that women hold primary responsibility for water use in the home, an account of drinking water scarcity would feature women more prominently than this account of scarcity in the fields does.

5. In summer months when water supplies are particularly limited, farmers time their irrigation turns literally down to the minute. In winter months, when water can be quite plentiful in some areas, the rotation schedules are not always so closely followed.

6. When farmers speak of buying water, they mostly mean renting a pump to tap water from another canal, at a rate of around LE50 per feddan for a day's irrigation. They can also mean buying water from a pump operating on a drainage ditch, at a cost of about LE30 an hour (see chapter 5). In rare cases, farmers purchase other farmers' irrigation turns.

7. The literal translation for this farmer's expression —*nahnu ta'banin akhir ta'ab*— is "We are tiring the last tiredness."

8. In colloquial Arabic, the adjective *tired (ta'ban)* is commonly used in reference to both people (who are weary or fed up) and things (which are old, in low supply, or of poor quality).

9. The drinking water and irrigation systems are linked. Most drinking water is sourced from irrigation canals or directly from the Nile, treated, and then distributed by pipes.

10. One of the goals of the USAID-funded Agricultural Policy Reform Program (1997–2001) was to "reduce mismatch of irrigation deliveries," in part by improving the flow of real-time information between the ministries of agriculture and irrigation. The project team challenged, for example, the Ministry of Agriculture's practice of local agricultural staff passing the crop data first to the high-level officials in the provincial agricultural administration, "to be reviewed and refined." Instead, they recommended that the fieldworkers pass the data directly to the district engineers (King et al. 2000, ch. 6, 3). There are, however, political reasons why government officials may wish to control the process of data transfer and, consequently, why this donor recommenda-

tion has had little impact. For a more detailed discussion of how the supply of irrigation water often fails to match farmers' demands at a local level and the problems of wastage and inefficiency that result, see Radwan (1998).

11. The use of water levels as a measure of flow has a long history in Egypt. Since the beginning of the First Dynasty, around 3000 BC, civilizations have recorded the rise and fall of the Nile flood through inscriptions on stone pillars, buildings, cliffs, and, from around the seventh and eighth centuries AD, on marble gauges, which the ancient Greeks described as Nilometers (Evans 1994).

12. The telemetry system was established through the Main System Management Program, which was a subproject of the USAID-funded Irrigation Management Systems Project (1981–95).

13. Efforts to encourage the ministry to shift to a discharge-based system of water allocation were part of Tranche III of the USAID-funded Agricultural Policy Reform Program (1997–2001).

14. The results of a national farmer survey are indicative of Egyptian farmers' limited knowledge of the broader Nile system. Although 98 percent of the 2,267 sampled male farmers and 85 percent of the 279 sampled female farmers knew that Egypt's main source of water is the Nile, only 3 percent and 1 percent, respectively, knew that ten countries (prior to the independence of South Sudan) share the Nile Basin (El-Zanaty 2001, 35).

15. Unlike other complaints about water scarcity that I heard time and again, there was only one occasion when I heard a Fayoumi farmer draw a link between his water supply and the operation of the High Dam, when he commented explicitly, "We should get more water from the High Dam."

16. The High Dam also generates hydropower, but the ministry considers this to be a by-product of the releases for irrigation, municipal, and industrial water supply. No releases take place exclusively for hydropower generation.

17. For a discussion of future Nile flows under different climate change scenarios, see Conway (2005) and Conway and Hulme (1996). For an analysis of how different actors within and outside Egypt are thinking about climate change impacts on the country's water resources, see Barnes (forthcoming).

18. After completion of the High Dam, ministry officials were initially more concerned about erosion of the riverbed than of the riverbank. They knew that the Nile, robbed of its sediment in Lake Nasser, would incise the channel downstream of the dam. They anticipated that this would reduce the water level and therefore impact both the outflow from the river into irrigation canals and the flow of drainage water into the river channel through the interlinked aquifer. Their concerns were borne out, and in the early years bed erosion was a problem. Since the late 1970s, though, bed conditions have stabilized and the dominant concern now is bank erosion (Saad 2002).

19. The Toshka Spillway should not be confused with the Sheikh Zayed Canal, which draws from Lake Nasser about 45km east of the spillway for the Toshka

land reclamation project (see chapter 4). Like the spillway, the canal also transfers water westward into the Toshka Depression, but this water is used for the irrigation of new lands, whereas the water from the spillway is left just to evaporate in the Toshka Lakes.

20. The Dutch-funded Lake Nasser Flood and Drought Control Project (2002–5) used models to explore different options for operating the reservoir system. The project staff's conclusion was that it would be best to operate the lake at a lower level.

21. Timothy Mitchell (2002, chap. 7) provides a valuable critique of how the naturalized framing of Egypt's resource problem masks questions about who is using those resources and what they are being used for.

22. A similar story is told by Tony Allan, a geographer who is prominent in international water management circles, when he recalls his repeated efforts to discuss Egypt's water shortage with high-level policy makers in the 1990s. "All I remember hearing was the reiteration of that unshakeable article of faith: there was no water shortage in Egypt" (Allan 2011, 245).

23. The workshop on scarcity was organized by the Advisory Panel Project on Water Management, a Dutch project that ran from 1976 to 2011.

24. The Irrigation Improvement Project consisted of several phases of funding for pilot initiatives aimed at improving the irrigation infrastructure. Phase I, funded by USAID and the World Bank, ran from 1985 to 1989; phase II, also funded by USAID and the World Bank, ran from 1989 to 1996; and phase III, funded by the World Bank and German Bank for Reconstruction, ran from 1996 to 2005. The successor to these projects, renamed the Integrated Irrigation Improvement and Management Project (2005–14), is also being funded by the World Bank and German Bank for Reconstruction. The Japanese International Cooperation Agency (JICA) funded a similar irrigation improvement project, the Water Management Improvement Project in the Nile Delta (2000–2007).

25. Personal communication from a consultant who was involved in the Irrigation Improvement Project, June 8, 2008.

26. This is also an idea that has been subject to considerable critique. Studies have demonstrated that local people are often not those responsible for resource degradation and that projects that seek to educate those people to use the resources more efficiently therefore produce very limited results. See, for example, Ferguson (1994); Fairhead and Leach (1996); Walley (2002).

27. The idea of charging for the use of a resource is part of the neoliberal agenda, which places faith in the power of free markets to bring about optimum economic outcomes, thereby necessitating the creation of such markets where they do not exist. International organizations and governments have widely promoted neoliberal policies for the management of resources ranging from conservation areas (Igoe and Brockington 2007) to forests (Kull, Ibrahim, and Meredith 2007), fisheries (Mansfield 2004), agricultural commodities (West

2010), and wetlands (Robertson 2004). For a review of neoliberal water management, see Furlong (2010).

28. At international water conferences, people often talk about water pricing as privatization. The two terms, however, are not equivalent. Privatization entails a much broader transfer of resource management responsibilities from the public to the private sector. (For valuable critiques of water privatization, see Bakker 2005; Swyngedouw 2005; Goldman 2007.) Charges for use of a resource, on the other hand, may be levied by public entities, in which case, although a price is put on a formerly freely available resource, the resource remains in the public realm.

29. Notably the resistance of many ministry officials is toward charging for water itself, not toward cost recovery in general. In fact there are already certain circumstances in which farmers have to pay for their irrigation infrastructure, like when the ministry carries out irrigation improvement works (as I discuss earlier in this chapter) or installs subsurface drainage (see chapter 5).

30. USAID's Public Awareness on Water Scarcity Project ran from 1995 to 1998.

31. There is a gender difference here. It is rare to see female farmers in the offices of the ministry making complaints. Instead, women commonly go to relatives, neighbors, or influential members of the community for help when they do not have enough water and ask them to campaign to the ministry on their behalf.

32. This type of "informal adjustment" is typical of farmers' efforts to ensure that their needs are met within state-run irrigation schemes (Lees 1986).

33. There is no aquifer underlying Fayoum, so farmers do not have the option of drilling deep wells to access groundwater.

34. Mike Davis (2002) makes a similar argument in *Late Victorian Holocausts*, although he traces the roots of late nineteenth-century famines not to mechanisms of food distribution but to international commodity markets and price speculation.

CHAPTER 3: FLUID GOVERNANCE

1. Participatory resource management, also known as community-based natural resource management, has been widely promoted by governments, donors, and nongovernmental organizations as a mechanism for managing a range of resources from forests (Gauld 2000; Li 2002; Ribot 2009) and fisheries (Pinkerton 1989; McCay and Jentoft 1996; Maliao, Pomeroy, and Turingan 2009) to grasslands (Banks et al. 2003) and conservation areas (Birkes 2004; Brosius, Tsing, and Zerner 2005).

2. A number of European countries, for example, have a tradition of water user associations (see the European Union of Water Management Associations at www.euwma.org, last accessed on June 7, 2013). The Dutch water boards date back over 1,000 years (Dolfing and Snellen 1999), and France's *wateringues* were established in the twelfth century (Le Bourhis 2005).

3. The acronym for water user association, WUA, is widely used in the literature on participatory water management and in discussions among international donors and consultants, whose speech is often peppered with acronyms. When ministry staff talk about water user associations (*rabita mustakhdami al-mai*), however, they generally shorten the term to "association" (*rabita*) rather than use the acronym. For simplicity, I use WUA except in quotations.

4. Previous donor-funded projects, implemented between 2000 and 2006, established 41 WUAs in Fayoum. Thus by the end of 2010, there were (on paper at least) 137 WUAs operating around the province. The project also created 19 main canal water user associations and five district water boards. However, since the project staff had yet to start working on establishing these larger organizations at the time of my fieldwork with the project in 2007–8, I focus here on the branch canal associations.

5. The Irrigation Advisory Service was established by the Irrigation Improvement Project, which ran from 1985 to 1996 and was funded by the USAID and World Bank.

6. The suggestion that the WUAs will play a similar service provision role to the cooperatives can be problematic in the expectations that it generates. I attended one awareness meeting, for example, where around 70 women were crammed into a village hall. Amira, the community organizer, started by asking a local teacher to write down the names of those present. This simple process caused a furor. Women pressed in on all sides of the teacher shouting, "Don't forget my name! Don't forget my name!" I began to wonder what the women were expecting, especially after a woman tapped me on the shoulder and asked me explicitly, "Miss, what will we get if he writes down our names?" Amira gave her speech and explained that a WUA is like an agricultural cooperative but on the canal. It was not until the question period that I understood. One woman raised her hand and asked if we would be giving loans. When Amira explained that the WUA would not be able to disburse money, many lost interest and started talking among themselves. As we drove away, Amira told me that in rural areas people automatically associate the words *project* (*mashru'*) and *cooperative* (*gam'iya*) with the idea of loans.

7. The Institutional Reform Vision was established through the German- and Dutch-funded Institutional Reform Vision and Strategy Development Project, 2004–5.

8. In their analysis of the Zimbabwe Bush Pump, de Laet and Mol (2000) make a similar argument about how a joint effort to access water for a particular purpose can build community.

9. The fact that communal structures of cooperation and management develop around the flow of water has been amply demonstrated in the literature on community-run irrigation systems. See Tang (1992); Mitchell and Guillet (1994); Ostrom et al. (1994); Lam (1998); Trawick (2001); Vavrus (2003).

10. The most recent data available on landownership in Fayoum come from IDSC (1998). According to this report, 20 percent of the landowners in Fayoum are female, and women own 17 percent of the land in the province.

11. The persistence of claims that women do not irrigate, even when they participate in a variety of irrigation-related activities, has been documented in studies around the world (see, for example, Meinzen-Dick and Zwarteveen 1998; Harris 2006).

12. This contrasts, for example, with the project of WUA establishment in South India analyzed by Mosse (2003), where advocates of participatory irrigation management framed the WUAS organized around village tanks (reservoirs) as the inheritors of kudimaramat, which were traditional village institutions of tank maintenance and communal labor.

13. Attention to the role played by those who coordinate the WUA establishment process (in this case, the community organizers) has been largely missing from many other studies of WUAS. For a more detailed analysis of this role, with a particular focus on the female community organizers, see Barnes (2013a).

14. These kinds of barriers to female participation in water user associations have been well documented in the literature (e.g., Meinzen-Dick and Zwarteveen 1998).

15. The "community" component of community-based natural resource management is never a given. Instead, what advocates of participatory management see to be a community is the outcome of a series of politicized assumptions (Agrawal and Gibson 1999).

16. The "water councils union" that this man leads is a district water board, which comprises several WUAS.

17. This is an argument that Beatrice Hibou (2004, 17) makes for the case of privatization. See also Cooke and Kothari's (2001) discussion of participation as "the new tyranny."

18. Steven Heydemann (2007) describes this process in programs of democratic reforms as being one of "authoritarian upgrading." Such reforms do not displace authoritarian modes of government, he argues, but merely create new forms of authoritarianism. Similarly, Tania Li (2002) argues that in the case of forest management, the shift to community-based management can actually intensify state control over upland resources, lives, and livelihoods.

CHAPTER 4: IRRIGATING THE DESERT

This chapter contains data previously presented in "Pumping Possibility: Agricultural Expansion through Desert Reclamation in Egypt," *Social Studies of Science* 42, no. 4 (2012): 517–38.

1. Egyptians use the word *gabl*, mountain, to describe the desert land that borders the agricultural zone. It is difficult to find an exact translation for this term. This land is higher, but sometimes just by a meter or two, and it is not

hilly or mountainous per se. I translate the word either as hills or desert, or a combination of the two, depending on the context.

2. While the term *land reclamation* in Egypt also refers to the draining of wetlands and remediation of saline soils, I focus on reclamation in the sense of bringing desert land into cultivation. In this usage, the term is somewhat misleading, since it is not a process of *re*-claiming something that has been lost but of creating something new. The Arabic term for reclamation—*istislah*—derived from the root *salaha*, to be good or useful, does not carry with it the same connotation of a return to a former state but, rather, means the process of making land useful. Yet this term is also problematic in its implication that desert land is *not* useful, since nomadic populations have resided in and lived off Egypt's desert for many years (see Murray 1935; Abu-Lughod 1986; Cole 2003).

3. For more on nineteenth-century land reclamation in Egypt, see Willcocks (1899, 238–54); Baer (1962); Allan (1983); Cuno (1992). On reclamation during the twentieth century, see Springborg (1979); Voll (1980); Meyer (1998); Alterman (2002); Barnes (2012a).

4. While some international agencies and bilateral donors have supported projects in the new lands, by far the majority of the funding for reclamation has come from the Egyptian government. Indeed, within the donor community there is considerable skepticism about the validity of Egypt's reclamation policy, and has been ever since the early 1980s, when a controversial USAID study concluded that reclamation was not economically feasible "except under the most heroic assumptions regarding yields" (Hesser et al. 1980, 23). Indicative of the continuing skepticism, one Dutch consultant commented to me during an interview in 2007, "I'm a bit afraid about this type of ongoing land reclamation, conquering the desert. It will always lead to disaster!"

5. Each of the government's arguments in favor of reclamation is open to critique. For instance, the idea that Egypt needs more land to accommodate its growing population is driven by a problematic assumption that the existing land is overpopulated (see Mitchell 2002, chap. 7, for a critical analysis of this assumption). It also ignores the fact that very few new settlements have actually emerged in reclaimed areas, as farmers more commonly remain in their old homes and commute to the new lands. Some more cynical observers suggest that the reason the government wants to expand the area of cultivated land is to generate more demand for water and thus justify its continuing calls for an increased allocation of Nile waters (Waterbury and Whittington 1998).

6. There are also a number of mega projects in the Western Desert that draw on water from the Nubian sandstone aquifer, which I do not discuss here.

7. See, for example, Lonergan and Wolf (2001); Wichelns (2003); El-Din (2006); Dannies (2009); Sowers (2011).

8. On the tendency for ambitious state-led projects to fail, see Scott (1998).

9. Personal communication from a consultant working in the ministry, November 25, 2011.

10. As much of this marginal reclamation is informal, it does not appear in government statistics. It is therefore impossible to give precise figures to demonstrate its significance. From an early survey, Tomich (1984, 19) estimated that private initiatives were responsible for the reclamation of at least 60,000 feddan in the Nile delta between 1967 and 1973. A more recent study found that informal reclamation accounted for about 15 percent of the total land reclaimed in the 1980s and 1990s (Zalla et al. 2000, 4). But in some areas, the contribution of informal reclamation to total reclamation may be much more considerable. In Fayoum, for example, ministry engineers estimate that about 80 percent of the land reclaimed in the last two decades has been reclaimed informally by farmers (FWMP 2006b, 5).

11. For more on the Graduate Scheme and life in the graduate reclamation areas, see Adriansen (2009) and Malm and Esmailian (2013).

12. Nomadic groups have traditionally used the desert lands for grazing livestock, but since the early nineteenth century, a series of government programs has encouraged the settlement of these groups (Awad 1954). The nomadic communities remaining today mostly live farther out in the desert rather than on the borders of the agricultural zone.

13. Although the term al-ard al-gadid, new land, is commonly used by policy makers to describe reclaimed land, it is not clearly distinguishable from al-ard al-qadim, old land. Officials use multiple definitions to distinguish old from new, which draw on various criteria—temporal (when the land was brought into production), physical (soil type), geographical (location), technological (irrigation system), and legal (land title) (Zalla et al. 2000, 17).

14. While in other contexts land that has been heavily exploited is referred to as being "exhausted"—a similar metaphor of tiredness—the land to which Abu Khaled is referring had not been cultivated before. Thus this land was not tired in the sense of being overcultivated. Rather, tiredness here is an allusion to the land's weak condition.

15. Lying just west of the Nile valley, the land of Fayoum was not submerged in the same way as the valley and delta during the annual Nile flood. During the time of the flood, however, more water flowed through the canals and the water became thick with sediment. As farmers channeled the water over the fields for irrigation, much of this sediment was deposited, creating a clay-rich soil.

16. The Egyptian-American Rural Improvement Service was a land reclamation and resettlement program that ran from 1953 to 1963. The project reclaimed 6,730 feddan in Fayoum and 28,850 feddan in Abis, just south of Alexandria. Jon Alterman (2002) provides a fascinating account of the project, drawing on archival material to explore the conflicting priorities of the Americans and Egyptians involved in it and charting how those different perspectives influenced project activities.

17. The land on the north shore of Lake Qaroun cannot be reclaimed, partly be-

cause it is too steeply sloping and partly because of its distance from a water source (the water of the lake itself is too saline for use in irrigation).

18. This figure comes from Hussein et al. (1999, 24). More recent figures for how much of this land the government has actually developed and is now in cultivation are not available.

19. This figure of 80 percent comes from FWMP (2006b, 5).

20. Illegality may refer either to the land being cultivated (the farmer does not formally own the land) or the water being used to cultivate it (the farmer does not have official water use rights). In fact, the system is such that farmers have no alternative but to act illegally, for they are only able to apply for formal property and water rights for land that is being cultivated. Thus they have no choice but to obtain water initially through unofficial means so as to bring the land into cultivation.

21. A number of people in Thania refer to the Egyptian-American Rural Improvement Service project as Nasser's program, clearly associating the foundation of their land with that president's socialist ambitions.

22. The efficiency of water use is a complex issue that depends on a number of factors. For example, in non-sandy soils, flood irrigation can be an efficient way of watering a crop because water that is not immediately taken up by the crop remains in the topsoil and is gradually taken up through the crop roots after the irrigation event. Policy discussions on irrigation efficiency often fail to take these complexities into account, though, leading to an overestimation of the potential savings from modern irrigation technologies (Perry 2007; Perry et al. 2009; Molden et al. 2010).

23. Drip irrigation, for example, requires a constant flow of water, which is not always available to new land farmers due to the rotation system.

24. While the conflict often plays out as a battle of old land versus new land, this overlooks the fact that many farmers cultivate land in both old and reclaimed areas.

25. As I discuss in chapter 2, efforts to increase irrigation efficiency through the irrigation improvement project have met with limited success. In terms of urban encroachment, policy makers estimate that about 26,000 feddan of agricultural land in the valley and delta are lost each year to urban development (MWRI 2005a, ch. 4, 8). Studies have yet to be done, however, to quantify precisely what this change in land use means for water demand.

26. Yields in desert farms can be significantly higher than in the old lands. On my tour around Helwa Farm, Engineer Yasser explained, "The desert land is better than the old lands. You get more production." Studies by the agricultural ministry found citrus yields in the new lands to be 60 percent higher than the national average (MALR 1994). For the case of onions, Abu Khaled told me that feddan of reclaimed land (land in the *gabl*) yields 25 tons, whereas a feddan of old land yields only 10 to 12 tons. There are some crops, though, which

are more suited to the clay-rich soil of the older lands, such as wheat. To gain a more comprehensive evaluation of yield differentials, it would be necessary to look at data on land productivity per unit input (in particular capital, labor, and water).

27. Verdant images of forests, waterfalls, pastures, and rivers are commonplace on the posters and calendars that adorn the walls of offices and homes in Egypt. Images of sand dunes and desert vistas, which are used in a similar way in the United States for picturesque greeting cards and posters, are not so common. Among my Egyptian colleagues and friends, I was struck by a marked preference for verdant landscapes. Enthusing to one friend about my visit to see the amazing 40 million-year-old whale fossils in Wadi Heitan in the Fayoum desert, his response was that the location would be nicer if there were a lake and some vegetation there. On another occasion, driving through one of the more lush areas of Fayoum where orchards of mangos and oranges line both sides of the road, a friend commented, "Green relaxes the eyes whereas the desert tires the eyes." He went on to tell me that some doctors say that it is better to look at green than at the desert. The fact that not many farmers wear glasses, he said, is evidence of this (as opposed to an indication that eye examinations and glasses may be prohibitively expensive for some).

CHAPTER 5: FLOWS OF DRAINAGE

1. I use the term *drain* throughout this chapter to distinguish the channels that carry drainage water from those that carry irrigation water, which I refer to as canals. To clarify, these drains are not point sources of waste disposal, like the drain in a sink, but channels that direct drainage water to an outlet.

2. This is a rough comparison of costs, which I offer merely to demonstrate the scale of the drainage project. The figure for Egypt's drainage program comes from a paper lead authored by a senior official within the ministry (Abdel-Dayem et al. 2007, S104). I compare this to the cost of $1 billion for the High Dam, which is cited by many sources (e.g., Nixon 2004). Without access to a more detailed breakdown on the budgets of the two projects and currency valuations at which those costs were calculated, it is impossible to offer a more precise cost comparison.

3. This figure is based on the monitoring study conducted by the National Drainage Project I (1992–2000), which was funded by the World Bank and the Dutch, German, and Japanese development agencies (Ali, van Leeuwen, and Koopmans 2001).

4. A 2004 World Bank report states, "Drainage has almost disappeared from international water discourse as a theme and a concern" (Abdel-Dayem et al. 2004, 1). Drainage is missing from many of the prominent global water policy documents from the past decade. Agricultural drainage is not mentioned once, for example, in the Global Water Partnership's 2007 report (GWP 2008), it receives only ten fleeting references in the 865-page Fourth UN World Water De-

velopment Report (WWAP 2012), and it is absent from the research strategy of a major research initiative, the Consultative Group on International Agricultural Research's Challenge Program on Water and Food (CPWF 2005). There was not a single panel on drainage at the Fifth or Sixth World Water Forums, and in all the sessions that I attended on water use in agriculture, participants did not once raise drainage as an issue of concern.

5. For example, World Bank lending for drainage dropped by nearly 50 percent between 1973 and 2002, falling from a peak of US$690 million in 1986 to only US$130 million in 2002 (World Bank 2004, 1).

6. Over two decades ago, William Kelly (1983) noted a tendency within the literature on irrigation to focus on water delivery roles and to overlook other phases of agricultural water use, including drainage. Despite this insight, subsequent influential works on irrigation (e.g., Lansing 1991; Guillet 1992; Trawick 2003; Mosse 2003) contain little analysis of drainage management.

7. In referring to drainage water as an excess, I also depart from hydrologists' concept of drainage as return flow (although notably this is not a term that I ever heard hydrologists working in Egypt use). Framed as return flow, drainage is not the management of surplus water but an integral part of the irrigation system. To hydrologists, the draining of water through the soil is an important process through which downstream farmers get their water; it is a flow that is taken into account by water managers when budgeting allocations from an irrigation network. Yet a considerable proportion of the water applied to Egyptian fields that is not taken up by crops does not return to flow on to the next farmer, but is drawn to the surface and evaporated off, contributing to soil salinization. Thus at the level of the field, drainage is a precise hydro-ecological decision that is critical to determining key soil characteristics. In this sense, it is a management of excess.

8. The proportion of the water that is lost to deep infiltration depends on the soil type. Amer (1994, 18) estimates a figure of 10 percent.

9. For a more detailed discussion of different techniques for drainage management and case studies of drainage programs around the world, see Tanji and Kielen (2002).

10. The degree to which the soil becomes saturated depends, in part, on the vertical layering of soils. If the soil is underlain by a very porous sandy layer, drainage tends not to be too much of a problem, as the soil water can percolate downward easily, so excess water does not accumulate. In Egypt, however, the soils of the cultivated land are alluvial, with no underlying sandy layer and a clay content ranging from 30 to 80 percent, resulting in a low to medium hydraulic conductivity (Amer and Abu Zeid 1989, 44–45). Drainage is therefore an important issue throughout Egypt's agricultural land. Since the clay content of the soil increases toward the north of the country, though, drainage is particularly problematic in the northern parts of the delta.

11. Electrical conductivity refers to the degree to which an electric current moves

through the water. The more dissolved salts in the water, the stronger the current flow and the higher the electrical conductivity.

12. Salinization has two secondary impacts on crops in addition to its impact on water uptake. First, certain ions (e.g., sodium and chloride) can be toxic to crops when in excess. Second, changes in the salt composition of the soil can negatively affect soil structure and therefore limit water, air, and root movement in the soil (Umali 1993).

13. For a detailed account of this irrigation system, see Willcocks (1899, 57–62).

14. The historical account in this and the following section draws on archival research at the British National Archives in London and the following secondary sources: Amer and Abu-Zeid (1989); Amer et al. (1989); Abdel-Dayem and El-Safty (1993); El-Kadi et al. (1995, 363–83).

15. This alarm was bolstered by research that confirmed the problems which could result from soil waterlogging caused by insufficient drainage. In the early twentieth century, two colonial scientists, Audebeau and Gibson, came up with a "water-table hypothesis," which linked the decline in cotton yields to rising water tables and resultant root asphyxiation (Balls 1918).

16. Quote cited in Willcocks (1899, 157).

17. Quote cited in Amer and Abu-Zeid (1989, 56–57).

18. Lord Cromer to the Marquess of Salisbury, February 26, 1899, p. 30, British National Archives, London, FO78/5022.

19. The degree to which drainage was responsible for the cotton yield declines in the early twentieth century is, however, a matter of scholarly debate. Alan Richards (1986) asserts that it was, but Ellis Goldberg (2004) rejects this idea and argues, instead, that this decline in yields was due to farmers shifting to a higher value, lower yielding variety of cotton.

20. See Goldberg (2004, 57).

21. Quote from Cotton Federation (1938, 63), cited in Goldberg (2004, 57).

22. The earliest experiments with subsurface drainage in Egypt actually date back to the start of the twentieth century. In his 1903 annual report, Lord Cromer described a "very interesting experiment" on an 80-acre plot of land in which a "system of subsoil drainage . . . produced healthy, well-grown plants." He contrasted this with the land within the plot that had surface drainage where "about one-fourth of the area remained completely barren" (Lord Cromer to the Marquess of Lansdowne, 1904, p. 22, British National Archives, London, FO78/5366). It was not until the 1930s and 1940s, though, that the ministry conducted trials of subsurface drainage on a larger scale.

23. This shift in approach to drainage in Egypt reflects a wider trend in work on drainage, in line with the increasingly popular paradigm of integrated water resources management. A recent World Bank report on drainage includes a section specifically on redefining drainage in a more integrated fashion. The alternative definition of drainage that the authors propose is: "Land and water management through the processes of managing excess surface water and

shallow water tables—by retaining and removing water—with the aim of achieving an optimal mix of *economic* and *social* benefits while safeguarding key *ecological* functions" (World Bank 2004, 15; emphasis added).

24. Maize has a much lower salt tolerance than these other crops (see table 5.1), hence the size of its yield increase after installation of the subsurface drains.

25. The ministry purchases the drainage installation machines from overseas and then sells them to contractors, who repay the cost in a series of installments.

26. Farmers pay for the installation of subsurface drainage on their land over a twenty-year period. They do not have to pay for the operation of the system, although the ministry raises the land tax slightly for those areas with subsurface drains to cover the maintenance costs. The ministry has not found farmers to be reluctant to pay for subsurface drainage, since they see the benefits in crop yields. Farmers generally recover their costs in just three to four years (Ali et al. 2001, 18).

27. By 1997, only 92,300 of the 430,000 cultivated feddan in Fayoum were fully equipped with subsurface drainage (FWMP 2002, 15). More up-to-date figures are not available, but a drainage engineer I interviewed in 2009 estimated that about 25 percent of Fayoum's land still does not have subsurface drainage.

28. On the High Dam, see Little (1965); Schalie (1974); Benedick (1979); Allan (1981); Fahim (1981); Walton (1981); Bishop (1997); White (1998); Shokr (2009); Reynolds (2013).

29. See, for example, Baviskar (1997); Roy (1999); McCully (2001); Sneddon and Fox (2008); Molle et al. (2009).

30. Quote from Postel (1999, 54).

31. An exception is the case of the Netherlands where, due to the low-lying nature of the country, drainage (in addition to flood protection and land reclamation) plays a key role in maintaining the country's territory. In a very material way, therefore, drainage has helped build the Dutch nation. Symbolically, also, the Dutch drainage program draws on a nationalist rhetoric. Indeed a book on drainage written by a former chief engineer in the Netherlands Ministry of Water Management is subtitled *The Art of a Nation* (van Veen 1962).

32. The only other places that receive Nile water but do not drain water back into the Nile catchment are the large reclamation projects outside the Nile valley and delta, like the Toshka Project (see chapter 4).

33. The idea of using Wadi Rayan as a reservoir for excess water was first proposed in the late nineteenth century. Cope Whitehouse, an American Egyptologist, conducted research in Wadi Rayan and suggested that this area could be used as a reservoir for controlling the Nile floods (Brown 1892, 5). The idea was further developed in the 1894 Irrigation Report, which included a specific plan with a detailed reservoir design (Willcocks 1899, 157–58, 443–48).

34. This figure is an average of the range of figures that Ismail (2011) presented for official reuse in the delta (between 5.5bcm and 7bcm) and Fayoum (between 1bcm and 1.5bcm). The range reflects the fact that official reuse varies

from year to year, as the ministry adjusts the operation of its pumping stations according to the water supply. Notably, ministry officials distinguish between two types of official reuse: main system reuse and intermediate reuse. In the former, which has been the ministry's primary focus, large pumping stations direct drainage water from the main drains back into the main canals or branches of the Nile. In the latter, smaller pumps operated by the regional irrigation directorates channel drainage water from the branch drains into the ends of the branch canals. For a more detailed discussion of these two approaches and their contrasting political implications, see Barnes (2012b).

35. This figure is based on the figure given by Ismail (2011) and the estimate that Egypt's total water use amounts to 72.4bcm a year (MWRI 2005a, ch. 4, 28).

36. In fact, the ministry has had to close four of its twenty-three mixing stations due to concerns about contamination of the drinking water supply; three other stations have never been put into operation due to anticipated concerns. In one case this was due to excess salinity; in the other cases it was due to different pollutants (WQU 2004).

37. Ppm stands for parts per million, which refers to the concentration of dissolved salts in the water. This is an alternative measure of salinity to the measure of electrical conductivity, which I explain in note 11 to this chapter (there is no simple equation to convert between the two). The FAO's guidelines suggest that a salinity of up to 450ppm in irrigation water will not cause any problems, 450–2,000ppm may cause slight to moderate problems, and over 2,000ppm will cause severe problems for use in irrigation (Ayers and Westcot 1994). Seawater, by means of a comparison, ranges in salinity from 31,000 to 39,000ppm.

38. While the term *free water* implies a degree of naturalness, the Nile receives discharge from drain outlets throughout the valley and so is far from pure. The volume of flow in the river is sufficiently large, though, that pollutants and salts are highly diluted, maintaining a good water quality (see table 5.3).

39. On the ways in which water quality is embedded in cultural beliefs, social relations, sensorial experiences, and technical practice, see Alley (2002) and Scaramelli (2013).

REFERENCES

Abbassy, M. S., H. Z. Ibrahim et al. 2003. "Persistent Organochlorine Pollutants in the Aquatic Ecosystem of Lake Manzala, Egypt." *Bulletin of Environmental Contamination and Toxicology* 70:1158–64.

Abdel-Aal, M. 2004. "Tenants, Owners, and Sugar Cane: Law 96/1992 in Qena and Aswan." In *Upper Egypt: Identity and Change*, ed. N. Hopkins and R. Saad, 251–67. Cairo: American University in Cairo Press.

Abdel-Dayem, S., S. Abdel-Gawad, and H. Fahmy. 2007. "Drainage in Egypt: A Story of Determination, Continuity and Success." *Irrigation and Drainage* 56:S101–S111.

Abdel-Dayem, S., and M. El-Safty. 1993. "Review of Egyptian Experience in Implementing Land Drainage Projects." *Irrigation and Drainage Systems* 6:311–24.

Abdel-Dayem, S., J. Hoevenaars, P. Mollinga et al. 2004. *Reclaiming Drainage: Toward an Integrated Approach*. Agriculture and Rural Development Report No. 1. Washington, DC: World Bank.

Abdel-Khalek, G. 2002. "Stabilization and Adjustment in Egypt: Sequencing and Sustainability." In *Counter-Revolution in Egypt's Countryside: Land and Farmers in the Era of Economic Reform*, ed. R. Bush. London: Zed Books.

Abu Edries Ali, A. 2011. "Egypt Seeks New Food and Water Security in Sudan." Associated Free Press, March 27.

Abu-Lughod, L. 1986. *Veiled Sentiments: Honor and Poetry in a Bedouin Society*. Berkeley: University of California Press.

ADB. 2000. *Project Completion Report: Drainage V Project, Arab Republic of Egypt*. Country Department, North Region, African Development Bank (ADB) and African Development Fund, October.

ADE. 2010. *Evaluation of European Commission's Support with Egypt—A Country Level Evaluation*. Aide à la Décision Économique Belgium (ADE), December.

Adriansen, H. 2009. "Land Reclamation in Egypt: A Study of Life in the New Lands." *Geoforum* 40:664–74.

Agarwal, B. 2001. "Participatory Exclusions, Community Forestry, and Gender: An Analysis for South Asia and a Conceptual Framework." *World Development* 29:1623–48.

Agrawal, A., and C. Gibson. 1999. "Enchantment and Disenchantment: The Role of Community in Natural Resource Conservation." *World Development* 27:629–49.

Ahmed, A., and U. Ismail. 2008. *Sediment in the Nile River System*. Report written for the UNESCO International Hydrological Programme—International Sediment Initiative, Khartoum.

Al-Bultagi, A., and E. Abu Hadeed. 2008. *The Main Pillars for the National Program for the Greatest Use of Water in the Old Lands*. Cairo: Ministry of Agriculture and Land Reclamation Committee for Research and Development, March. Al-raka'iz al-asasia lil-barnamig al-qawmi li-t'athim al-istifada min al-mai fi al-aradi al-qadima (in Arabic).

Alatout, S. 2000. "Water Balances in Palestine: Numbers and Political Culture in the Middle East." In *Water Balances in the Eastern Mediterranean*, ed. D. Brooks and O. Mehmet, 59–84. Ottawa: IDRC Books.

Alatout, S. 2008. " 'States' of Scarcity: Water, Space, and Identity Politics in Israel, 1948–59." *Environment and Planning D: Society and Space* 26:959–82.

Alatout, S. 2009. "Bringing Abundance into Environmental Politics: Constructing a Zionist Network of Water Abundance, Immigration, and Colonization." *Social Studies of Science* 39:363–94.

Ali, A., H. van Leeuwen, and R. Koopmans. 2001. "Benefits of Draining Agricultural Land in Egypt: Results of Five Years' Monitoring of Drainage Effects and Impacts." *Water Resources Development* 17:633–46.

Allan, J. 1981. "High Aswan Dam Is a Success Story." *Geographical Magazine* 53:393–96.

Allan, J. 1983. "Some Phases in Extending the Cultivated Area in the Nineteenth and Twentieth Centuries in Egypt." *Middle Eastern Studies* 19:470–81.

Allan, J. 2002a. *The Middle East Water Question: Hydropolitics and the Global Economy*. London: I. B. Tauris.

Allan, J. 2002b. "Hydro-Peace in the Middle East: Why No Water Wars? A Case Study of the Jordan River Basin." *SAIS Review* 22:255–72.

Allan, T. 2011. *Virtual Water: Tackling the Threat to Our Planet's Most Precious Resource*. London: I. B. Tauris.

Alley, K. 2002. *On the Banks of the Ganga: When Wastewater Meets a Sacred River*. Ann Arbor: University of Michigan Press.

Alterman, J. 2002. EARIS. *Egypt and American Foreign Assistance, 1952–1956: Hopes Dashed*, 63–95. New York: Palgrave Macmillan.

Amer, M. 1994. Principles of Land Drainage in Arid and Semi-Arid Regions. Refresher Course on Land Drainage in Egypt, December 10–19, Qanatir, Egypt.

Amer, M, S. Abdel-Dayem, M. Osman et al. 1989. "Recent Developments of Land Drainage in Egypt." In *Land Drainage in Egypt*, ed. M. Amer and N. de Ridder, 67–92. Cairo: Drainage Research Institute.

Amer, M., and M. Abu-Zeid. 1989. "History of Land Drainage in Egypt." In *Land Drainage in Egypt*, ed. M. Amer and N. de Ridder, 43–66. Cairo: Drainage Research Institute.

Amery, H., and A. Wolf. 2000. *Water in the Middle East: A Geography of Peace*. Austin: University of Texas Press.

Anand, N. 2011. "Pressure: The PoliTechnics of Water Supply in Mumbai." *Cultural Anthropology* 26:542–63.

Anderson, B. 1991. *Imagined Communities: Reflections on the Origin and Spread of Nationalism*. London: Verso.

Anwar, M. 2011. *Public-Private Participation in Large-Scale Irrigation Systems*. http://www.solutionsforwater.org.

APP. 1995. Report on the 29th Meeting of the Dutch-Egyptian Advisory Panel Project (APP) on Land Drainage and Drainage Related Water Management, Alexandria, March 7–9.

AQUASTAT. 2010. *Egypt: Average Water Resources by Country*. http://www.fao.org/nr/water/aquastat/main/index.stm.

Arnstein, S. 1969. "A Ladder of Citizen Participation." *Journal of the American Institute of Planners* 35:216–24.

Attia, B., A. Saleh, K. Abu-Zeid et al. 2009. *Middle East and North Africa and Arab Countries: Regional Document*. Report prepared by the Arab Water Council for the Fifth World Water Forum, Istanbul, March.

Attia, F. 2005. *Water Boards*. Report produced for the 39th Meeting of the Egyptian-Dutch Advisory Panel on Water Management, Egypt, April 10–14.

Attia, F., H. Fahmy, M. Eid et al. 2007. *Resettlement Policy Framework*. The West Delta Water Conservation and Irrigation Rehabilitation Project, Ministry of Water Resources and Irrigation, Cairo, April 30.

Awad, M. 1954. "The Assimilation of Nomads in Egypt." *Geographical Review* 44:240–52.

Ayers, R., and D. Westcot. 1994. *Water Quality for Agriculture*. Food and Agriculture Organization of the United Nations, FAO Irrigation and Drainage Paper No. 29.

Bach, K. 2002. "Rural Egypt under Stress." In *Counter-Revolution in Egypt's Countryside: Land and Farmers in the Era of Economic Reform*, ed. R. Bush. London: Zed Books.

Bach, K. 2004. "Changing Family and Marriage Patterns in an Aswan Village." In *Upper Egypt: Identity and Change*, ed. N. Hopkins and R. Saad, 169–90. Cairo: American University of Cairo Press.

Baer, G. 1962. *A History of Landownership in Modern Egypt, 1800–1950*. London: Oxford University Press.

Baker, J. 2005. *The Kuhls of Kangra: Community-Managed Irrigation in the Western Himalaya*. Seattle: University of Washington Press.

Bakker, K. 2000. "Privatizing Water, Producing Scarcity: The Yorkshire Drought of 1997." *Economic Geography* 76:4–27.

Bakker, K. 2002. "From State to Market: Water *Mercantilización* in Spain." *Environment and Planning A* 34:767–90.

Bakker, K. 2004. *An Uncooperative Commodity: Privatizing Water in England and Wales.* New York: Oxford University Press.

Bakker, K. 2005. "Neoliberalizing Nature? Market Environmentalism in Water Supply in England and Wales." *Annals of the Association of American Geographers* 95:542–65.

Bakker, K. 2012. "Water: Political, Biopolitical, Material." *Social Studies of Science* 42, no. 4:616–23.

Bakker, K., and G. Bridge. 2006. "Material Worlds? Resource Geographies and the 'Matter of Nature.'" *Progress in Human Geography* 30:5–27.

Ball, J. 1939. *Contributions to the Geography of Egypt.* Cairo: Government Press.

Balls, L. 1918. "Analyses of Agricultural Yield. Part III. The Influence of Natural Environmental Factors upon the Yield of Egyptian Cotton." *Philosophical Transactions of the Royal Society of London. Series B, Containing Papers of a Biological Character* 208:157–223.

Banks, T., C. Richard, L. Ping et al. 2003. "Community-Based Grasslands Management in Western China: Rationale, Pilot Project Experience, and Policy Implications." *Mountain Research and Development* 23:132–40.

Barnes, J. 2009. "Managing the Waters of Ba'th Country: The Politics of Water Scarcity in Syria." *Geopolitics* 14:510–30.

Barnes, J. 2012a. "Expanding the Nile's Watershed: The Science and Politics of Land Reclamation in Egypt." In *Water on Sand: Environmental Histories of the Middle East and North Africa*, ed. A. Mikhail, 251–72. New York: Oxford University Press.

Barnes, J. 2012b. "Mixing Waters: The Reuse of Agricultural Drainage Water in Egypt." *Geoforum.* http://dx.doi.org/10.1016/j.geoforum.2012.1011.1019.

Barnes, J. 2013a. "Who Is a Water User? The Politics of Gender in Egypt's Water User Associations." In *Contemporary Water Governance in the Global South: Scarcity, Marketization, and Privatization*, ed. L. Harris, J. Goldin, and C. Sneddon, 183–196. London: Routledge.

Barnes, J. 2013b. "Water, Water Everywhere but Not a Drop to Drink: The False Promise of Virtual Water." *Critique of Anthropology* 33, no. 4:369–87.

Barnes, J. (forthcoming). "Scale and Agency: Climate Change and the Future of Egypt's Water." In *Climate Cultures: Anthropological Perspectives on Climate Change*, ed. J. Barnes and M. Dove. New Haven: Yale University Press.

Barnes, J., and S. Alatout. 2012. "Water Worlds: Introduction to the Special Issue." *Social Studies of Science* 42, no. 4:483–88.

Barry, A. 2013. *Material Politics: Disputes along the Pipeline.* Chichester: John Wiley and Sons, Ltd.

Baviskar, A. 1997. *In the Belly of the River: Tribal Conflicts over Development in the Narmada Valley.* New York: Oxford University Press.

Bear, C., and J. Bull. 2011. "Water Matters: Agency, Flows, and Frictions." *Environment and Planning A* 43:2261–66.

Belt, D. 2010. "Parting the Waters: The Middle East Could Be a Model for Averting Water Wars." *National Geographic* 217:154–72.

Benedick, R. 1979. "The High Dam and the Transformation of the Nile." *Middle East Journal* 33:119–44.

BIC. 2010. *CSO Exchanges Letters with World Bank and Egypt's Ministry of Water Resources re Controversial West Delta Project*. Bank Information Center. http://www.bicusa.org.

Biersack, A., and J. Greenberg. 2006. *Reimagining Political Ecology*. Durham, NC: Duke University Press.

Bijker, W. 1995. *Of Bicycles, Bakelites, and Bulbs: Toward a Theory of Sociotechnical Change*. Cambridge, MA: MIT Press.

Bijker, W. 2007. "Dikes and Dams, Thick with Politics." *Isis* 98:109–23.

Birkenholtz, T. 2009. "Irrigated Landscapes, Produced Scarcity, and Adaptive Social Institutions in Rajasthan, India." *Annals of the Association of Amercian Geographers* 99:118–37.

Birkes, F. 2004. "Rethinking Community-Based Conservation." *Conservation Biology* 18:621–30.

Biro, A. 2007. "Water Politics and the Construction of Scale." *Studies in Political Economy* 80:9–30.

Bishop, E. 1997. "Talking Shop: Egyptian Engineers and Soviet Specialists at the Aswan High Dam." PhD diss., University of Chicago.

Biswas, A., and C. Tortajada, eds. 2009. *Impacts of Megaconferences on the Water Sector*. New York: Springer.

Boak, A. 1926. "Irrigation and Population in the Faiyum, the Garden of Egypt." *Geographical Review* 16:353–64.

Boelens, R., and G. Davila. 1998. *Searching for Equity: Conceptions of Justice and Equity in Peasant Irrigation*. Assen: Van Gorcum.

Bonnardeaux, D. 2009. "Water Wars and Water Woes." *Daily News Egypt*, March 17.

Bowman, A., and E. Rogan. 1999. *Agriculture in Egypt: From Pharaonic to Modern Times*. London: British Academy.

Brosius, J. P., A. Tsing, and C. Zerner. 2005. *Communities and Conservation: Histories and Politics of Community-Based Natural Resource Management*. Walnut Creek, CA: AltaMira Press.

Brouwer, C., and M. Heibloem. 1986. *Irrigation Water Management: Irrigation Water Needs*. FAO Training Manual No. 3. Rome: FAO.

Brown, H. 1892. *The Fayum and Lake Moeris*. London: Edward Stanford.

Brown, P., F. El Gohary, M. Tawfic et al. 2003. *Nile River Water Quality Management Study*. Egypt Water Policy Reform Project, Report No. 67. USAID, Ministry of Water Resources and Irrigation, June.

Bruce, J. 1804. *Travels to Discover the Source of the Nile, in the Years 1768, 1769, 1770, 1771, 1772, and 1773*. London: Longman.

Budds, J. 2008. "Whose Scarcity? The Hydrosocial Cycle and the Changing Waterscape of La Ligua River Basin, Chile." In *Contentious Geographies: Environmental*

Knowledges, Meaning, and Scale, ed. M. Goodman, K. Evered, and M. Boykoff, 59–78. Abingdon, UK: Ashgate.

Bull, J. 2011. "Encountering Fish, Flows, and Waterscapes through Angling." *Environment and Planning A* 43:2267–84.

Bulloch, J., and A. Darwish. 1993. *Water Wars: Coming Conflicts in the Middle East.* London: Gollancz.

Bush, R. 2002. "More Losers than Winners in Egypt's Countryside: The Impact of Changes in Land Tenure." In *Counter-Revolution in Egypt's Countryside: Land and Farmers in the Era of Economic Reform*, ed. R. Bush. London: Zed Books.

Butzer, K. 1976. *Early Hydraulic Civilization in Egypt: A Study in Cultural Ecology.* Chicago: University of Chicago Press.

Callon, M. 1986a. "Some Elements of a Sociology of Translation: Domestication of the Scallops and Fishermen of St. Brieuc Bay." In *Power, Action, and Belief: A New Sociology of Knowledge?*, ed. J. Law, 196–223. London: Routledge.

Callon, M. 1986b. "The Sociology of an Actor-Network: The Case of the Electric Vehicle." In *Mapping the Dynamics of Science and Technology*, ed. M. Callon, J. Law, and A. Rip, 19–34. London: Palgrave Macmillan.

Callon, M., P. Lascoumes, and Y. Barthe. 2009. *Acting in an Uncertain World: An Essay on Technical Democracy.* Translated by Graham Burchell. Cambridge, MA: MIT Press.

Callon, M. and V. Rabeharisoa. 2004. "Gino's Lesson on Humanity: Genetics, Mutual Entanglements, and the Sociologist's Role." *Economy and Society* 33:1–27.

CAPMAS. 2009. "Agriculture Statistics, Planted Area, 1960–2007." *Egypt in Figures 2009.* Arab Republic of Egypt, Central Agency for Public Mobilization and Statistics (CAPMAS), 71.

Cascão A. 2008. "Ethiopia—Challenges to Egyptian Hegemony in the Nile Basin." *Water Policy* 10:13–28.

Cascão, A. 2009. "Changing Power Relations in the Nile River Basin: Unilateralism vs. Cooperation?" *Water Alternatives* 2:245–68.

Castree, N. 1995. "The Nature of Produced Nature: Materiality and Knowledge Construction in Marxism." *Antipode* 27:12–48.

Chambers, R. 1988. *Managing Canal Irrigation: Practical Analysis from South Asia.* New York: Cambridge University Press.

Cheeseman, R. 1936. *Lake Tana and the Blue Nile.* London: Macmillan.

Chipman, J., and T. Lillesand. 2007. "Satellite-Based Assessment of the Dynamics of New Lakes in Southern Egypt." *International Journal of Remote Sensing* 28:4365–79.

Choy, T. 2011. *Ecologies of Comparison: An Ethnography of Endangerment in Hong Kong.* Durham, NC: Duke University Press.

Cole, D. 2003. "Where Have the Bedouin Gone?" *Anthropological Quarterly* 76:235–67.

Collins, R. 1994. "History, Hydropolitics, and the Nile: Nile Control—Myth or

Reality?" In *The Nile—Sharing a Scarce Resource: An Historical and Technical Review of Water Management and of Economical and Legal Issues*, ed. P. Howell and J. Allan, 109–37. Cambridge: Cambridge University Press.

Conca, K. 2006. *Governing Water: Contentious Transnational Politics and Global Institution Building*. Cambridge, MA: MIT Press.

Conway, D. 2005. "From Headwater Tributaries to International River: Observing and Adapting to Climate Variability and Change in the Nile Basin." *Global Environmental Change* 15:99–114.

Conway, D., and M. Hulme. 1996. "The Impacts of Climate Variability and Future Climate Change in the Nile Basin on Water Resources in Egypt." *International Journal of Water Resources Development* 12:261–80.

Cooke, B., and U. Kothari. 2001. *Participation: The New Tyranny?* London: Zed Books.

Cornwall, A. 2002. *Making Spaces, Changing Places: Situating Participation in Development*, IDS Working Paper No. 170. Brighton, UK: Institute for Development Studies.

Cosgrove, W., and F. Rijsberman. 2000. *World Water Vision: Making Water Everybody's Business*. London: Earthscan.

Cotton Federation. 1938. *Official Report of the XVIII International Cotton Congress*. International Federation of Master Cotton Spinners' and Manufacturers' Associations. Manchester, UK: Cloister Press.

Coward, E. 1980. *Irrigation and Agricultural Development in Asia: Perspectives from the Social Sciences*. Ithaca, NY: Cornell University Press.

CPWF. 2005. *CGIAR Challenge Program on Water and Food: Research Strategy 2005–2008*. Colombo, Sri Lanka: Challenge Program on Water and Food (CPWF).

Cuno, K. 1992. *The Pasha's Peasants: Land, Society, and Economy in Lower Egypt, 1740–1858*. Cambridge: Cambridge University Press.

Dannies, K. 2009. "Egypt to Reclaim 3.4 Million Feddans to Meet Food Needs." *Daily News Egypt*, August 16, 2009.

Davis, D., and E. Burke. 2011. *Environmental Imaginaries of the Middle East and North Africa*. Athens: Ohio University Press.

Davis, M. 2002. *Late Victorian Holocausts: El Niño Famines and the Making of the Third World*. London: Verso.

Dawoud, M., M. Darwish, and M. El-Kady. 2005. "GIS-Based Groundwater Management Model for the Western Nile Delta." *Water Resources Management* 19:585–604.

de Laet, M., and A. Mol. 2000. "The Zimbabwe Bush Pump: Mechanics of a Fluid Technology." *Social Studies of Science* 30, no. 2:225–63.

Delaney, D., and H. Leitner. 1997. "The Political Construction of Scale." *Political Geography* 16:93–97.

Demeritt, D. 2002. "What Is the 'Social Construction of Nature'? A Typology and Sympathetic Critique." *Progress in Human Geography* 26, no. 6:767–90.

Derr, J. 2009. "Cultivating the State: Cash Crop Agriculture, Irrigation, and the Geography of Authority in Colonial Southern Egypt, 1868–1931." PhD diss., Stanford University.

Dolfing, B., and W. Snellen. 1999. *Sustainability of Dutch Water Boards: Appropriate Design Characteristics for Self-Governing Water Management Organizations*. Wageningen, Netherlands: ILRI.

Dove, M. 2004. "Anthropogenic Grasslands in Southeast Asia: Sociology of Knowledge and Implications for Agroforestry." *Agroforestry Systems* 61:423–35.

Drydyk, J. 2005. "When Is Development More Democratic?" *Journal of Human Development* 6:247–67.

Economist. 2010. "To the Last Drop: How to Avoid Water Wars." *Economist: Special Report on Water* (May 22): 2017–19.

Eid, E., K. Shaltout et al. 2010. "Effects of Abiotic Conditions on *Phragmites Australis* Along Geographic Gradients in Lake Burullus, Egpyt." *Aquatic Botany* 92:86–92.

El-Bastawesy, M., S. Arafat, and F. Khalaf. 2007. "Estimation of Water Loss from Toshka Lakes Using Remote Sensing and GIS." *10th AGILE International Conference on Geographic Information Science*. Aalborg University, Denmark.

El-Din, G. 2006. "Parliament to Scrutinize Toshka." *Al-Ahram Weekly*, April 12.

El-Guindy, S., and M. Amer. 1979. *Reuse of Drainage Water*. Progress report submitted to the Dutch-Egyptian Advisory Panel on Land Drainage, September.

El-Kadi, M., M. Abdel-Ghani Seoudi, M. El-Bahei Esawy et al. 1995. *The Nile and History of Irrigation in Egypt*. Cairo: Egyptian National Committee of Irrigation and Drainage, Ministry of Public Works and Water Resources.

El-Zanaty, F. 2001. *Knowledge, Attitudes, and Practices of Egyptian Farmers Towards Water Resources: National Survey 2001*. EPIQ Water Policy Reform Program Report No. 7. Prepared by El-Zanaty and Associates for the Agricultural Policy Reform Project, USAID, Cairo.

Elgood, P. 1928. *The Transit of Egypt*. London: Edward Arnold.

Elhance, A. 1999. *Hydropolitics in the Third World: Conflict and Cooperation in International River Basins*. Washington, DC: U.S. Institute of Peace.

Elyachar, J. 2005. *Markets of Dispossession. NGOs, Economic Development, and the State in Cairo*. Durham, NC: Duke University Press.

Escobar, A. 1999. "After Nature: Steps to an Anti-Essentialist Political Ecology." *Current Anthropology* 40:1–30.

Escobar, A. 2008. *Territories of Difference: Place, Movements, Life, Redes*. Durham, NC: Duke University Press.

Evans, T. 1994. "History of Nile Flows." In *The Nile—Sharing a Scarce Resource: An Historical and Technical Review of Water Management and of Economical and Legal Issues*, ed. P. Howell and J. Allan, 27–65. Cambridge: Cambridge University Press.

Ezzat, S. 2011. "Post-Revolutionary Trail-Blazing Egypt Farmers." *Egyptian Gazette*, September 9.

Fahim, H. 1981. *Dams, People, and Development: The Aswan High Dam Case.* New York: Pergamon Press.

Fairhead, J., and M. Leach. 1996. *Misreading the African Landscape: Society and Ecology in the Forest-Savanna Mosaic.* Cambridge: Cambridge University Press.

Falkenmark, M., J. Lundqvist, and C. Widstrand. 1989. "Macro-Scale Water Scarcity Requires Micro-Scale Approaches: Aspects of Vulnerability in Semi-Arid Development." *Natural Resources Forum* 13:258–67.

Falkenmark, M., and J. Rockström. 2006. "The New Green and Blue Water Paradigm: Breaking New Ground for Water Resources Planning and Management." *Journal of Water Resources Planning and Management* (May/June): 129–32.

FAOSTAT. 2008. "Statistics on Egypt's Cultivated Area by Crop. Country Production Statistics. Food and Agriculture Organization of the United Nations." Accessed February 17, 2009. http://faostat.fao.org.

Faruqi, N. 2001. "Islam and Water Management: Overview and Principles." In *Water Management in Islam,* ed. N. Faruqi, A. Biswas, and M. Bino, 1–32. New York: United Nations University Press.

Fathi, M., and A. M. Hamza. 2000. "Development of Land Drainage in Egypt and the Role of the Egyptian Public Authority for Drainage Projects." In *Drainage Along the River Nile,* ed. H. Nijland, 20–53. Cairo: Ministry of Public Works and Water Resources.

FaWUOP. 2007. *Project Inception Report.* Fayoum Water Users Organization Project (FaWUOP), Ministry of Water Resources and Irrigation, Fayoum, March.

FaWUOP. 2010. *Assessment of Level of Involvement of BCWUAs and Level of Cooperation Between IWMD and BCWUAs.* Report for the Fayoum Water Users' Organization Project, October.

Ferguson, J. 1994. *The Anti-Politics Machine: "Development," Depoliticization, and Bureaucratic Power in Lesotho.* Minneapolis: University of Minnesota Press.

Ferry, E., and M. Limbert, eds. 2008. *Timely Assets: The Politics of Resources and Their Temporalities.* Santa Fe, NM: School for Advanced Research Press.

Fletcher, L. 1996. *Egypt's Agriculture in a Reform Era.* Ames: Iowa State University Press.

Flower, R., C. Stickley, N. Rose et al. 2006. "Environmental Changes at the Desert Margin: An Assessment of Recent Paleolimnological Records in Lake Qaroun, Middle Egypt." *Journal of Paleolimnology* 35:1–24.

Forsyth, T. 2003. *Critical Political Ecology: The Politics of Environmental Science.* London: Routledge.

Furlong, K. 2010. "Neoliberal Water Management: Trends, Limitations, Reformulations." *Environment and Society: Advances in Research* 1:46–75.

FWMP. 2002. *Drainage Water Reuse.* Technical Report No. 29. Fayoum Water Management Project (FWMP), Ministry of Water Resources and Irrigation, Fayoum, May.

FWMP. 2006a. *Water Management Allowing for Cultivation of Rice.* Technical Report

No. 40. Fayoum Water Management Project (FWMP), Ministry of Water Resources and Irrigation, Fayoum, November.

FWMP. 2006b. *Study on Land Reclamation.* Technical Report No. 41. Fayoum Water Management Project (FWMP), Ministry of Water Resources and Irrigation, Fayoum, November.

FWMP. 2006c. *Management of the Lakes in Fayoum.* Technical Report No. 42. Fayoum Water Management Project (FWMP), Ministry of Water Resources and Irrigation, Fayoum, November.

Garces-Restrepo, C., D. Vermillion, and G. Munoz. 2007. *Irrigation Management Transfer: Worldwide Efforts and Results.* FAO Water Reports No. 32. Rome: Food and Agriculture Organization of the United Nations.

Gauld, R. 2000. "Maintaining Centralized Control in Community-Based Forestry: Policy Construction in the Philippines." *Development and Change* 31:229–54.

Geertz, C. 1983. "Organization of the Balinese Subak." In *Irrigation and Agricultural Development in Asia: Perspectives from the Social Sciences,* ed. E. Coward, 70–90. Ithaca, NY: Cornell University Press.

Gelles, P. 2000. *Water and Power in Highland Peru.* New Brunswick: Rutgers University Press.

Gidwani, V. 2002. "The Unbearable Modernity of 'Development'? An Essay on Canal Irrigation and Development Planning in Western India." *Progress in Planning* 58:1–80.

Gleick, P. 1994. "Water, War, and Peace in the Middle East." *Environment* 36:6.

Gleick, P. 2006. *The World's Water 2006–2007: The Biennial Report on Freshwater Resources.* Washington, DC: Island Press.

Gleick, P., E. Chalecki, and A. Wong. 2002. "Measuring Water Well-Being: Water Indicators and Indices." In *World's Water: The Biennial Report on Freshwater Resources 2002–2003,* ed. P. Gleick, 87–113. Washington, DC: Island Press.

Gleick, P., and J. Lane. 2005. "Large International Water Meetings: Time for a Reappraisal." *Water International* 30, no. 3:410–14.

Goldberg, E. 2004. *Trade, Reputation, and Child Labor in Twentieth-Century Egypt.* New York: Palgrave Macmillan.

Goldman, M. 2007. "How 'Water for All!' Policy Became Hegemonic: The Power of the World Bank and Its Transnational Policy Networks." *Geoforum* 38:786–800.

Goldman, M., P. Nadasdy, and M. Turner, eds. 2011. *Knowing Nature: Conversations at the Intersection of Political Ecology and Science Studies.* Chicago: University of Chicago Press.

Gouda, D. 2007. *Preliminary Findings of Monitoring Farmers' Perceptions of the IIIMP Pilot Area.* Agricultural Water Mangement Project. Ministry of Agriculture and Land Reclamation, Cairo, February.

Groenfeldt, D. 2000. "Introduction: A Global Consensus on Participatory Irrigation Management." In *Case Studies in Participatory Irrigation Management,* ed.

D. Groenfeldt and M. Svendsen, 1–3. Washington, DC: World Bank Institute Learning Resources Series.

Guillet, D. 1992. *Covering Ground: Communal Water Management and the State in the Peruvian Highlands*. Ann Arbor: University of Michigan Press.

Gupta, A., and J. Ferguson. 2002. "Spatializing States: Toward an Ethnography of Neoliberal Governmentality." *American Ethnologist* 29:981–1002.

GWP. 2008. *GWP in Action 2007*. London: Global Water Partnership.

Gyawali, D., and A. Dixit. 2010. "The Construction and Destruction of Scarcity in Development: Water and Power Experiences in Nepal." In *The Limits to Scarcity: Contesting the Politics of Allocation*, ed. L. Mehta, 233–52. London: Earthscan.

Hardin, G. 1968. "The Tragedy of the Commons." *Science* 162:1243–48.

Harris, L. 2005. "Negotiating Inequalities: Democracy, Gender, and Politics of Difference in Water User Groups of Southeastern Turkey." In *Environmentalism in Turkey: Between Democracy and Development?*, ed. F. Adaman and M. Arsel, 185–201. Aldershot, UK: Ashgate.

Harris, L. 2006. "Irrigation, Gender, and the Social Geographies of the Changing Waterscape in Southeastern Anatolia." *Environment and Planning D: Society and Space* 24:187–213.

Harris, L., and S. Alatout. 2010. "Negotiating Hydro-Scales, Forging States: Comparison of the Upper Tigris/Euphrates and Jordan River Basins." *Political Geography* 29:148–56.

Harvey, D. 2003. *The New Imperialism*. Oxford: Oxford University Press.

Helmreich, S. 2011. "Nature/Culture/Seawater." *American Anthropologist* 113:132–44.

Hesser, L., I. Asmon, F. Hedlund et al. 1980. *New Lands Productivity in Egypt: Technical and Economic Feasibility Study*. Written by Pacific Consultants on contract from USAID, January.

Heydemann, S. 2007. *Upgrading Authoritarianism in the Arab World*. Analysis Paper No. 13. Washington, DC: Saban Center for Middle East Policy at the Brookings Institute.

Hibou, B. 2004. "From Privatising the Economy to Privatising the State." In *Privatising the State*. Edited by B. Hibou. Translated by Jonathan Derrick, 1–46. New York: Columbia University Press.

Hillel, D. 1994. *Rivers of Eden: The Struggle for Water and the Quest for Peace in the Middle East*. Oxford: Oxford University Press.

Hoekstra, A., and P. Hung. 2005. "Globalisation of Water Resources: International Virtual Water Flows in Relation to Crop Trade." *Global Environmental Change* 15:45–56.

Hoevenaars, J., F. Attia, F. Hussam et al. 2007. *Environmental and Social Impacts Assessment and Framework Management Plan*. West Delta Water Conservation and Irrigation Rehabilitation Project, Ministry of Water Resources and Irrigation, Cairo, April 30.

Hollings, M. 1917. *The Life of Sir Colin Scott-Moncrieff*. London: John Murray.

Hopkins, N. 1987. *Agrarian Transformation in Egypt*, Boulder, CO: Westview Press.

Hopkins, N. 1999. "Irrigation in Contemporary Egypt." In *Agriculture in Egypt: From Pharaonic to Modern Times*, ed. A. Bowman and E. Rogan, 367–87. London: British Academy.

Hopkins, N. 2005. "The Rule of Law and the Rule of Water." *Égypte / Monde Arabe*, 173–86. Paris: Troisième série.

Hopkins, N., and R. Saad. 2004. *Upper Egypt: Identity and Change*. Cairo: American University in Cairo Press.

Hopkins, N., and K. Westergaard. 1998. "Introduction: Directions of Change in Rural Egypt." In *Directions of Change in Rural Egypt*, ed. N. Hopkins and K. Westergaard, 1–18. Cairo: American University in Cairo Press.

Howell, P., and T. Allan. 1994. *The Nile: Sharing a Scarce Resource. An Historical and Technical Review of Water Management and of Economical and Legal Issues*. Cambridge: Cambridge University Press.

Hughes, D. 2010. "Commentary on Water." *Cultural Anthropology*. Interview with authors by Ashley Carse, September. Accessed January 2012. http://www.culanth.org/.

Hughes, T. 1987. "The Evolution of Large Technological Systems." In *The Social Construction of Technological Systems*, ed. W. Bijker, T. Hughes, and T. Pinch, 51–82. Cambridge, MA: MIT Press.

Hunt, R. 1989. "Appropriate Social Organization? Water Users Associations in Bureaucratic Canal Irrigation Systems." *Human Organization* 48:79–90.

Hussein, M. 2011. "From Liberalization to Self-Sufficiency: Egypt Charts a New Agricultural Policy." *Al Ahram Online*, April 28.

Hussein, M. 2012. "Experts Question New Agriculture Minister's Land Reclamation Plan." *Al Ahram Online*, August 9.

Hussein, S., J. Gleason, E. El-Kholy et al. 1999. *Study of New Land Allocation Policy in Egypt*. Report No. 65. Reform Design and Implementation Unit of the Agricultural Policy Reform Program (APRP), Ministry of Agriculture and Land Reclamation, Cairo, February.

Hvidt, M. 1998. *Water, Technology, and Development: Upgrading Egypt's Irrigation System*. London: Tauris Academic Studies.

ICWE. 1992. *The Dublin Statement on Water and Sustainable Development*. Statement adopted at the International Conference on Water and the Environment (ICWE), Dublin, January 31.

IDSC. 1998. *National Indicators on the Situation of Egyptian Women in Aswan and Fayoum, Fayoum Document*. Information and Decision Support Center, Egypt.

IEG. 2009. *Egypt: Positive Results from Knowledge Sharing and Modest Lending—An IEG Country Assistance Evaluation 1999–2007*. Washington, DC: Independent Evaluation Group (IEG), World Bank.

IFAD. 2005. *Arab Republic of Egypt Country Program Evaluation*. Document of the International Fund on Agricultural Development (IFAD). Report No. 1658-EG.

Igoe, J., and D. Brockington. 2007. "Neoliberal Conservation: A Brief Introduction." *Conservation and Society* 5:432–49.

Ingold, T. 2007. "Materials Against Immateriality." *Archaeological Dialogues* 14:1–16.

IPRSID. 2007a. *Nile Dam Poses No Risk to Egypt, High Dam Is Safe.* Report from the IPR Strategic Business Information Database (IPRSID), August 20.

IPRSID. 2007b. *Minister of Water Resources Asserts Flood Receding This Year.* Report from the IPR Strategic Business Information Database (IPRSID), October 24.

Ismail, A. 2011. "Egyptian Drainage Water Reuse Practices and Measures to Alleviate the Risk of Failure." Second Arab Water Forum, November 20–23, 2011, Cairo.

Jairath, J. 2010. "Advocacy of Water Scarcity: Leakages in the Argument." In *The Limits to Scarcity: Contesting the Politics of Allocation,* ed. L. Mehta, 215–32. London: Earthscan.

Johnson, P., A. El Dahry, R. Dekmejian et al. 1983. *Egypt: The Egyptian American Rural Improvement Service, a Point Four Project, 1952–63.* AID Project Impact Evaluation, No. 43. Washington, DC: Agency for International Development.

Kaika, M. 2003. "Constructing Scarcity and Sensationalising Water Politics: 170 Days That Shook Athens." *Antipode* 35:919–54.

Kelly, W. 1983. "Concepts in the Anthropological Study of Irrigation." *American Anthropologist* 85, no. 4:880–86.

Kim, J., and M. Sultan. 2002. "Assessment of the Long-Term Hydrologic Impacts of Lake Nasser and Related Irrigation Projects in Southwestern Egypt." *Journal of Hydrology* 262:68–83.

King, L., R. Abdel Azim et al. 2000. *Reducing Mismatch of Irrigation Deliveries Phase I: Pilot Program.* Agricultural Policy Reform Project, Report No. 33, December. Cairo: Ministry of Water Resources and Irrigation.

Kline, R., and T. Pinch. 1996. "Users as Agents of Technological Change: The Social Construction of the Automobile in the Rural United States." *Technology and Culture* 37:763–95.

Kliot, N. 1994. *Water Resources and Conflict in the Middle East.* London: Routledge.

Kotb, T., T. Watanabe, Y. Ogino et al. 2000. "Soil Salinization in the Nile Delta and Related Policy Issues in Egypt." *Agricultural Water Management* 43:239–61.

Kull, C., C. Ibrahim, and T. Meredith. 2007. "Tropical Forest Transitions and Globalization: Neo-Liberalism, Migration, Tourism, and International Conservation Agendas." *Society and Natural Resources* 20:723–37.

Lam, W. F. 1998. *Governing Irrigation Systems in Nepal: Institutions, Infrastructure, and Collective Action.* Oakland, CA: Institute for Contemporary Studies Press.

Lansing, S. 1991. *Priests and Programmers: Technologies of Power in the Engineered Landscape of Bali.* Princeton, NJ: Princeton University Press.

Latour, B. 1992. "Where Are the Missing Masses? The Sociology of a Few Mundane Artifacts." In *Shaping Technology/Building Society: Studies in Sociotechnical Change,* ed. W. Bijker and J. Law, 225–58. Cambridge, MA: MIT Press.

Latour, B. 1999. *Pandora's Hope: Essays on the Reality of Science Studies.* Cambridge, MA: Harvard University Press.

Latour, B. 2005. *Reassembling the Social: An Introduction to Actor-Network-Theory.* Oxford: Oxford University Press.

LCHR. 2002. "Farmer Struggles Against Law 96 of 1992." In *Counter-Revolution in Egypt's Countryside: Land and Farmers in the Era of Economic Reform,* ed. R. Bush. Chapter by the Land Center for Human Rights (LCHR). London: Zed Books.

LCHR. 2009. *Case Filed on West Delta Project.* Land Center for Human Rights press release, September 15.

Le Bourhis, J.-P. 2005. "Water Parliaments: Some Examples." In *Making Things Public: Atmospheres of Democracy,* ed. B. Latour and P. Weibel, 482–85. Cambridge, MA: MIT Press.

Leach, M., R. Mearns, and I. Scoones. 1999. "Environmental Entitlements: Dynamics and Institutions in Community-Based Natural Resource Management." *World Development* 27:225–47.

Lees, S. 1986. "Coping with Bureaucracy: Survival Strategies in Irrigated Agriculture." *American Anthropologist* 88:610–22.

Leila, R. 2007. "Safe Waters." *Al-Ahram Weekly* 865, October 4–10.

Leila, R. 2008. "Water War: Egypt's Precious Nile Water Is Wanted by Outsiders." *Al-Ahram Weekly* 896, May 8–14.

Li, T. 2002. "Engaging Simplifications: Community-Based Resource Management, Market Processes, and State Agendas in Upland Southeast Asia." *World Development* 30:265–83.

Li, T. 2007. "Practices of Assemblage and Community Forest Management." *Economy and Society* 36:263–93.

Libiszewski, S. 1999. "International Conflicts over Freshwater Resources." In *Ecology, Politics, and Violent Conflict,* ed. M. Suliman, 115–38. New York: Zed.

Limbert, M. 2001. "The Senses of Water in an Omani Town." *Social Text* 19, no. 3:35–55.

Little, T. 1965. *High Dam at Aswan: The Subjugation of the Nile.* New York: John Day.

Lonergan, S., and A. Wolf. 2001. "Moving Water to Move People: The Toshka Project in Egypt." *Water International* 26:589–96.

Luzi, S. 2010. "Driving Forces and Patterns of Water Policy Making in Egypt." *Water Policy* 12:92–113.

Maliao, R., R. Pomeroy, and R. Turingan. 2009. "Performance of Community-Based Coastal Resource Management Programs in the Philippines: A Meta-Analysis." *Marine Policy* 33:818–25.

Malm, A., and S. Esmailian. 2013. "Ways in and out of Vulnerability to Climate Change: Abandoning the Mubarak Project in the Northern Nile Delta, Egypt." *Antipode* 45, no. 2:474–92.

MALR. 1994. *New Lands Development Study,* vol. 1. Main Report. Ministry of Agriculture and Land Reclamation and USAID, Cairo, April.

Mansfield, B. 2004. "Neoliberalism in the Oceans: 'Rationalization,' Property Rights, and the Commons Question." *Geoforum* 35:313–26.

Mansour, S. 2011. "Egypt Rice Update." Global Agricultural Information Network Report, USDA Foreign Agricultural Service, August 2.

Mansour, S., S. Sherif, and C. Guven. 2010. "Egypt Rice Update." Global Agricultural Information Network Report, USDA Foreign Agricultural Service, June 29.

Mansour, S., and M. Beillard. 2012. "Egypt Lifts Rice Export Ban." Global Agricultural Information Network Report, USDA Foreign Agricultural Service, October 1.

Marston, S., J. Jones, and K. Woodward. 2005. "Human Geography Without Scale." *Transactions of the Institute of British Geographers*, 416–32.

McCay, B., and S. Jentoft. 1996. "From the Bottom Up: Participatory Issues in Fisheries Management." *Society and Natural Resources* 9:237–50.

McCully, P. 2001. *Silenced Rivers: The Ecology and Politics of Large Dams*. London: Zed Books.

McKinnon, R. 1996. "Issues in Financial Reforms and Sequencing in Economic Transitions." In *Egypt's Agriculture in a Reform Era*, ed. L. Fletcher. Ames: Iowa State Press.

Mehta, L. 2005. *The Politics and Poetics of Water: Naturalizing Scarcity in Western India*. New Delhi: Orient Longman.

Meinzen-Dick, R., and M. Zwarteveen. 1998. "Gendered Participation in Water Management: Issues and Illustrations from WUAs in South Asia." *Agriculture and Human Values* 15:337–45.

Mekonnen, D. 2010. "The Nile Basin Cooperative Framework Agreement Negotiations and the Adoption of a "Water Security" Paradigm: Flight into Obscurity or a Logical Cul-de-sac?" *European Journal of International Law* 21:421–40.

Meyer, G. 1998. "Economic Changes in the Newly Reclaimed Lands: From State Farms to Small Holdings and Private Agricultural Enterprises." In *Directions of Change in Rural Egypt*, ed. N. Hopkins and K. Westergaard, 334–57. Cairo: American University in Cairo Press.

Mikhail, A. 2010. "An Irrigated Empire: The View from Ottoman Fayoum." *International Journal of Middle East Studies* 42:569–90.

Mikhail, A., ed. 2012. *Water on Sand: Environmental Histories of the Middle East and North Africa*. New York: Oxford University Press.

Mitchell, T. 2002. *The Rule of Experts: Egypt, Technopolitics, Modernity*. Berkeley: University of California Press.

Mitchell, T. 2011. *Carbon Democracy: Political Power in the Age of Oil*. London: Verso.

Mitchell, W., and D. Guillet. 1994. *Irrigation at High Altitudes: The Social Organization of Water Control Systems in the Andes*. Washington, DC: American Anthropological Association.

Moharram, I. 2003. *Fayoum Human Development Report 2003*. Participation for Development Project, Ministry of Local Development, Cairo.

Molden, D., T. Oweis, P. Steduto et al. 2010. "Agricultural Water Productivity: Between Optimism and Caution." *Agricultural Water Management* 97:528–35.

Molle, F., T. Foran, and M. Käkönen. 2009. *Contested Waterscapes in the Mekong Region: Hydropower, Livelihoods, and Governance.* London: Earthscan.

Mollinga, P. 2003. *On the Waterfront: Water Distribution, Technology, and Agrarian Change in a South Indian Canal System.* Hyderabad, India: Orient Longman.

Momani, B. 2003. "Promoting Economic Liberalization in Egypt: From U.S. Foreign Aid to Trade and Investment." *Middle East Review of International Affairs* 7:88–100.

Moorehead, A. 1960. *The White Nile.* New York: Harper and Row.

Moorehead, A. 1962. *The Blue Nile.* New York: Harper and Row.

Mosse, D. 2003. *The Rule of Water: Statecraft, Ecology, and Collective Action in South India.* New Delhi: Oxford University Press.

Muehlmann, S. 2013. *Where the River Ends: Contested Indigeneity in the Mexican Colorado Delta.* Durham, NC: Duke University Press.

Murray, G. 1935. *Sons of Ishmael: A Study of the Egyptian Bedouin.* London: George Routledge.

MWRI. 2005a. *National Water Resources Plan for Egypt—2017.* Report prepared through the National Water Resources Plan Project, Ministry of Water Resources and Irrigation, Cairo.

MWRI. 2005b. *Vision and Strategy for MWRI Institutional Reform.* Strategy developed as part of the Institutional Reform Project, Ministry of Water Resources and Irrigation, Cairo.

NAWQAM. 1999. *Inception Report for the National Water Quality and Availability Management Project (NAWQAM),* Ministry of Water Resources and Irrigation and Canadian International Development Agency.

Nicol, A., and A. Cascão. 2011. "Against the Flow—New Power Dynamics and Upstream Mobilisation in the Nile Basin." *Review of African Political Economy* 38:317–25.

Nixon, S. 2004. "The Artificial Nile." *American Scientist* 92:158.

NSV. 2011. *Jonglei Canal Project May Hold Great Potential for South Sudan:* New Sudan Vision (NSV), August 2, Accessed on September 20, 2011. http://www.newsudanvision.com.

NWRP. 2001. *Groundwater in the Nile Valley and Delta.* Technical Report No. 16. National Water Resources Plan (NWRP) for Egypt Project, Ministry of Water Resources and Irrigation, Cairo, June.

Nyberg, A., S. Barghouti, and S. Rehman. 1990. *Arab Republic of Egypt Land Reclamation Subsector Review.* World Bank, Middle East and North Africa Region, Agricultural Operations Division, Report No. 8047-EGT, February 1.

Orlove, B. 2002. *Lines in the Water: Nature and Culture at Lake Titicaca.* Berkeley: University of California Press.

Orlove, B., and S. Caton. 2010. "Water Sustainability: Anthropological Approaches and Prospects." *Annual Review of Anthropology* 39:401–15.

Ostrom, E., R. Gardner, and J. Walker. 1994. *Rules, Games, and Common-Pool Resources.* Ann Arbor: University of Michigan Press.

Özyürek, E. 2006. *Nostalgia for the Modern: State Secularism and Everyday Politics in Turkey*. Durham, NC: Duke University Press.

Padoch, C., and N. Peluso. 2003. *Borneo in Transition*. 2nd ed. Kuala Lumpur: Oxford University Press.

Peet, R., P. Robbins, and M. Watts, eds. 2011. *Global Political Ecology*. London: Routledge.

Pellissery, S., and S. Bergh. 2007. "Adapting the Capability Approach to Explain the Effects of Participatory Development Programs: Case Studies from India and Morocco." *Journal of Human Development* 8:283–302.

Perry, C. 1996. *Alternative Approach to Cost Sharing for Water Services to Agriculture in Egypt*. Research Report No. 2. International Irrigation Management Institute, Colombo, Sri Lanka.

Perry, C. 2007. "Efficient Irrigation: Inefficient Communication; Flawed Recommendations." *Irrigation and Drainage* 56:367–78.

Perry, C., P. Steduto, R. Allen et al. 2009. "Increased Productivity in Irrigated Agriculture: Agronomic Constraints and Hydrological Realities." *Agricultural Water Management* 96:1517–24.

Peterson, N. 2010. "Excluding to Include: (Non)participation in Mexican Natural Resource Management." *Agriculture and Human Values*, 27.

Peterson, N., K. Broad, B. Orlove et al. 2010. "Participatory Processes and Climate Forecast Use: Socio-Cultural Context, Discussion, and Consensus." *Climate and Development* 2:14–29.

Pfaffenberger, B. 1990. "The Harsh Facts of Hydraulics: Technology and Society in Sri Lanka's Colonization Schemes." *Technology and Culture* 31:361–97.

Pickering, A. 1992. *Science as Practice and Culture*. Chicago: University of Chicago Press.

Pinch, T., and W. Bijker. 1984. "The Social Construction of Facts and Artifacts: Or, How the Sociology of Science and the Sociology of Technology Might Benefit Each Other." *Social Studies of Science* 14:399–441.

Pinkerton, E. 1989. *Co-operative Management of Local Fisheries: New Directions for Improved Management and Community Development*. Vancouver: University of British Colombia Press.

Postel, S. 1999. *Pillar of Sand: Can the Irrigation Miracle Last?* New York: Norton.

Pretty, J. 1995. "Participatory Learning for Sustainable Agriculture." *World Development* 23:1247–63.

Price, D. 1995. "The Cultural Effects of Conveyance Loss in Gravity-Fed Irrigation Systems." *Ethnology* 34:273–91.

Pritchard, S. 2011. *Confluence: The Nature of Technology and the Remaking of the Rhone*. Cambridge, MA: Harvard University Press.

Quintero-Pinto, L. 2000. "Benefits and Second-Generation Problems of Irrigation Management Transfer in Colombia." In *Case Studies in Participatory Irrigation Management*, ed. D. Groenfeldt and M. Svendsen, 89–113. Washington, DC: World Bank Institute Learning Resources Series.

Raby, N. 2000. "Case Studies in Participatory Irrigation Management." In *Case Studies in Participatory Irrigation Management*, ed. D. Groenfeldt and M. Svendsen, 113–39. Washington, DC: World Bank Institute Learning Resource Series.

Rademacher, A. 2011. *Reigning the River: Urban Ecologies and Political Transformation in Kathmandu*. Durham, NC: Duke University Press.

Radwan, H. 2007. *Female Farmers in Egypt: Their Water Management Interests and Coping Mechanisms*. Technical Report No. 45. Water Boards—Integrated Irrigation Improvement and Management Project, Ministry of Water Resources and Irrigation, Cairo.

Radwan, L. 1998. "Water Management in the Egyptian Delta: Problems of Wastage and Inefficiency." *The Geographical Journal* 164, no. 2:129–38.

Raffles, H. 2002. *In Amazonia: A Natural History*. Princeton, NJ: Princeton University Press.

Rasmussen, E., O. Petersen et al. 2009. "Hydrodynamic-Ecological Model Analyses of the Water Quality of Lake Manzala (Nile Delta, Northern Egypt)." *Hydrobiologia* 662, no. 1:195–220.

Ribot, J. 2009. "Authority over Forests: Empowerment and Subordination in Senegal's Democratic Decentralization." *Development and Change* 40:105–29.

Richards, A. 1986. *Egypt's Agricultural Development, 1800–1980*. Boulder, CO: Westview Press.

Richardson, T., and G. Weszkalnys. 2014. "Resource Materialities." *Anthropological Quarterly* 87, no. 1:5–30.

Rijsberman, F. 2006. "Water Scarcity: Fact or Fiction?" *Agricultural Water Management* 80:5–22.

Robbins, P. 2004. *Political Ecology: A Critical Introduction*. Oxford: Blackwell.

Roberts, R., and J. Emel. 1992. "Uneven Development and the Tragedy of the Commons: Competing Images for Nature-Society Analysis." *Economic Geography* 68, no. 3:249–71.

Robertson, M. 2004. "The Neoliberalization of Ecosystem Services: Wetland Mitigation Banking and Problems in Environmental Governance." *Geoforum* 35:361–73.

Rocheleau, D., B. Thomas-Slayter, and E. Wangari. 1996. *Feminist Political Ecology: Global Perspectives and Local Experience*. New York: Routledge.

Rodríguez, S. 2006. *Acequia: Water Sharing, Sanctity, and Place*, Santa Fe, NM: School for Advanced Research Press.

Roy, A. 1999. "The Greater Common Good." *Algebra of Infinite Justice*. Delhi: Penguin Books.

Saad, M. 2002. "Nile River Morphology Changes Due to the Construction of High Aswan Dam in Egypt." Report by the head of the Planning Sector, Ministry of Water Resources and Irrigation, Cairo.

Saad, R. 1999. "State, Landlord, Parliament, and Peasant: The Story of the 1992 Tenancy Law in Egypt." In *Agriculture in Egypt: From Pharaonic to Modern Times*, ed. A. Bowman and E. Rogan. London: British Academy.

Saad, R. 2004. "Social Reproduction and Social Transformation: Trade and Exchange Relations in the Rural South." In *Upper Egypt: Identity and Change*, ed. N. Hopkins and R. Saad, 233–50. Cairo: American University in Cairo Press.

Sadowski, Y. 1991. *Political Vegetables? Businessman and Bureaucrat in the Development of Egyptian Agriculture*. Washington, DC: Brookings Institution.

Said, R. 1993. *The River Nile—Geology, Hydrology, and Utilization*. Oxford: Pergammon.

Salman, S. 2003. "From Marrakech through The Hague to Kyoto: Has the Global Debate on Water Reached a Dead End? Part 1." *Water International* 28, no. 4:491–500.

Salman, S. 2004. "From Marrakech through The Hague to Kyoto: Has the Global Debate on Water Reached a Dead End? Part 2." *Water International* 29, no. 1:11–19.

Sayre, N. 2005. "Ecological and Geographical Scale: Parallels and Potential for Integration." *Progress in Human Geography* 29:276–90.

Scaramelli, C. 2013. "Making Sense of Water Quality: Multispecies Encounters on the Mystic River." *Worldviews* 17:150–60.

Schalie, H. 1974. "Aswan Dam Revisited." *Environment* 16:18–26.

Scheumann, W., and M. Schiffler. 1998. *Water in the Middle East: Potential for Conflicts and Prospects for Cooperation*, Berlin: Springer.

Scott, J. C. 1987. *Weapons of the Weak. Everyday Forms of Peasant Resistance*. New Haven, CT: Yale University Press.

Scott, J. C. 1998. *Seeing Like a State: How Certain Schemes to Improve the Human Condition Have Failed*. New Haven, CT: Yale University Press.

Selby, J. 2005. "The Geopolitics of Water in the Middle East: Fantasies and Realities." *Third World Quarterly* 26:329–49.

Sen, A. 1983. *Poverty and Famines: An Essay on Entitlement and Deprivation*. Oxford: Oxford University Press.

Shalash, S. 1980. "The Effect of the High Aswan Dam on the Hydrological Regime of the River Nile." Proceedings of the Helsinki Symposium, June, 244–50. IAHS-AISH Publ. No. 130.

Shokr, A. 2009. "Hydropolitics, Economy, and the Aswan High Dam in Mid-Century Egypt." *Arab Studies Journal* 17:9–31.

Sid-Ahmed, M. 1998. "The Opening Shot in the Water War." *Al-Ahram Weekly* 407, December 10–16.

SIS. 2007. *Nile Flood Stable, High Dam in No Danger*. http://new.sis.gov.eg.

Smith, N. 1984. *Uneven Development: Nature, Capital, and the Production of Space*. Oxford: Basil Blackwell.

Smith, N. 1992. "Contours of a Spatialized Politics: Homeless Vehicles and the Production of Geographical Scale." *Social Text* 33:54–81.

Sneddon, C. 2007. "Nature's Circuitous Paths of Accumulation: Dispossession of Freshwater Fisheries in Cambodia." *Antipode* 39:167–93.

Sneddon, C., and C. Fox. 2006. "Rethinking Transboundary Waters: A Critical Hydropolitics of the Mekong Basin." *Political Geography* 25:181–202.

Sneddon, C., and C. Fox. 2008. "Struggles over Dams as Struggles for Justice: The World Commission on Dams (WCD) and Anti-Dam Campaigns in Thailand and Mozambique." *Society and Natural Resources* 21:625–40.

Sowers, J. 2011. "Remapping the Nation, Critiquing the State: Narrating Land Reclamation for Egypt's 'New Valley.'" In *Environmental Imaginaries of the Middle East*, ed. D. Davis and T. Burke, 158–91. Athens: Ohio University Press.

Sowers, J., and C. Toensing. 2010. "Running Dry: Editorial." *Middle East Report* 254.

Springborg, R. 1979. "Patrimonialism and Policy Making in Egypt: Nasser and Sadat and the Tenure Policy for Reclaimed Lands." *Middle Eastern Studies* 15:49–69.

Starr, J. 1991. "Water Wars." *Foreign Policy* 82:17–36.

Steward, J. 1955. *The Theory of Culture Change: The Methodology of Multilinear Evolution.* Urbana: University of Illinois Press.

Stoner, R. 1994. "Future Irrigation Planning in Egypt." In *The Nile: Sharing a Scarce Resource. An Historical and Technical Review of Water Management and of Economical and Legal Issues*, ed. P. Howell and J. Allan, 195–205. Cambridge: Cambridge University Press.

Strang, V. 2004. *The Meaning of Water.* Oxford: Berg.

Sultana, F. 2013. "Water, Technology, and Development: Transformations of Development Technonatures in Changing Waterscapes." *Environment and Planning D: Society and Space* 31, no. 2:337–53.

Sutcliffe, J., and Y. Parks. 1999. *The Hydrology of the Nile.* Wallingford, UK: International Association of Hydrological Sciences.

Swyngedouw, E. 2004. *Social Power and the Urbanization of Water: Flows of Power.* Oxford: Oxford University Press.

Swyngedouw, E. 2005. "Dispossessing H_2O: The Contested Terrain of Water Privatization." *Capitalism, Nature, Socialism* 16:81–98.

Tang, S. Y. 1992. *Self-Governing Organizations and Irrigation.* San Francisco: Institute for Contemporary Studies Press.

Tanji, K., and N. Kielen. 2002. *Agricultural Drainage Water Management in Arid and Semi-Arid Areas.* FAO Irrigation and Drainage Paper 61. Rome: Food and Agriculture Organization of the United Nations.

Tomich, T. 1984. "Private Land Reclamation in Egypt: Studies of Feasibility and Adaptive Behavior." PhD diss., Stanford University.

Toset, H., N. Gleditsch, and H. Hegre. 2000. "Shared Rivers and Interstate Conflict." *Political Geography* 19:971–96.

Trawick, P. 2001. "Successfully Governing the Commons: Principles of Social Organization in an Andean Irrigation System." *Human Ecology* 29:1–25.

Trawick, P. 2003. *The Struggle for Water in Peru: Comedy and Tragedy in the Andean Commons.* Palo Alto: Stanford University Press.

Tsing, A. 1993. *In the Realm of the Diamond Queen: Marginality in an Out-of-the-Way Place.* Princeton, NJ: Princeton University Press.

Tsing, A. 2005. *Friction: An Ethnography of Global Connection*. Princeton, NJ: Princeton University Press.

Tvedt, T. 2004a. *The Nile: An Annotated Bibliography*. New York: I. B. Tauris.

Tvedt, T. 2004b. *The River Nile in the Age of the British: Political Ecology and the Quest for Economic Power*. New York: I. B. Tauris.

Umali, D. 1993. *Irrigation-Induced Salinity: A Growing Problem for Development and the Environment*. World Bank Technical Paper No. 215. Washington, DC: World Bank.

Uphoff, N. 1986. *Improving International Irrigation Management with Farmer Participation: Getting the Process Right*. Boulder, CO: Westview Press.

Uphoff, N., P. Ramamurthy, and R. Steiner. 1991. *Managing Irrigation: Analyzing and Improving the Peformance of Bureaucracies*. New Delhi: Sage.

van Achthoven, T., Z. Merabet, K. Shalaby et al. 2004. *Balancing Productivity and Environmental Pressure in Egypt: Towards an Interdisciplinary and Integrated Approach to Agricultural Drainage*. Agriculture and Rural Development Working Paper No. 13. Washington, DC: World Bank.

van Steenbergen, F., and S. Abdel-Dayem. 2007. "Making the Case for Integrated Water Resources Management: Drainage in Egypt." *Water International* 32:674–85.

van Veen, J. 1962. *Dredge, Drain, Reclaim: The Art of a Nation*. The Hague: Martinus Nijhoff.

Varady, R., K. Meehan, and E. McGovern. 2009. "Charting the Emergence of 'Global Water Initiatives' in World Water Governance." *Physics and Chemistry of the Earth* 34:150–55.

Vavrus, F. 2003. "'A Shadow of the Real Thing': Furrow Societies, Water User Associations, and Democratic Practices in the Kilimanjaro Region of Tanzania." *Journal of African American History* 88:393–412.

Vayda, A., and B. Walters. 1999. "Against Political Ecology." *Human Ecology* 27:167–79.

Viney, S. 2012. "Abandoned by the System, Egypt's Farmers Suffer Discrimination, Violence, and Poverty." *Egypt Independent*, September 16.

Voll, S. 1980. "Egyptian Land Reclamation since the Revolution." *Middle East Journal* 34:127–48.

Von Schnitzler, A. 2013. "Traveling Technologies: Infrastructure, Ethical Regimes, and the Materiality of Politics in South Africa." *Cultural Anthropology* 28, no. 4:670–93.

Walley, C. 2002. "'They Scorn Us Because We Are Uneducated': Knowledge and Power in a Tanzanian Marine Park." *Ethnography* 3:265–98.

Walton, S. 1981. "Egypt—After the Aswan Dam." *Environment* 23:30–36.

Waterbury, J. 1979. *Hydropolitics of the Nile Valley*. Syracuse, NY: Syracuse University Press.

Waterbury, J. 2002. *The Nile Basin: National Determinants of Collective Action*. New Haven, CT: Yale University Press.

Waterbury, J., and D. Whittington. 1998. "Playing Chicken on the Nile: The Implications of Microdam Development in the Ethiopian Highlands and Egypt's New Valley Project." *Natural Resources Forum* 22:155–63.

Watts, M., and R. Peet. 2004. "Liberating Political Ecology." In *Liberation Ecologies: Environment, Development, Social Movements*, ed. R. Peet and M. Watts, 3–44. New York: Routledge.

West, P. 2006. *Conservation Is Our Government Now: The Politics of Ecology in Papua New Guinea*. Durham, NC: Duke University Press.

West, P. 2010. "Making the Market: Specialty Coffee, Generational Pitches, and Papua New Guinea." *Antipode* 42:690–718.

White, G. 1988. "The Environmental Effects of the High Dam at Aswan." *Environment* 30:4–11, 34–40.

White, R. 1996. *The Organic Machine: The Remaking of the Colorado River*. New York: Hill and Wang.

Wichelns, D. 2001. "The Role of 'Virtual Water' in Efforts to Achieve Food Security and Other National Goals, with an Example from Egypt." *Agricultural Water Management* 49:131–51.

Wichelns, D. 2003. "Moving Water to Move People: Evaluating the Success of the Toshka Project in Egypt." *Water International* 28:52–56.

Willcocks, W. 1899. *Egyptian Irrigation*. 2nd ed. London: E and F Spon.

Williams, G. 2004. "Evaluating Participatory Development: Tyranny, Power, and (Re)politicization." *Third World Quarterly* 25:557–78.

Winner, L. 1980. "Do Artifacts Have Politics?" *Daedalus* 109:121–36.

Wolf, A. 1998. "Conflict and Cooperation along International Waterways." *Water Policy* 1, no. 2:251–65.

Wolters, W., N. Ghobrial, H. Van Leeuwen et al. 1989. "Managing the Water Balance of the Fayoum Depression." *Irrigation and Drainage Systems* 3:103–23.

World Bank. 2004. *Drainage for Gain: Integrated Solutions to Drainage in Land and Water Management*. Washington, DC: Agriculture and Rural Development Department, World Bank.

World Bank. 2007. *Making the Most of Scarcity: Accountability for Better Water Management Results in the Middle East North Africa Region*. MENA Development Report. Washington DC: World Bank.

World Bank. 2011. *Implementation Status and Results: West Delta Water Conservation and Irrigation Rehabilitation Project*. Report No. ISR3738. Washington, DC: World Bank, June.

Worster, D. 1992. *Rivers of Empire: Water, Aridity, and the Growth of the American West*. New York: Oxford University Press.

WQU. 2004. *Reuse of Drainage Water: Alternative Solutions for Stopped Reuse Stations*. Water Quality Unit (WQU), Ministry of Water Resources and Irrigation, Cairo, December.

WWAP. 2012. *The United Nations World Water Development Report 4: Managing Water*

Under Uncertainty and Risk. World Water Assessment Programme (WWAP). Paris: UNESCO.

Zalla, T., M. Fawzy, A. Saad et al. 2000. *Availability and Quality of Agricultural Data for the New Lands in Egypt.* Impact Assessment Report No. 12. Report written by Abt Associates for the Monitoring, Verification, and Evaluation Unit of the Agricultural Policy Reform Project (APRP), Ministry of Agriculture and Land Reclamation, Cairo, June.

Zhu, Z., I. Elassiouti, A. Khattab et al. 1998. *National Policy for Drainage Water Reuse.* Agricultural Policy Reform Program, USAID, Ministry of Public Works and Water Resources, Report No. 8, June.

Zimmerer, K. 2000. "Rescaling Irrigation in Latin America: The Cultural Images and Political Ecology of Water Resources." *Ecumene* 7, no. 2:150–75.

Zwarteveen, M., P. Udas, and J. Delgado. 2010. "Gendered Dynamics of Participation in Water Management in Nepal and Peru: Revisiting the Linkages Between Membership and Power." In *Social Participation in Water Governance and Management: Critical and Global Perspectives*, ed. K. Berry and E. Mollard, 69–94. London: Earthscan.

INDEX

Page numbers in italics refer to illustrations.

abundance, 58–59, 138–39, 162

access to water: along canals, 15, 61–63, 164, 174; drainage water, 155, 162–64, 167, 168; illegal, 69–70, 77, 121–22, 176–77, 193n20; rights to, 6, 65–66; technology, 23, 119–20, 132, 162–64, 175–76

accumulation by dispossession: Harvey's definition, 109, 112; land reclamation and, 122, 125, 133–35; nature of resources and, 113, 135

agency: of farmers, 69, 77, 134, 174; flow of water and, 3, 44, 71, 78, 138, 158, 173; participation and, 96–97, 104

Agreement for the Full Utilization of Nile Waters, 6

agricultural cooperatives, 12, 77–78, 189n6

agricultural production: contribution to Egypt's GDP, 18; control of water for, 3, 9–10; desert irrigation and, 135–36; expansion, 107–9, 108, 112, 118–19, 125, 132–33, 160; seasonal patterns, 6–9, 180n11; state intervention in, 11–12, 181n14; subsurface drainage and, 151–52, 158; in the west delta, 126–28. *See also* crops; farmers

agricultural reform, 12, 41–42, 181n14

aid: international donors, 17–20; total received by Egypt, 18, 181n21

Alatout, Samer, 138, 162

Allan, Tony, 187n22

aquifers: Nile, 116, 128, 144, 144–45, 147; west delta, 128; Western Desert, 179n1; Fayoum, 188n33

Arab Spring, xii

Arab Water Council, 56

Arab Water Forum, 34, 57, 64–65, 184n1

Aswan High Dam: cost of, 137, 194n2; drainage and, 147–48, 156–58; funding for, 17, 157; hydropower generation, 186n16; impact on downstream discharge, 9–10, 11; location (map), 10; purpose, 9, 51; releases from, 50, 52–53, 56, 178, 186n15; security at, 55; significance of, xi, 26, 147, 156–58; water level measurement, 55

Asyut Barrage, 22, 180n12; location (map), 10

awareness (*taw'iya*): meetings, 78, 89, 92, 189n6; of water scarcity, 66–67, 71

bahhar (gatekeeper): reporting violations, 121–22; responsibilities, 46–48

Bahr Hassan Wasif, 21, 22

Bahr Yusuf, 21, 22–23

Bakker, Karen, 26
barrages, 5, 9, 15, 44, 170, 180n12;
    Delta, 9, 22, 145, 180n11; location
    (map), 10
Bijker, Wiebe, 26
Blue Nile: course, 4, 179n1; dam con-
    struction, x, 6; location (map), 2; rain-
    fall over, 5
blue water, 184n1

Callon, Michel, 20, 95–96
canals: access to water along, 15, 61–63,
    164, 174; blockages, 43, 69; converted
    into drains, 146; daily operations, 44–
    45; inequality along, 39–41, 92, 124,
    164, 176–78; maintenance work, 16,
    43, 73, 79–80, 80, 98–103; overview of
    Egypt's, 22, 22–23; rotation system,
    23, 61, 182n28; water level manage-
    ment in, 45–50, 55, 69; water quality
    in, 15, 88, 135, 136; water users, 88–
    90; WUAs for, 90–93
Castree, Noel, 29
Caton, Steven, 19
Central Administration for Water Distri-
    bution, 44–45
climate change, 1, 52, 186n17
clover (birsim), 8, 142, 180n9
community: boundaries, 90–93; build-
    ing, 86–87, 190n15; leaders, 94; par-
    ticipation, 76–78, 95–96. See also
    "global water community"
community organizers: election coor-
    dination, 93–94; establishment of
    WUAS, 38–39, 78–79, 86–87, 90–93,
    190n13; female, 89–90, 94, 190n13
Comprehensive Framework Agreement,
    6, 179n6
connections (wasta): farmers' use of, 68,
    97, 131, 134, 173–74; impact on WUA
    effectiveness, 102–3; within the min-
    istry, 16
conservation. See water conservation
consultants, 19–20, 79–81, 85
cooperatives. See agricultural
    cooperatives

cotton, 17, 122–23, 146, 196n19; salinity
    threshold, 12, 142, 166
covered drainage. See subsurface
    drainage
crisis of water, 1, 35, 57, 60, 178. See also
    scarcity
Cromer, Lord, 146, 196n22
crops: choice in planting, 12, 39, 41;
    data, 45, 185n10; in Fayoum, 6–8,
    180n9; irrigation efficiency and,
    193n22; salinization/salinity, 12, 142,
    142–43, 166, 196n12; seasonal pat-
    terns, 6–9, 180n11; water-intensive,
    39, 41–42, 76, 147, 155; water require-
    ments, 12; in the west delta, 126–28;
    yields, 132, 138, 142, 151, 166, 193n26

dams, 4–5, 156–58; earthen, 37–38, 44,
    71, 87, 155, 173–74. See also Aswan
    High Dam; barrages; Hidase Dam
decision making: by farmers, 73, 77, 81–
    82, 84, 103, 105; participatory forms
    of, 84–85; water scarcity and, 37, 40;
    by women, 97; by WUAS, 98–100,
    102–3, 105
delta, the. See Nile delta; west delta
Delta Barrages, 9, 22, 145, 180n11
demand: in the delta, 131; in Fayoum,
    44; for land reclamation initiatives,
    64, 191n5; measures to reduce, 64–
    67, 71
democracy, 77, 83, 85, 104
desalination, 60
desert: agriculture, 106–7, 113–16, 126–
    27, 132, 193n26; nomadic groups in,
    191n2, 192n12; soil, 114; translation of
    term, 190n1
desert reclamation. See land reclamation
dispossession. See accumulation by
    dispossession
district engineers (muhandis): issuing of
    fines, 69, 121–22; role of, 16, 45–48,
    177; and WUAS, 79–80, 82, 98–99,
    102
diversion of water: dispossession
    through, 134–35; of drainage water,

161, 163; into El-Salam Canal, 108; for land reclamation, 123–25, 130–31, 133; into Toshka Spillway, 53–55; for the Toshka Project, 107–8; water quality and, 109, 130

donor projects (*mashari‘*), 18, 181n23; in Fayoum, 33–34, 73, 118; Dutch, 18, 74–75, 129, 149, 187n20, 187n23, 189n7; German, 61, 75, 149, 187n24, 189n7, 194n3; Japanese, 61, 66, 75, 149, 187n24, 194n3. *See also* United States Agency for International Development (USAID); World Bank

donors. *See* international donors

drainage: "controlled," 155; costs, 137, 146, 148, 153–54, 194n2; government administration of, 15, 145–47, 152; history of, 144–50; importance of, 137–38; integrated approach to, 150, 196n23; international funding for, 148, 149, 157, 195n5; lack of donor and academic interest in, 138, 194n4, 195n6; maintenance, 154–55, 162; "natural," 144–45; in the Netherlands, 157, 197n31; outlets, 131, 139, 143, 158–62; process, 139–41; return flow, 195n7. *See also* subsurface drainage; surface or open drainage

drainage ditches, 139–40, 143, 150; digging of, 114, 147, 153; maintenance, 154; pumping from, 43, 69, 163–64, 185n6

drainage systems. *See* subsurface drainage; surface or open drainage

drainage water: disposal of, 158–62; quality of, 165, 165–67; reuse of, 139, 163–64

drinking water, 17, 43, 88, 185n9; pollutants in, 165, 198n36; scarcity, 185n4

Dublin Statement on Water and Sustainable Development, 20, 65, 73

Egypt: agricultural expansion, 107–9, 108; genealogy of WUAS in, 73, 74–75; importance of Aswan High Dam, xi, 156–57; political transition, xii;

rainfall, 180n10; relations with Nile Basin states, x, 6, 179n6; total drainage water reuse, 164, 198n35; water supply, 3, 5–6, 59–60, 179nn1–2; water availability per capita, 184n1

Egyptian-American Rural Improvement Service, 110, 118, 122, 192n16, 193n21

Egyptian Public Authority for Drainage Projects, 152–53

electrical conductivity, 12, 142, 195n11, 198n37

Ethiopian Highlands, ix, 4

European Union, 17

evaporation: salt accumulation from, 141–42, 145; water losses through, 53–55, 60

evapotranspiration, 11, 40, 158–59

everyday politics, x, 26–27, 71, 138–39, 173–75

everyday practices, xi, 1, 3, 44, 77, 87, 107, 171–73; to obtain more water, 69, 96–97, 119–20, 123, 129, 163–64; to control drainage, 154–55

excess water, 139. *See also* drainage water

Falkenmark, Malin, 35, 57, 184n1

farmers: awareness of water scarcity, 66–67; complaints, 39, 48, 63, 68–69, 96, 101, 104–5, 177–78, 186n15, 188n31; crop choice, 12, 39, 41, 133; dispossession, 122–25, 133–35; Egyptian term for, 13, 114; farm size, 12–13; female, 13–14, 32, 39, 88–89, 177–78, 188n31, 190n10; knowledge of water sources, 50, 186n14; participation in WUAS, 78–81, 95–97, 104–5; payment for water, 66; role in land reclamation, 112–14; reuse of drainage water, 162–67; subsurface drainage and, 150, 153–54, 197n26. *See also* investors

Fayoum: crops, 6–8, 180n9; drainage system, 154, 159–61, 197n27; irrigation system, 22–23; landownership, 88–90, 190n10; land reclamation, 117–19, 122–25, 192n10; location and

Fayoum (continued)
population, 21, 21, 182n25; rice cultivation, 39, 41, 41–42; scarcity, 40–44,
46, 124–25, 163–64, 177–78; soils,
192n15; water sources, 21–22, 164,
188n33; WUAS, 73, 76, 84, 90–91,
104–5, 189n4
Fayoum Irrigation Directorate: drainage management, 160–61, 164; farmer
complaints to, 67–68; position on rice
cultivation, 42; role of, 22; WUAS and,
76, 104
fertilizers, 10, 12, 113, 116, 165
"free water" (mai hurra), 166, 198n38
funding, 17–19; for Aswan High Dam,
17, 157; for drainage projects, 148,
195n5; for land reclamation projects,
191n4; for WUA projects, 73, 82.
See also international donors; donor
projects

gatekeepers. See bahhar
gender: assumptions, 33–34; farming
and, 13–14, 32, 39, 188n31; water user
categories and, 88–90; participation
in WUAS and, 93–95
German Development Agency (BMZ)
and Development Bank (KfW), 61, 75,
149, 187n24, 189n7, 194n3
Gish Abay, ix, 179n1
"global water community," 19–20; international meetings, 56, 181n24; lack
of attention to drainage, 138, 194n4;
paradigms and buzzwords of, 64–65,
73, 85, 175. See also donor projects;
World Water Forum
graduates (kharigin), 107, 109, 114, 123
Graduate Scheme (Project for Developing and Serving the Land Allocated to
Youth Graduates), 109, 114, 119, 123,
125; reclamation area (map), 114, 127
Grand Renaissance Dam. See Hidase Dam
green water, 184n1
groundwater: for irrigation, 116–17, 128,
130, 188n33, 191n6; link with surface

water, 128, 144, 144–45; resources,
60, 179n1. See also aquifers

Harvey, David, 109, 112
Hidase Dam, 6, 179n5, 179n6; location
(map), 2
hydropolitics, 26

Ibrahimia Canal, 10, 22
Institutional Reform Vision, 81, 189n7
international donors ("the donors"):
agricultural policy reform projects,
12; drainage projects, 138, 148, 149,
194n4; investment in dams, 17, 156–
57; irrigation projects, 61–63, 129;
promotion of participation, 73, 74–
75, 81–83; reports, 34, 73, 184n38;
role, 17–21; skepticism of land reclamation, 191n4; water distribution improvement, 45, 48–49. See also donor
projects (mashari'); "global water community"; and individual donors
investors (mustathmirin): 13, 109, 114,
116–17, 128–32
irrigation: center pivot systems, 126,
127, 127; community-run, 87, 189n9;
directorates, 16, 45, 67–68; drainage
water for, 162–67; drip and sprinkler,
13, 116, 119, 124, 130, 133, 193n23;
efficiency, 133, 193n22, 193n25; in
Fayoum, 22–23; flood, 7, 7, 37–38,
193n22; improvement, 61–64, 187n24;
Japanese system, 66; maintenance, 16,
43, 79–80, 87, 98–103, 176–77; modern, 124, 133, 135, 193n22; network in
Egypt (map), 10; participatory management, 73; perennial, 9, 180n11;
public-private partnerships for, 129–
32; rights, 6, 180n8, 193n20; rotation,
23, 61, 87, 182n28, 185n5; scholarship
on, 25; total Nile water used for, 1,
179n2; in the west delta, 126, 127–32;
women's role in, 89, 190n11
Irrigation and Drainage Law, 6, 74, 100
irrigation ditches. See mesqas

Japanese International Cooperation Agency (JICA), 61, 66, 75, 149, 187n24, 194n3
Jonglei Canal, 2, 60

Lahun Regulator, 21, 22, 43
Land Center for Human Rights, 131
landowners, 13, 118, 133, 146–47, 181n15; female, 88–90, 190n10; influence of, 68, 97, 102, 174
land reclamation: accumulation through, 112–13; diversion of water for, 123–25, 130–31, 133; donors' position on, 191n4; in Fayoum borderlands, 117–19, 192n16; government promotion of, 107–8, 132, 191nn4–5; history of, 107; key actors involved in, 113–14; marginal and informal, 109, 192n10; modern irrigation and, 135; projects, 107–9, 192n16; term usage, 191n2; totals, 108, 109, 110–11, 192n10; transformation process, 113–14, 115, 116–17; use of pumps in, 116–17, 119–21, 128–30; water demand and, 64; water dispossession and, 112–13, 122, 125, 133–35; water quality and, 135; in the west delta, 126–32; yields, 193n26
land reform, 12–13, 181n15; Law No. 96 (1992), 13, 109, 111
Latour, Bruno, 28, 49
laws: on irrigation and drainage, 6, 15, 100; on land reclamation, 111; on land reform, 13, 109, 181n16; on subsurface drainage, 148; on water quality, 15, 165; WUAS and, 74, 100
Li, Tania, 97, 190n18

mafish mai ("no water"), 37, 38–39, 185n3. See also scarcity
maintenance: of drainage system, 154, 162, 197n26; identifying priorities for, 73, 98–99, 101–3; of irrigation canals, 43, 99–100, 176–77; of mesqas, 87; winter closure (al-sadde al-shitwiya), 16, 79–80, 98–99

maize, 7, 12, 68; yields, 142, 151, 197n24
making of Egypt's water, x–xi, 3, 169–71, 173, 175; Aswan High Dam and, xi, 50; international donors and, 19, 34; and making of Egypt's land, 109; materiality and, 29–30; scarcity and, 37, 44; through everyday practices, x–xi, 3, 44, 71, 120, 167–68, 175, 178; WUAS and, 98, 104, 105; vertical dimension to, 139, 167
marwa (field ditch), 62–63
materiality of water, 25, 29–30, 172, 174, 183n34; accumulation through reclamation and, 113, 133, 135; dissolution and transportation of salts, 109, 140–41, 143, 145; erosive power, 43, 52–53, 186n18; fluidity, 91, 98, 135; transformation of land, 107; water scarcity and, 36, 70–71; water excess and, 139
mesqas (irrigation ditches): irrigation improvement and, 61–62; maintenance, 87; management of, 15, 22–23, 87; rotation system of, 23, 182n28; term usage, 182n27; water flow in, 37–38, 69, 178; water scarcity in, 39–41; WUAS, 74, 90–91
Ministry of Agriculture and Land Reclamation, 12, 45, 78, 132–33, 185n10; responsibilities, 17
Ministry of Foreign Affairs, 17
Ministry of Water Resources and Irrigation ("the ministry"): Arabic abbreviation, 16; canal maintenance, 43, 101–3; complaints to, 68–69, 96, 104, 188n31; control over drainage, 155–56, 163; drain maintenance, 154; hierarchical structure, 16, 101; Irrigation Advisory Service, 18, 72, 76, 93, 104, 189n5; National Water Resources Plan, 18, 181n22; offices, 15, 67–68, 152; offtake installation and reconstruction, 37, 42, 69, 79, 123, 176–78; management of Aswan High Dam, 52–55; position on water scarcity, 58–59; pricing of water, 65–66; relation-

Ministry of Water Resources and Irrigation ("the ministry") (*continued*) ship with donors, 18–19; relationship with WUAS, 78–83, 100–103, 105; responsibilities and objectives, 15–17; rice cultivation policy, 42–43; water level monitoring, 48–49; water reuse program, 163–64, 166–67, 198n34. *See also* district engineers

Mitchell, Timothy, 156, 158, 187n21

mixed water (*mai khalat*), 165–66, 198n36

Moeris, Lake, 159

Mohamed Ali, 9, 17

Mubarak, Hosni, xii, 11

Nasser, Gamal Abdel, 9, 11, 12, 123, 157

Nasser, Lake, 4, 50–51; evaporative losses from, 55–56, 60; location (map), 2; water levels, 50–56, 51, 187n20

Nasser Canal, 129–30; location, 127

nature: production and construction of, 36, 184n2; and society, 24, 182n29

Netherlands: drainage projects, 149, 152, 157, 197n31; irrigation projects, 129; water management projects, 18, 187n20, 187n23, 189n7; WUA projects, 74–75

new lands. *See* old vs. new lands

Nile Basin: farmer knowledge of, 186n14; flow of water through, 4–5, 108, 179n1; map of, 2; politics within the, x, 6, 52–53, 58, 60, 179nn5–6, 180n7, 184n1, 191n5

Nile delta: drainage projects, 146, 148, 149, 151, 153; drainage reuse, 163–64, 197n34; flow of water through, 5, 9; irrigation, 9, 23, 61–64, 131, 132–33, 180n11; map of, 10; reclamation on borders of, 109, 110–11, 171, 192n10; soils, 142, 144, 153, 195n10; topography of, 128; urbanization, 131, 193n25; water quality in, 158, 165, 165; WUAS in the, 75. *See also* west delta

Nile River: agricultural history of, 9; allocation between basin states, x, 6, 52, 179n6; aquifer linkage, 144, 144–

45; bank erosion, 52, 186n18; climate change impact on, 52, 186n17; course, 1, 2, 4–5; drain discharge into, 159–60; flood, 9–10, 11, 22, 43, 114, 144–45, 146, 159, 163, 186n11, 192n15; mean monthly discharge, 10, 11; source, ix, 4, 179n1; treaty, 6, 179n6; water quality, 165, 165, 198n38

Nile valley, 21–22, 61, 109, 144, 158–59, 171

offtakes, 7, 37, 40–41; rebuilding of, 79, 102, 176–78; widening of, 42, 68–70, 77, 119–20, 123

old vs. new lands, 125, 192n13, 193n24; in Fayoum, 118; irrigation techniques, 114, 116, 119, 133, 135–36; soil, 114, 116; in the west delta, 127, 128; yields, 132, 193n26

onions, 8, 32, 180n9; transplanting, 139–40, 140; water shortages and, 46–47; yields, 142, 193n26

Orlove, Ben, 19

participation: as a buzzword, 20, 73; and democratic governance, 83; as a form of control, 103–4, 190n17; ladder of, 81; understandings of, 77–85. *See also* water user associations (WUAS)

pipes: to increase water access, 69, 120–21, 173; subsurface drainage, 15, 137, 148, 151–56, 157; subsurface irrigation, 62–63

policy: agricultural, 11–12; Aswan High Dam operation, 52, 55–56; drainage water reuse, 163, 166–67; land reclamation, 107, 124, 191n4; participatory water management, 73, 78–79, 81; on rice cultivation, 42–43; water pricing, 65; for water scarcity, 59, 71

political ecology, 23–24, 29, 175, 182n29

politics of water. *See* everyday politics

pricing, water, 20, 64–66, 71, 187n27, 188nn28–29

privatization: of state farms, 111, 181n14; of water, 36, 188n28 projects. *See* donor projects

property rights. *See* rights to water

protests, xii, 68, 103

Public Works Department, 17, 145–47

pumps (*makina*): buying or renting, 42, 185n6; on canals, 23, 61–62, 69–70, 106–7, 114, 119–20, 123; diesel *vs.* electric, 62, 64, 119, 120; for drainage water reuse, 43, 155, 163–64, 167, 174, 197n34; for groundwater, 116, 128, 130; legality and illegality, 120–21, 193n20; pumping stations, 15, 159; technique and technology, 25, 119–20

Qaroun, Lake, 21, 162, 164, 192n17; location (map), 21, 117; photo of, 118; water level, 159–62, 160

quality. *See* water quality (*no'ia*)

Quta Canal, 122–23; location (map), 21, 117

rainfall, 3, 5, 179n1, 180n10; in Fayoum, 35; rainwater harvesting, 60; variability, 51–52

reclamation. *See* land reclamation

rice cultivation, 7–8, 39, 41, 41–43, 142, 174; drainage flows and, 155, 161

rights to water, 6, 130, 180n8, 193n20

rotation system (*mutarfa*), 23, 61, 87, 182n28, 185n5

Sadat, Anwar al-, 11, 110

salinity/salinization: impact on crops, 12, 142, 142–43, 166, 196n12; metrics of, 195n11, 198n37; of soil, 138, 142–43, 145, 153, 191n2, 195n7; of water, 109, 128–29, 135, 159, 162, 165, 165–66, 193n17, 198nn36–37

scale: of action, 44, 50, 55, 59, 108, 113, 137, 173; agency and, 71, 101; "jumping" scales, 16; limitations of single-scale analysis, 27, 183n33; literature on, 27–29; multiscaled approach, xii, 3, 36–37, 169, 175–76; production of, 28–29

scarcity: awareness of, 66–67; causes of, 40–44, 50–53; construction and production of, 36, 71, 184n2; excess and, 162, 172, 178; Falkenmark Water Stress Index on, 184n1; in the home, 185n4; literature on, 35–36; material dimension of, 70–71; ministry position on, 58–59; pricing water and, 65; regional dialog on, 56–58; seasonal patterns to, 40, 185n5; solutions to, 59–60, 63–67, 68–69; water level and, 48, 50

Sen, Amartya, 70

Sheikh Zayed Canal, 107, 186n19; location (map), 10, 54

Smith, Neil, 28

Sneddon, Chris, 113, 135, 183n33

soil: flow of water through, 140–41; of old and new lands, 114, 116, 193n26; permeability, 144, 152, 195n8, 195n10; salinization, 138, 141, 142–43, 145, 153, 191n2, 195n7; saturation, 142, 195n10

sorghum, 12, 41, 142

South Sudan, 60, 180n6

Soviet Union, 17, 157

subsurface drainage: Arabic term, 147–48; compared to dams, 156–58; and control of flows, 154–56, 158; donor-funded projects, 148–49, 149, 150; farmer requests for, 72, 153; field trials, 147–48, 196n22; installation, 152–54, 197nn25–26; maintenance, 154, 197n26; ministry responsibility for, 15; system overview, 143, 143, 148; unequal access to, 151–53

Sudan, 4–6, 52, 60, 180n6

surface or open drainage: history of, 145–47; remodeling of, 149, 150; system overview, 143, 143

Tana, Lake, 179n1; location (map), 2

technology: access to, 116, 119, 151, 174; and society, 24–25, 63, 119–20, 132, 156; subsurface drainage, 150–51, 154

telemetry system, 48–49, 186n12

Thania, 122–25, 134, 193n21; location (map), 117

tiredness: expression, 39, 185n7; temporality of, 40; term usage, 185n8, 192n14
Toshka: land reclamation project, 107–9, 197n32; location (map), 10; spillway, 53–55, 54, 186n19
Tsing, Anna, 85, 183n35

United States Agency for International Development (USAID): Agriculture Policy Reform Project, 11–12, 49, 181n14, 185n10, 186n13; drainage project, 149; irrigation improvement project, 61–64, 187n24; land reclamation study, 191n4; Public Awareness on Water Scarcity Project, 67, 188n30; telemetry system, 48–49, 186n12; water pricing study, 65–66; WUA projects, 74–75

violations (mukhalafat), 69, 121–22, 156

Wadi Rayan, 161–62, 164, 197n33; location (map), 21
Warda (pseud.), 30–33, 117–18, 183n36
water conservation, 60, 66, 132, 187n26
water distribution: level-based system of, 45–48; discharge-based system of, 49, 186n13; the ministry's role in, 15
water level (mansub al-mai): of Lake Qaroun, 159–61; of Lake Nasser, 50–53, 51; measuring and managing, 45–48; monitoring system, 48–49, 55; scarcity and, 48, 50
waterlogging, 3, 138, 146, 151, 153, 158, 196n15
water quality (no'ia): in canals, 88, 135; of drainage water, 158–59, 162–67, 165; of drinking water, 185n4; ministry's responsibility for, 15; of Nile River, 130, 165, 172–73, 198n38; urban pollution and, 88
water table, 153, 196n15, 197n23; in Nile floodplain, 144, 144, 145; in the west delta, 128
water user associations (WUAS): agricultural cooperatives and, 78, 189n6;

as assemblages, 97; awareness of, 84; for branch canals, 90–93, 100; community building process, 86–88; democracy and, 83; donor projects, 73, 74–75, 189n4; elections, 83, 93–95; exclusion from or nonparticipation in, 76, 89, 95–97; legal status, 100; leadership of, 99–100; for mesqas, 90; in other countries, 73, 85, 188n2, 190n12; rabita term for, 78, 84, 189n3; relations with the ministry, 78–83, 100–103, 105. See also participation
water user categories, 88–90
water wars, 1, 26, 183n32
weirs, 37, 40, 47, 49; level measurements at, 45–46
west delta: cultivation areas (map), 127; irrigation techniques, 126, 127–28; water diversion project, 128–32, 129
Western Desert, 53, 60, 107, 110, 179n1, 191n6
wheat, 7–8, 12, 125, 180n9, 193n26; yields, 142, 151, 166
White Nile, 4–5, 60, 179n1; location (map), 2
Willcocks, William, 146
winter closure (al-sadde al-shitwiya), 16, 79–80, 98–99
women: farmers, 13–14, 32, 39, 177–78, 188n31; landowners, 88–89, 190n10; participation in WUAS, 93, 95, 96–97, 190n14; role in irrigation, 89, 190n11; water users, 88–90, 185n4
World Bank: drainage projects, 148, 149, 194n3, 195n5, 196n23; irrigation projects, 61, 74–75, 129, 131, 187n24, 189n5; reclamation projects, 111; relations with Egypt, 17; structural adjustment, 11–12
World Water Forum: Fifth, 20, 34, 56, 57, 64, 67, 73, 83, 181n24, 195n4; Sixth, 34, 64, 131, 181n24, 195n4
World Water Council, 20, 64, 73. See also World Water Forum

Yusuf Siddique, 107, 117, 123–24